Teach Yourself®
Microsoft®
FrontPage® 2000

Teach Yourself®
Microsoft®
FrontPage® 2000

David Crowder and Rhonda Crowder

IDG Books Worldwide, Inc.
An International Data Group Company

Foster City, CA • Chicago, IL • Indianapolis, IN • New York, NY

IDG BOOKS WORLDWIDE

Teach Yourself® Microsoft® FrontPage® 2000

Published by
IDG Books Worldwide, Inc.
An International Data Group Company
919 E. Hillsdale Blvd., Suite 400
Foster City, CA 94404
www.idgbooks.com (IDG Books Worldwide Web site)

ISBN: 0-7645-7523-6

Printed in the United States of America

10 9 8 7 6 5 4 3 2 1

1P/SZ/QW/ZZ/IN

Distributed in the United States by IDG Books Worldwide, Inc.

Distributed by CDG Books Canada Inc. for Canada; by Transworld Publishers Limited in the United Kingdom; by IDG Norge Books for Norway; by IDG Sweden Books for Sweden; by IDG Books Australia Publishing Corporation Pty. Ltd. for Australia and New Zealand; by TransQuest Publishers Pte Ltd. for Singapore, Malaysia, Thailand, Indonesia, and Hong Kong; by ICG Muse, Inc. for Japan; by Norma Comunicaciones S.A. for Colombia; by Intersoft for South Africa; by Eyrolles for France; by International Thomson Publishing for Germany, Austria and Switzerland; by Distribuidora Cuspide for Argentina; by Livraria Cultura for Brazil; by Ediciones ZETA S.C.R. Ltda. for Peru; by WS Computer Publishing Corporation, Inc., for the Philippines; by Contemporanea de Ediciones for Venezuela; by Express Computer Distributors for the Caribbean and West Indies; by Micronesia Media Distributor, Inc. for Micronesia; by Grupo Editorial Norma S.A. for Guatemala; by Chips Computadoras S.A. de C.V. for Mexico; by Editorial Norma de Panama S.A. for Panama; by American Bookshops for Finland. Authorized Sales Agent: Anthony Rudkin Associates for the Middle East and North Africa.

For general information on IDG Books Worldwide's books in the U.S., please call our Consumer Customer Service department at 800-762-2974. For reseller information, including discounts and premium sales, please call our Reseller Customer Service department at 800-434-3422.

For information on where to purchase IDG Books Worldwide's books outside the U.S., please contact our International Sales department at 317-596-5530 or fax 317-596-5692.

For consumer information on foreign language translations, please contact our Customer Service department at 800-434-3422, fax 317-596-5692, or e-mail rights@idgbooks.com.

For information on licensing foreign or domestic rights, please phone +1-650-655-3109.

For sales inquiries and special prices for bulk quantities, please contact our Sales department at 650-655-3200 or write to the address above.

For information on using IDG Books Worldwide's books in the classroom or for ordering examination copies, please contact our Educational Sales department at 800-434-2086 or fax 317-596-5499.

For press review copies, author interviews, or other publicity information, please contact our Public Relations department at 650-655-3000 or fax 650-655-3299.

For authorization to photocopy items for corporate, personal, or educational use, please contact Copyright Clearance Center, 222 Rosewood Drive, Danvers, MA 01923, or fax 978-750-4470.

Library of Congress Cataloging-in-Publication Data
    Teach Yourself Microsoft FrontPage 2000
        p.   cm.
    ISBN 0-7645-7523-6 (alk. paper)
    1. Microsoft FrontPage.   2. Web sites--Design.   3. Web publishing.
TK5105.8885.M53T43 1999
005.7'2--dc21   99–10958
                                                                         CIP

ABOUT IDG BOOKS WORLDWIDE

Welcome to the world of IDG Books Worldwide.

IDG Books Worldwide, Inc., is a subsidiary of International Data Group, the world's largest publisher of computer-related information and the leading global provider of information services on information technology. IDG was founded more than 30 years ago by Patrick J. McGovern and now employs more than 9,000 people worldwide. IDG publishes more than 290 computer publications in over 75 countries. More than 90 million people read one or more IDG publications each month.

Launched in 1990, IDG Books Worldwide is today the #1 publisher of best-selling computer books in the United States. We are proud to have received eight awards from the Computer Press Association in recognition of editorial excellence and three from Computer Currents' First Annual Readers' Choice Awards. Our best-selling ...For Dummies® series has more than 50 million copies in print with translations in 31 languages. IDG Books Worldwide, through a joint venture with IDG's Hi-Tech Beijing, became the first U.S. publisher to publish a computer book in the People's Republic of China. In record time, IDG Books Worldwide has become the first choice for millions of readers around the world who want to learn how to better manage their businesses.

Our mission is simple: Every one of our books is designed to bring extra value and skill-building instructions to the reader. Our books are written by experts who understand and care about our readers. The knowledge base of our editorial staff comes from years of experience in publishing, education, and journalism — experience we use to produce books to carry us into the new millennium. In short, we care about books, so we attract the best people. We devote special attention to details such as audience, interior design, use of icons, and illustrations. And because we use an efficient process of authoring, editing, and desktop publishing our books electronically, we can spend more time ensuring superior content and less time on the technicalities of making books.

You can count on our commitment to deliver high-quality books at competitive prices on topics you want to read about. At IDG Books Worldwide, we continue in the IDG tradition of delivering quality for more than 30 years. You'll find no better book on a subject than one from IDG Books Worldwide.

John Kilcullen
Chairman and CEO
IDG Books Worldwide, Inc.

Steven Berkowitz
President and Publisher
IDG Books Worldwide, Inc.

WINNER

Eighth Annual Computer Press Awards ≥1992

WINNER

Ninth Annual Computer Press Awards ≥1993

WINNER

Tenth Annual Computer Press Awards≥1994

WINNER

Eleventh Annual Computer Press Awards ≥1995

IDG is the world's leading IT media, research and exposition company. Founded in 1964, IDG had 1997 revenues of $2.05 billion and has more than 9,000 employees worldwide. IDG offers the widest range of media options that reach IT buyers in 75 countries representing 95% of worldwide IT spending. IDG's diverse product and services portfolio spans six key areas including print publishing, online publishing, expositions and conferences, market research, education and training, and global marketing services. More than 90 million people read one or more of IDG's 290 magazines and newspapers, including IDG's leading global brands — Computerworld, PC World, Network World, Macworld and the Channel World family of publications. IDG Books Worldwide is one of the fastest-growing computer book publishers in the world, with more than 700 titles in 36 languages. The "...For Dummies®" series alone has more than 50 million copies in print. IDG offers online users the largest network of technology-specific Web sites around the world through IDG.net (http://www.idg.net), which comprises more than 225 targeted Web sites in 55 countries worldwide. International Data Corporation (IDC) is the world's largest provider of information technology data, analysis and consulting, with research centers in over 41 countries and more than 400 research analysts worldwide. IDG World Expo is a leading producer of more than 168 globally branded conferences and expositions in 35 countries including E3 (Electronic Entertainment Expo), Macworld Expo, ComNet, Windows World Expo, ICE (Internet Commerce Expo), Agenda, DEMO, and Spotlight. IDG's training subsidiary, ExecuTrain, is the world's largest computer training company, with more than 230 locations worldwide and 785 training courses. IDG Marketing Services helps industry-leading IT companies build international brand recognition by developing global integrated marketing programs via IDG's print, online and exposition products worldwide. Further information about the company can be found at www.idg.com.   1/24/99

Credits

Acquisitions Editor
Kathy Yankton

Development Editors
Valerie Perry
Katharine Dvorak

Technical Editor
Dennis Cohen

Copy Editors
Nancy Rapoport
William F. McManus

Book Designers
Daniel Ziegler Design
Cátálin Dulfu, Kurt Krames

Production
IDG Books Worldwide

Proofreading and Indexing
York Production Services

About the Authors

David Crowder and **Rhonda Crowder** run Far Horizons Software, a Web site design firm, and created the LinkFinder and NetWelcome sites. David founded three Internet mailing lists: Delphi Talk (for Borland Delphi programmers), JavaScript Talk (for Web designers), and Java Talk (for Java programmers). They also converted the Dade County version of the South Florida Building Code to hypertext in the wake of Hurricane Andrew. They are the authors of *Setting Up An Internet Site For Dummies* and recently finished *Teach Yourself the Internet*, both published by IDG Books Worldwide.

To Foxx

Welcome to
Teach Yourself

Welcome to *Teach Yourself,* a series read and trusted by millions for nearly a decade. Although you may have seen the *Teach Yourself* name on other books, ours is the original. In addition, no *Teach Yourself* series has ever delivered more on the promise of its name than this series. That's because IDG Books Worldwide recently transformed *Teach Yourself* into a new cutting-edge format that gives you all the information you need to learn quickly and easily.

Readers told us that they want to learn by doing and that they want to learn as much as they can in as short a time as possible. We listened to you and believe that our new task-by-task format and suite of learning tools deliver the book you need to successfully teach yourself any technology topic. Features such as our Personal Workbook, which lets you practice and reinforce the skills you've just learned, help ensure that you get full value out of the time you invest in your learning. Handy cross-references to related topics and online sites broaden your knowledge and give you control over the kind of information you want, when you want it.

More Answers . . .

In designing the latest incarnation of this series, we started with the premise that people like you, who are beginning to intermediate computer users, want to take control of their own learning. To do this, you need the proper tools to find answers to questions so you can solve problems now.

In designing a series of books that provide such tools, we created a unique and concise visual format. The added bonus: *Teach Yourself* books actually pack more information into their pages than other books written on the same subjects. Skill for skill, you typically get much more information in a *Teach Yourself* book. In fact, *Teach Yourself* books, on average, cover twice the skills covered by other computer books — as many as 125 skills per book — so they're more likely to address your specific needs.

...In Less Time

We know you don't want to spend twice the time to get all this great information, so we provide lots of time-saving features:

- ▶ A modular task-by-task organization of information: Any task you want to perform is easy to find and includes simple-to-follow steps.
- ▶ A larger size than standard makes the book easy to read and convenient to use at a computer workstation. The large format also enables us to include many more illustrations — 500 screen illustrations show you how to get everything done!
- ▶ A Personal Workbook at the end of each chapter reinforces learning with extra practice, real-world applications for your learning, and questions and answers to test your knowledge.
- ▶ Cross-references appearing at the bottom of each task page refer you to related information, providing a path through the book for learning particular aspects of the software thoroughly.

- ▶ A Find It Online feature offers valuable ideas on where to go on the Internet to get more information or to download useful files.
- ▶ Take Note sidebars provide added-value information from our expert authors for more in-depth learning.
- ▶ An attractive, consistent organization of information helps you quickly find and learn the skills you need.

These Teach Yourself features are designed to help you learn the essential skills about a technology in the least amount of time, with the most benefit. We've placed these features consistently throughout the book, so you quickly learn where to go to find just the information you need — whether you work through the book from cover to cover or use it later to solve a new problem.

You will find a Teach Yourself book on almost any technology subject — from the Internet to Windows to Microsoft Office. Take control of your learning today, with IDG Books Worldwide's Teach Yourself series.

Teach Yourself
More Answers in Less Time

Go to this area if you want special tips, cautions, and notes that provide added insight into the current task.

Search through the task headings to find the topic you want right away. To learn a new skill, search the contents, chapter opener, or the extensive index to find what you need. Then find — at a glance — the clear task heading that matches it.

Learn the concepts behind the task at hand and, more important, learn how the task is relevant in the real world. Time-saving suggestions and advice show you how to make the most of each skill.

After you learn the task at hand, you may have more questions, or you may want to read about other tasks related to the topic. Use the cross-references to find different tasks to make your learning more efficient.

Creating Lists

Lists are a common method of organizing information on Web pages. FrontPage offers five different kinds of lists: bulleted, numbered, definition, directory, and menu lists. Of these five, bulleted lists and numbered lists are often used on a regular basis, while definition lists are very specialized. Directory lists and menu lists are never used at all, and don't work properly in either of the major browsers, anyway.

The two most commonly used lists are bulleted lists and numbered lists (known in HTML parlance as *unordered lists* and *ordered lists*). Both kinds are available in FrontPage by just clicking a button on the toolbar (see the upper-left figure, facing page).

Once you've clicked the numbered list button, the numeral 1 will appear on the Web page. Type an entry and hit the Enter key. The next line will show the numeral 2. Continue to type entries until you're done. When you've made the last entry in the list, just hit the Enter key on the final line without typing an entry. The entries don't have to be text — you can use images or hyperlinks in lists as well.

The bulleted list works the same way, except that the lines show bullets instead of numbers.

Definition lists are meant for dictionaries or glossaries. Place the cursor on the line where you want to put the first term, and then select Defined Term from the Paragraph Styles drop-down list. Type the term you want to define and hit the Enter key. The next line will be automatically indented and set with the

Definition style. Type the definition and hit the Enter key again. The next line will be set for the Defined Term style. To end the list, hit the Enter key instead of typing a term.

The remaining two types of lists, the directory list and menu list (both available from the Paragraph Styles drop-down menu), are *deprecated* by the World Wide Web Consortium (W3C). They work identically to bulleted lists and have no real purpose of their own.

TAKE NOTE

WHAT IS DEPRECATION, ANYWAY?
Deprecation is the first step toward discontinuing a feature in HTML. Deprecated features are supposed to be supported by browsers which adhere to the HTML standard, but their usage is officially frowned upon. There's no enforcement capability in the W3C, so Web developers just go on using whatever works, regardless of the official position.

AND WHAT'S THE W3C?
The World Wide Web Consortium is a group composed of any organization with $150,000 to spare ($50,000 dues per year with a three-year commitment). If you're interested in joining as an individual, the cost is "only" one-tenth that of organizational membership. There are no membership requirements other than the dues. The W3C has done a creditable job, nonetheless, of developing a series of standards which attempt to keep the World Wide Web organized.

CROSS-REFERENCE
See the preceding section for more information on paragraph styles.

FIND IT ONLINE
You can view the W3C specs on lists at **http://www. w3.org/TR/REC-html40/struct/lists.html.**

Use the Find It Online element to locate Internet resources that provide more background, take you on interesting side trips, and offer additional tools for mastering and using the skills you need. (Occasionally you'll find a handy shortcut here.)

The current chapter name and number always appear in the top right-hand corner of every task spread, so you always know exactly where you are in the book.

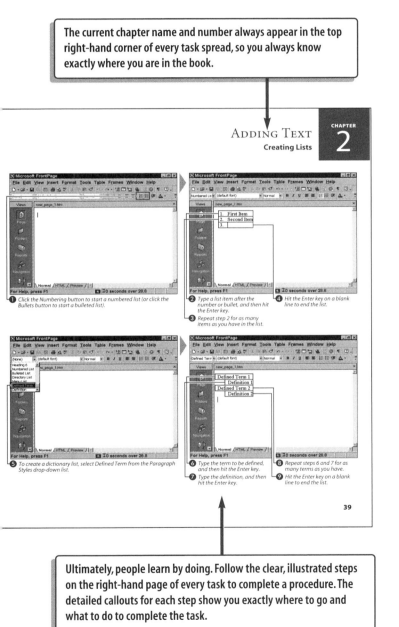

Who This Book Is For

This book is written for you, a beginning to intermediate PC user who isn't afraid to take charge of his or her own learning experience. You don't want a lot of technical jargon; you *do* want to learn as much about PC technology as you can in a limited amount of time. You need a book that is straightforward, easy to follow, and logically organized, so you can find answers to your questions easily. And, you appreciate simple-to-use tools such as handy cross-references and visual step-by-step procedures that help you make the most of your learning. We have created the unique *Teach Yourself* format specifically to meet your needs.

Ultimately, people learn by doing. Follow the clear, illustrated steps on the right-hand page of every task to complete a procedure. The detailed callouts for each step show you exactly where to go and what to do to complete the task.

Personal Workbook

It's a well-known fact that much of what we learn is lost soon after we learn it if we don't reinforce our newly acquired skills with practice and repetition. That's why each *Teach Yourself* chapter ends with your own Personal Workbook. Here's where you can get extra practice, test your knowledge, and discover ideas for using what you've learned in the real world. There's even a Visual Quiz to help you remember your way around the topic's software environment.

Feedback

Please let us know what you think about this book, and whether you have any suggestions for improvements. You can send questions and comments to the *Teach Yourself* editors on the IDG Books Worldwide Web site at **www.idgbooks.com.**

Personal Workbook

Q&A

❶ How do you enter special characters not found on your keyboard?

_____
_____
_____

❷ What if special characters are not found in FrontPage either?

_____
_____
_____

❸ What is the purpose of horizontal lines?

_____
_____
_____

❹ How many sizes of headings are there in HTML?

_____
_____
_____
_____

❺ What kind of font does the formatted paragraph style use?

_____
_____
_____

❻ What are the two most common kinds of lists?

_____
_____
_____

❼ What does red underlining mean on your Web page?

_____
_____
_____

❽ What does a validation program do?

_____
_____
_____

ANSWERS: PAGE 322

44

After working through the tasks in each chapter, you can test your progress and reinforce your learning by answering the questions in the Q&A section. Then check your answers in the Personal Workbook Answers appendix at the back of the book.

Another practical way to reinforce your skills is to do additional exercises on the same skills you just learned without the benefit of the chapter's visual steps. If you struggle with any of these exercises, it's a good idea to refer to the chapter's tasks to be sure you've mastered them.

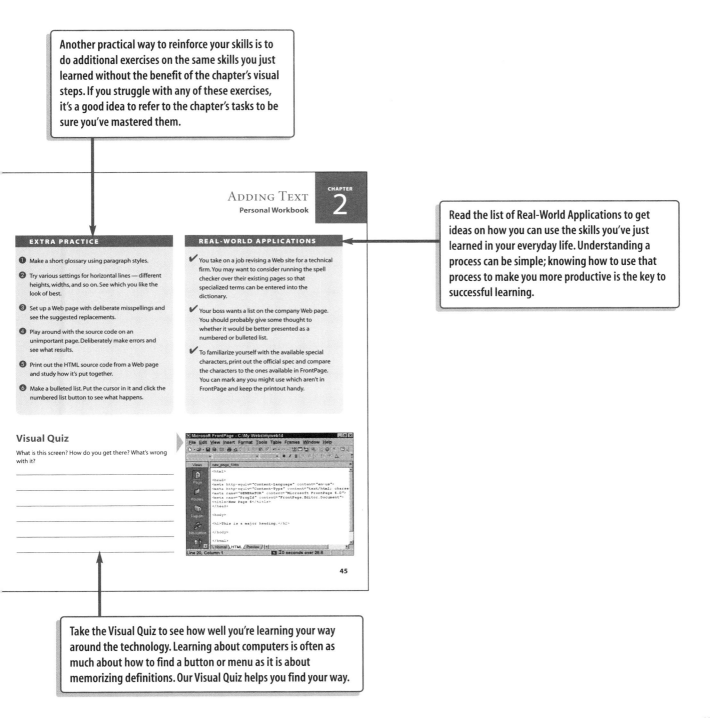

ADDING TEXT
Personal Workbook

CHAPTER 2

Read the list of Real-World Applications to get ideas on how you can use the skills you've just learned in your everyday life. Understanding a process can be simple; knowing how to use that process to make you more productive is the key to successful learning.

EXTRA PRACTICE

1. Make a short glossary using paragraph styles.
2. Try various settings for horizontal lines — different heights, widths, and so on. See which you like the look of best.
3. Set up a Web page with deliberate misspellings and see the suggested replacements.
4. Play around with the source code on an unimportant page. Deliberately make errors and see what results.
5. Print out the HTML source code from a Web page and study how it's put together.
6. Make a bulleted list. Put the cursor in it and click the numbered list button to see what happens.

REAL-WORLD APPLICATIONS

✔ You take on a job revising a Web site for a technical firm. You may want to consider running the spell checker over their existing pages so that specialized terms can be entered into the dictionary.

✔ Your boss wants a list on the company Web page. You should probably give some thought to whether it would be better presented as a numbered or bulleted list.

✔ To familiarize yourself with the available special characters, print out the official spec and compare the characters to the ones available in FrontPage. You can mark any you might use which aren't in FrontPage and keep the printout handy.

Visual Quiz

What is this screen? How do you get there? What's wrong with it?

Take the Visual Quiz to see how well you're learning your way around the technology. Learning about computers is often as much about how to find a button or menu as it is about memorizing definitions. Our Visual Quiz helps you find your way.

Acknowledgments

We'd like to thank Kathy Yankton, Katharine Dvorak, Valerie Perry, Dennis Cohen, Nancy Rapoport, Karen York, and all the other folks who work ceaselessly behind the scenes at IDG Books Worldwide. And, as always, we are grateful to have such a good agent in David Fugate of Waterside Productions.

Contents

Contents

CONTENTS

CONTENTS

Teach Yourself
Microsoft®
FrontPage® 2000

PART

I

FrontPage Webs

The chapters in this section provide information on the basic features necessary to create FrontPage webs and the Web pages that they contain. The first chapter covers the creation of the webs themselves, the addition of Web pages to them (whether by importation or addition), and the web publication process.

The second chapter covers how to add text to your Web pages. You'll find information on entering special symbols, using horizontal lines, applying paragraph styles, and using lists and the spell checker. This chapter also covers viewing, editing, and printing the HTML source code of Web pages.

In the third chapter, you learn about some of the more sophisticated features of FrontPage, including aligning and indenting textual elements, changing font faces and size, and altering text style and color. You'll also learn about background color.

The fourth chapter covers how URLs and hyperlinks work together to connect the different parts of the World Wide Web.

CHAPTER 1

MASTER
THESE
SKILLS

▶ Creating New Webs

▶ Adding and Deleting Pages

▶ Importing Existing Pages

▶ Importing Existing Webs from the WWW

▶ Importing Existing Webs from Files

▶ Opening Webs and Pages

▶ Publishing Your Webs

Creating FrontPage Webs

While anyone with a text editor and a modicum of programming knowledge can crank out an acceptable Web page in pretty short order, it's a different matter when it comes to managing a Web site. Web sites — collections of several interrelated Web pages — can rapidly reach a challenging level of complexity. That's where FrontPage really shines. Although it's versatile enough so that you can also use it to create single, stand-alone Web pages, it's designed to handle an entire Web site.

In the parlance of the program, a Web site is known as a *FrontPage web*. FrontPage webs include all aspects of the Web pages in the site. Blank pages, text, images, sounds, JavaScript programs — all the myriad of items you can put into the World Wide Web — can be managed as a single entity in a FrontPage web. It doesn't matter to FrontPage if the site includes a thousand pages with all the trimmings or if it's composed of just one page with nothing but simple text on it.

There are four basic ways to get a web going in FrontPage: create one from scratch, import the files from an existing Web site (either on the World Wide Web or a local folder), or use wizards or templates. *Wizards* are short programs built into FrontPage that walk you through the Web site creation process, asking you pertinent questions about design and content one step at a time. Templates are predesigned webs where all you need to do is fill in the particulars after the Web pages are generated by FrontPage.

The same basic options hold when you're creating a single Web page in FrontPage. In this chapter, we'll cover how to create both individual pages and entire webs, how to add ones that were made with other Web creation programs, and how to open them once you've made them or imported them into your local system.

After your webs are created, you'll want to publish them — upload them to the World Wide Web or another storage device on your system or local network. Once again, FrontPage makes the job easy for you. You don't have to wrestle with hard-to-use FTP programs anymore — just push a button and tell FrontPage where to put the files.

Creating New Webs

For each Web site you want to create, you'll need to make a new FrontPage web. Doing this sets aside a separate folder for the Web pages that will go into it. FrontPage offers a variety of assistance to you in creating new webs. Importing files and webs is covered later in this chapter, and web creation wizards are covered in Chapter 5. For now, we'll look at creating your own FrontPage web from scratch.

There are two ways to do this — the *blank web* and the *one-page web*. The blank web option creates a web with nothing in it, while the one-page web option creates a web with a single blank Web page in it. In either case, you'll be adding your own material to the web, but the one-page web starts you off with the home page already in place.

To start a new web, click the arrow next to the New button and select Web from the drop-down menu (in some views, the New button is sufficient by itself). Alternately, you can select File ➪ New ➪ Web from the main menu.

Any of these approaches takes you to the New dialog box (see the figure in the upper-right corner of the facing page). Once you've chosen one of the types of webs available, you can specify the location for the files. FrontPage will suggest one, and you can ignore this detail if you don't care about it. From here, click the OK button and FrontPage will take care of the rest, including creating the folder for the files.

TAKE NOTE

START OUT LOCALLY

Although you can use FrontPage to create, manage, or make changes to a Web site that's on a remote server, it's best to keep a local copy and make any alterations on it, and then upload (or "publish") the Web pages and other files to the remote Web server when you're done. This gives you an extra layer of protection — if something should happen to the files on the Web server, you'll still have your own up-to-date copy at hand.

WHERE DOES IT GO?

When you installed FrontPage, a folder called "My Webs" was automatically created, and your own webs will be placed there by default unless you specify otherwise. Also, the first web you create will be named "myweb" and go into C:\My Webs\myweb unless you tell FrontPage somewhere else to place it. (The name of the web is the name of the folder.) Subsequent webs will be named "myweb2," "myweb3," and so on.

WEBS AND SUBWEBS

You can build a FrontPage web that's subsidiary to the main web. When you create a new web, select the Add to current Web check box in the New dialog box, and a subweb will be created.

CROSS-REFERENCE

See Chapter 5 for details on specialized web creation wizards.

FIND IT ONLINE

The FrontPage home page is at http://www.microsoft.com/frontpage/default.htm.

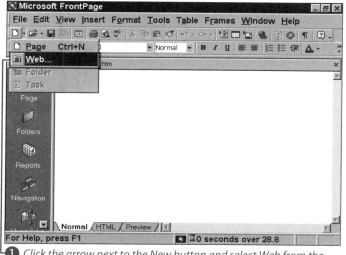

1 *Click the arrow next to the New button and select Web from the drop-down menu.*

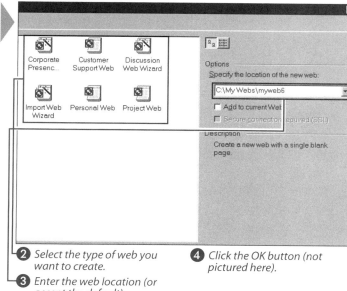

2 *Select the type of web you want to create.*

3 *Enter the web location (or accept the default).*

4 *Click the OK button (not pictured here).*

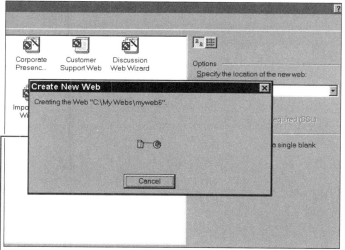

■ *FrontPage displays a message that it is creating the web.*

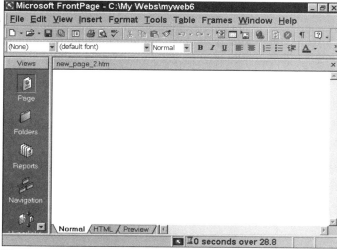

■ *The new web is created, and its location appears in the title bar.*

Adding and Deleting Pages

Whether you create a blank web or use one of the templates or wizards that generates a web with populated pages, you'll no doubt want to add and delete pages to and from your web from time to time.

FrontPage has two basic methods for creating new pages: the New Page button and the File ⇨ New ⇨ Page menu option. If you use the New Page button to create new pages, you can create only a blank page (see the figures on the upper left and upper right of the facing page). To utilize any of FrontPage's page creation templates and wizards, you have to select File ⇨ New ⇨ Page from the menu.

In the New dialog box (see the lower-right figure on the facing page), FrontPage offers a variety of templates and wizards to assist you in creating new pages, just as it does for creating entire webs. A *template* offers a one-step process that makes a new page with all the basic elements already in place for you, but where you need to replace the suggested elements with specifics of your own.

A *wizard*, on the other hand, is a small program that uses a series of dialog boxes to present you with specific choices, the answers to which will give it the information it needs to construct a ready-to-go Web page. Even with a wizard, you'll probably still need to do a little bit of customization before you're totally satisfied, but it's a much bigger step in the right direction than a mere template.

You might want to take a moment to explore the various options available to you here. Click each of the page icons in the New dialog box and take a look at the Preview window on the right side of it. FrontPage has a wide variety of page designs available covering a lot of different design possibilities. Even though you won't be using all of them at the moment, it's a really good idea to be familiar with them.

Continued

TAKE NOTE

BLANK WEB PAGES REALLY AREN'T
Web pages have lots of things on them that never get displayed by Web browsers. If you click the HTML tab in the Page view, you'll see that there's actually a fair amount of HTML code that goes into the structure of a Web page before anything ever shows up on it that'll be visible to a person viewing the page in a Web browser.

A VIEW TOWARD CREATING NEW PAGES
You can only create new pages under the Page, Folders, and Navigation views.

CROSS-REFERENCE
See Chapter 13 for more information on customizing FrontPage.

FIND IT ONLINE
You'll find lots of articles on FrontPage at
http://www.microsoft.com/workshop/
c-frame.htm#/workshop/languages/fp/default.asp.

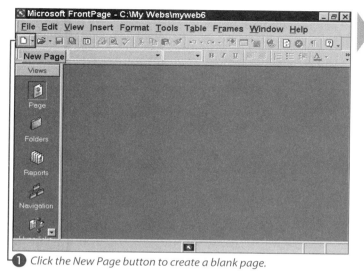

❶ Click the New Page button to create a blank page.

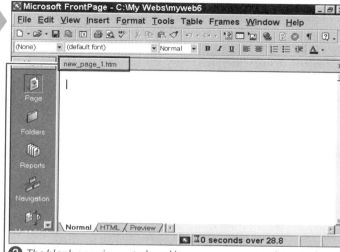

❷ The blank page is created, and its name appears at the top of your document window.

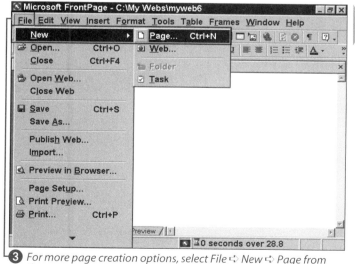

❸ For more page creation options, select File ➪ New ➪ Page from the menu.

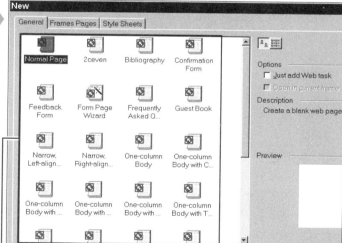

❹ The General tab of the New dialog box shows several templates and wizards.

Adding and Deleting Pages

Continued

The default Normal Page design (the one that's selected when you first look at the New dialog box) is not really of much interest — it's just the same old blank page you'd get if you had simply clicked on the New Button. Others, however, like the Bibliography or Frequently Asked Questions (FAQ) templates, can give you a real boost in getting your page going the way you want.

Once you've settled on the page design you want, just click the OK button and FrontPage will take over from there. The basic page design is created, but you still have to fill in the exact details (and, of course, you'll have to delete the instructions from the top of the page when you're done).

What about getting rid of pages from your FrontPage web? If you've created a Web page that you don't really like and you haven't yet saved it, simply select File ⇨ Close to delete it from the main menu. If you've already saved it, you'll have to switch to a view that shows the file listings (like the Folders or Hyperlinks view), and then select the filename (or names) in the listings. You can then press the Delete key. Alternately, you can right-click the filename and select the Delete option from the popup menu as shown in the figure on the lower left. With either approach, FrontPage will ask if you really want to delete the file or files (see the lower-right figure on the facing page). To delete one file, click the Yes button. If you've selected several files and don't want to have to confirm each deletion, click the Yes to All button. Clicking the No button spares one file from deletion, and the Cancel button, of course, aborts the operation.

TAKE NOTE

MAKE SURE YOU SAVE THOSE PAGES

Creating a FrontPage web is all you need to do for it. Since the actual FrontPage web is basically nothing but a series of folders with preassigned names, there's no option to save a web – the folders are created, and that's that. Individual pages are another matter entirely. When you create a new page or make changes to an existing page, you need to save the page even though it's a part of an existing web. Make it a practice to save your pages early, regularly, and often.

SAVING FILES TO AVOID THE FILE CLOSE TRAP

FrontPage will double check with you if you use the Delete key or the Delete option from the popup menu to try to delete a file that's been saved. Unfortunately, this is not the case with the main menu's File ⇨ Close option. If you use that approach, you'll receive no warning or second chance. If you close a file that hasn't been saved, it's just plain gone, right away, no questions asked.

CROSS-REFERENCE

See Chapter 11 for more information on page templates.

FIND IT ONLINE

You can find the FrontPage User Group at **http://www.fpug.com/**.

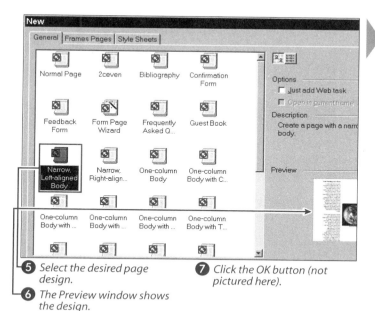

5 Select the desired page design.

6 The Preview window shows the design.

7 Click the OK button (not pictured here).

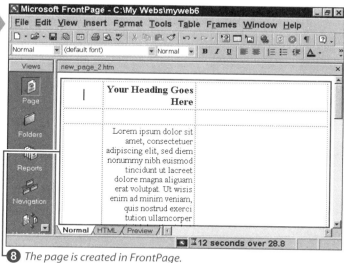

8 The page is created in FrontPage.

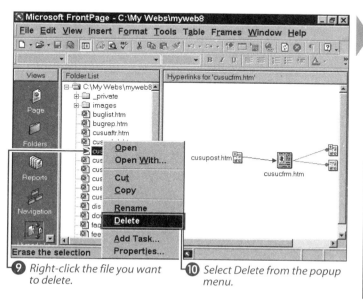

9 Right-click the file you want to delete.

10 Select Delete from the popup menu.

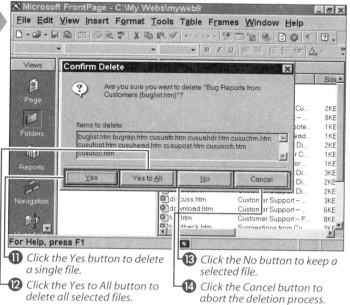

11 Click the Yes button to delete a single file.

12 Click the Yes to All button to delete all selected files.

13 Click the No button to keep a selected file.

14 Click the Cancel button to abort the deletion process.

Importing Existing Pages

If you have a FrontPage web, and you want to add one or more pages to it that were created with some other Web page design program, FrontPage provides a handy solution: the file importation feature. You can also use this feature to import pages from another FrontPage web.

First, make sure that the FrontPage web to which you want to add the old pages is open, and then select File ⇨ Import from the menu. This will bring up the Import File to FrontPage Web dialog box as shown in the figure in the upper-right corner of the facing page. At first, of course, the file listing is empty. There are three basic options in file importation, represented by the three top buttons on the right-hand side of this dialog box. The first two buttons are for adding individual files or entire folders from your local hard drive, floppy disk, or other storage medium. The third button is for importing files from a World Wide Web site. This third button invokes the Import Web Wizard, which is covered in the next section of this chapter, "Importing Existing Webs from the WWW."

Clicking on the Add File button brings up a standard file dialog box as shown in the lower-left figure on the facing page. Use it to navigate to the folder that contains the file or files you want to import. Then select the filename(s) and click the Open button to add them to the file listing in the Import File to FrontPage Web dialog box.

Clicking on the Add Folder button puts you in a similar situation, except that, of course, the dialog box is geared toward locating folders instead of files. At first, in fact, it doesn't even reach down to the folder level, but lists all the elements of the desktop. You'll need to click the icon for the drive you want to access before looking for the folder.

Continued

TAKE NOTE

▶ DON'T JUST COPY THE FILES

You have to import the files into the web via FrontPage. If you just copy the files into the web's folder with Windows Explorer, they haven't been added to the web at all; they're just occupying the same area on your hard drive. Without the importation feature, FrontPage won't recognize them as part of the web.

▶ MAKE SURE THAT WEB IS OPEN

If you try to use the File ⇨ Import menu option from FrontPage without having a web open, you'll have a totally different experience from the one you wanted. Under those circumstances, FrontPage assumes you want to import a web, not a file, and it will bring up the New Web dialog box with the Import Web Wizard selected.

CROSS-REFERENCE

See the following two sections in this chapter on importing entire webs.

FIND IT ONLINE

You can find the FrontPage Network at http://www.frontpagenetwork.com/.

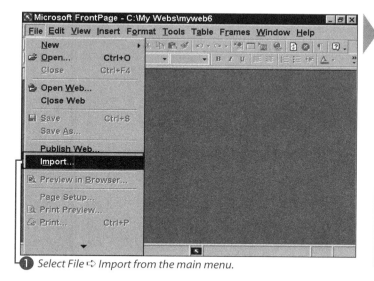

① Select File ➪ Import from the main menu.

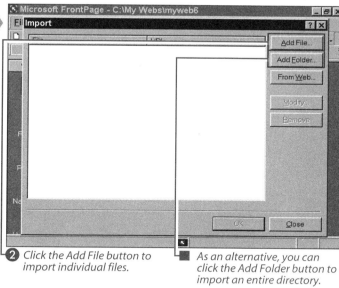

② Click the Add File button to import individual files.

As an alternative, you can click the Add Folder button to import an entire directory.

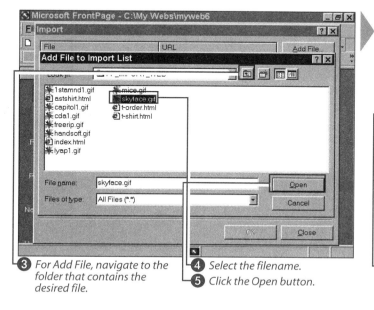

③ For Add File, navigate to the folder that contains the desired file.

④ Select the filename.

⑤ Click the Open button.

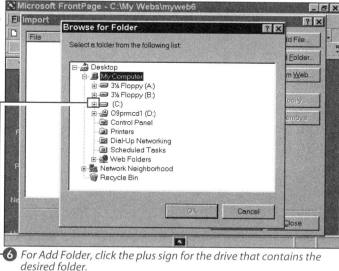

⑥ For Add Folder, click the plus sign for the drive that contains the desired folder.

Once you've got the folder listing for the drive that holds the folder you want, scroll until you find the desired folder. Select it as shown in the figure in the upper-left corner of the next page, and then click the OK button.

Whether you were going for a single file with the Add File button or an entire folder with the Add Folder button, the chosen file or files are now listed in the Import File to FrontPage Web dialog box (upper-right figure, facing page). If everything's just the way you want it, then all you have to do is click the OK button.

If there is a problem, however, FrontPage gives you the opportunity to fix it without having to start all over again. Specifically, there are two things you can do at this point. Your first option is to delete files from the listing. If you're importing a single file, odds are that you won't need to do this, of course, but you might well realize at this point that you don't really want every file that was in a folder you're importing. To delete a file from the listing, select it and click the Remove button (this only removes the filename from the listing; it does not delete the actual file).

The other option, Edit URL, is not so obvious. When you import files into FrontPage, they normally go into the main web folder. However, if you've been using one of the views that shows files for other purposes prior to importing a folder or files, you may have selected a FrontPage web folder other than the top one. If you did, and you didn't mean to do this, then the Edit URL button can be your salvation. Select a filename, and then click the Edit URL button. This brings up the Edit URL dialog box as shown in the figure in the lower-left corner of the next page. In this example, the file in question is headed for the images subfolder (a regular part of a FrontPage web) instead of the main web folder. To fix that, you'd just delete the "images/" part of the URL and then click the OK button.

TAKE NOTE

YOU MIGHT WANT TO START OVER ANYWAY

If you're importing a folder full of files and you find, via the Edit URL button, that they're headed for the wrong FrontPage web folder, you might not want to take the time to change the destination folder for each individual file. In that case, you'd probably be better off to just click the Close button and start over again.

CROSS-REFERENCE

See Chapter 13 for more information on how to customize FrontPage.

FIND IT ONLINE

Mike's FrontPage FAQ Archive is located at http://www.simplenet.com/frontpage/.

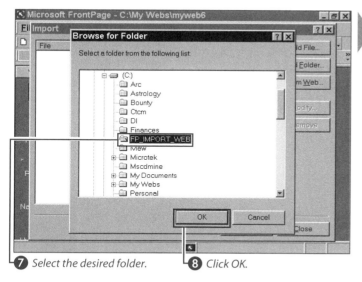

7 Select the desired folder.

8 Click OK.

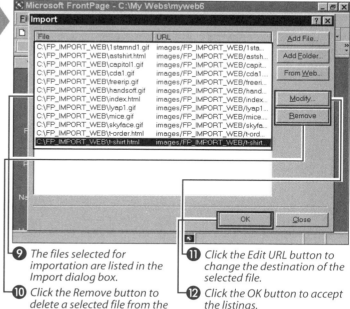

9 The files selected for importation are listed in the Import dialog box.

10 Click the Remove button to delete a selected file from the listing.

11 Click the Edit URL button to change the destination of the selected file.

12 Click the OK button to accept the listings.

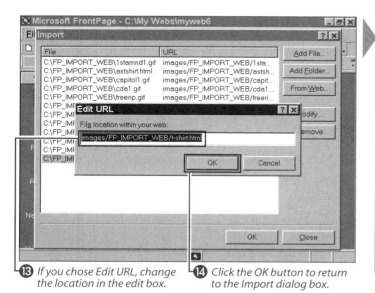

13 If you chose Edit URL, change the location in the edit box.

14 Click the OK button to return to the Import dialog box.

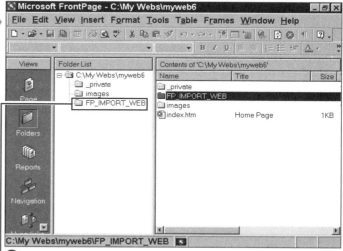

15 The imported file or folder is added to the FrontPage web.

Importing Existing Webs from the WWW

Although you may be new to using FrontPage, you may already have one or more Web sites you'd like to use it with. Or perhaps you're an old hand with it, but need to work with existing Web sites that were originally developed with other page creation systems. Either way, the Import Web Wizard is just the ticket. With it, you can effortlessly convert an entire Web site into the FrontPage way of doing things.

You're likely using this book as a cookbook — flipping to particular sections to find specific solutions — and haven't looked into the preceding and succeeding sections of this chapter. If so, you should be aware that those sections cover how to import individual files or folders into FrontPage as well as how to import Web sites from disk as opposed to from the World Wide Web.

To get started with a WWW Web site importation, click the New Web button. If you're in a view that shows the New Page button instead, then click the arrow next to the New Page button and select Web from the drop-down menu (see the upper-left figure, facing page).

In the New dialog box, select the Import Web Wizard. If you want to set a particular location for the web you're going to import, then enter it. Otherwise, just accept FrontPage's designation for the web location. Click the OK button to proceed.

At this point, if you're putting the web into a new folder, you'll be asked if you want to create the folder. Click the Yes button (unless you want to abort the importation process, in which case you should click the No button). The Import Web Wizard is now launched.

Continued

Continued

TAKE NOTE

IMPORTING WHAT?

Actually, the phrase "importing a web" is a bit of a misnomer. If a Web site is already structured as a FrontPage web, there's no need to import it at all; you just open it like any other web. When you're importing into FrontPage, you're actually importing a nonweb.

USING THE MENU

You can get into the Import Web Wizard from the main menu in two ways. The first, and obvious course is to select File ➪ New ➪ Web from the menu, and then to choose the Import Web Wizard from the New dialog box. The other option is a bit trickier. You can select File ➪ Import from the menu, and this will bring up the New dialog box with the Import Web Wizard already selected for you. But this doesn't work unless you do it when you first start FrontPage, or right after you've deleted a web, because the File ➪ Import command, if used with a web open, invokes a file importation process instead of a web importation one.

CROSS-REFERENCE
See "Creating New Webs" at the beginning of this chapter.

FIND IT ONLINE
Dynamic Net has a FrontPage tech support site at http://dynamicnet.net/support/frontpage.htm.

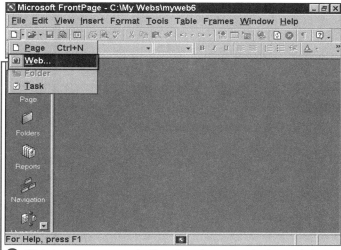

❶ Click the arrow next to the New Page button and select Web from the drop-down menu.

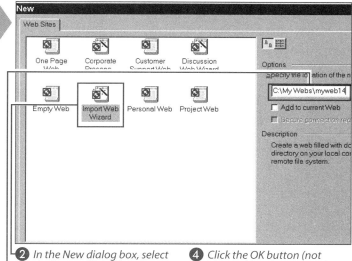

❷ In the New dialog box, select the Import Web Wizard.

❸ If you want to set a particular location for the web you're going to import, enter it.

❹ Click the OK button (not pictured here) to proceed.

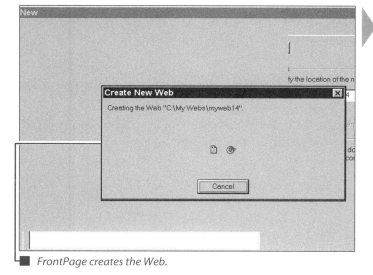

■ FrontPage creates the Web.

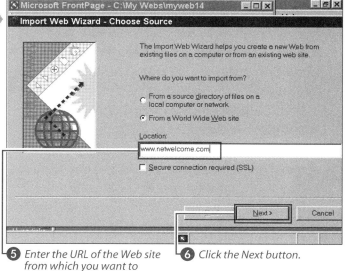

❺ Enter the URL of the Web site from which you want to import.

❻ Click the Next button.

Importing Existing Webs from the WWW *Continued*

The next screen in the Import Web Wizard is the Import Web Wizard - Choose Download Amount dialog box (see the upper-left figure, facing page). This comes in handy if you're importing a very large Web site. However, it has its limitations, like any automatic system does when compared to human supervision of the process. If you absolutely, definitely want to download everything in the entire Web site, regardless of how large it is or what type of file it is, then make sure all the check boxes in this dialog box are cleared. Otherwise, you can select how many levels down the Import Web Wizard will go to find files (the default is five levels) and the largest file size in kilobytes to be downloaded (the default is 500K). You can also choose to download only text and image files. (The default in this case is to download all files of any type, since the check box is unchecked.)

The next screen (the upper-right figure on the facing page) is the final one. Your only options here are to go back and change your responses on earlier screens, to cancel, or to click the Finish button to initiate the Web site importation process.

Once the importation begins, an Import Web Progress dialog box will keep you informed of what is being downloaded, where it's coming from, and where it's going to (see the lower-left figure). You can abort the download process by clicking the Cancel button if you wish.

When the download process is completed, all the files which fit the criteria you established will be in a FrontPage web on your local system.

TAKE NOTE

LONG FILENAME EXTENSIONS AND FRONTPAGE

FrontPage has one incredibly irritating feature that is absolutely inexplicable. It automatically renames imported files ending in the .html file extension so that they end in the .htm file extension instead. Since there isn't a modern computer system in common usage that isn't capable of handling a four character file extension, and since the proper file extension for Web pages is .html, there seems to be no valid reason in the world for this. After all, there just aren't that many DOS-based Web browsers out there, and Windows has been through two incarnations since version 3.1.

THERE'S MORE THAN TEXT AND IMAGES TO THE WWW

If you choose to download only text and image files in the Choose Download Amount dialog box, you could end up with a pretty useless copy of a Web site. Many sites on the World Wide Web today use sound files or video clips, and quite a lot of them use Perl or other program files as a part of their form processing repertoire.

CROSS-REFERENCE
See the next section on importing existing webs from local files.

FIND IT ONLINE
Ziff-Davis has a FrontPage tip-of-the-week page at http://www.cobbtips.com/mfp/zdt-f.htm.

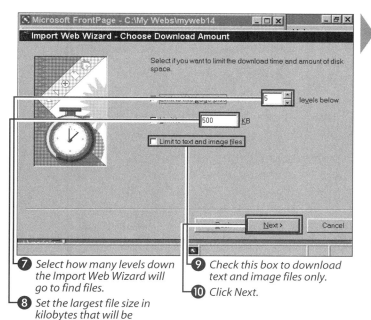

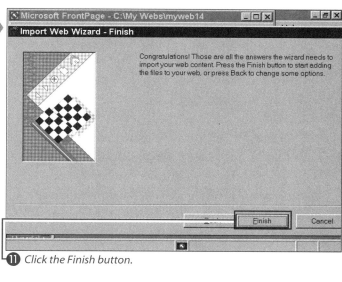

7 Select how many levels down the Import Web Wizard will go to find files.

8 Set the largest file size in kilobytes that will be downloaded.

9 Check this box to download text and image files only.

10 Click Next.

11 Click the Finish button.

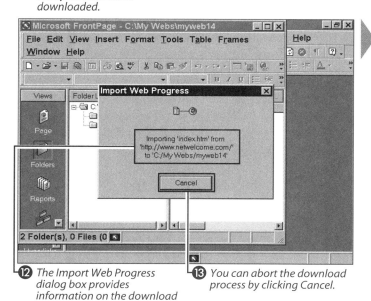

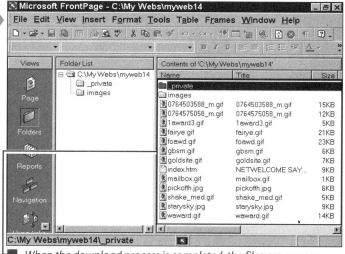

12 The Import Web Progress dialog box provides information on the download process.

13 You can abort the download process by clicking Cancel.

■ When the download process is completed, the files are on your local system.

Importing Existing Webs from Files

If a Web site exists as a set of files on your hard drive, floppy disk, or other storage medium, then the procedure you need to follow to import that site into FrontPage, while similar to the one for importing a Web site from the World Wide Web, has significant differences.

The first few steps are the same as for WWW importation. You click the New Web button to get things started. If you're in a view that shows the New Page button instead, then click the down arrow next to the New Page button and select Web from the drop-down menu (see the figure in the upper-left corner of the facing page).

In the New dialog box, select the Import Web Wizard (see the upper-right figure). If you want to set the location of the folder for the web you're going to import, enter it. Otherwise, just click the OK button.

If you're putting the web into a new folder, you'll be asked if you want to create the folder (see the lower-left figure). Click Yes (unless you want to abort the importation process, in which case you should click No). The Import Web Wizard is now launched.

Now the process begins to differ from the one above (see the lower-right figure). This time, you'll need to select the top radio button on the opening screen, the one that says "From a source directory of files on a local computer or network." This changes the prefix in the Location edit box from **http://** to **C:** (or whatever your local drive designation is). If you

know the location, you can just type it in, or you can click the Browse button to search for the folder on your local drive.

Continued

Continued

TAKE NOTE

▶ NO DOWNLOAD LIMITS HERE

This version of the Import Web Wizard doesn't offer the option of limiting the types or sizes of files which you choose to import. With the speed of local or network disk access as compared to downloading from the World Wide Web, this is not a problem; but it also doesn't give you the option to limit the depth of importation, which could mean you'll spend some time deleting unwanted files.

▶ EXCEPT IN ONE WAY

You can limit the depth of importation — sort of. By choosing whether to click the Include Subfolders check box (see the figure on the lower right), you can increase or decrease the number of files coming in. This is not really the same thing as levels of Web page links, but it's as close as you'll get with a file Web importation. Of course, if there are files in a subfolder that are important to the web's functioning, make sure to include them!

CROSS-REFERENCE

See the preceding section on importing webs from the WWW.

FIND IT ONLINE

You'll find lots of FrontPage tips at **http://www. v-page.com/fptips3.htm**.

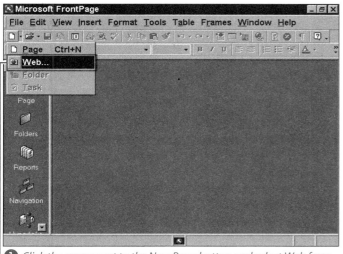

❶ Click the arrow next to the New Page button and select Web from the drop-down menu.

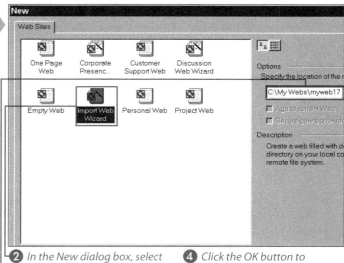

❷ In the New dialog box, select the Import Web Wizard.

❸ If you want to set a particular location for the web you're going to import, enter it.

❹ Click the OK button to proceed (not pictured here).

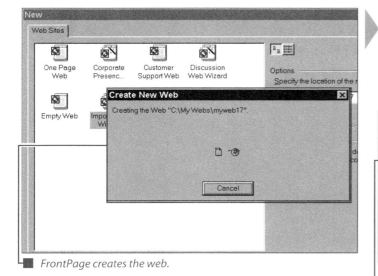

■ FrontPage creates the web.

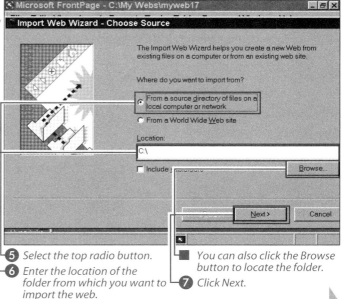

❺ Select the top radio button.

❻ Enter the location of the folder from which you want to import the web.

■ You can also click the Browse button to locate the folder.

❼ Click Next.

21

Importing Existing Webs
from Files *Continued*

If you do click the Browse button, the Browse for Folder dialog box appears (as illustrated in the upper-left figure on the facing page). Scroll down until you see the name of the folder from which you want to import the Web site (you may need to click the plus sign to expand the view and find a sub-folder). Once you've found the folder, select it and click the OK button to return to the Import Web Wizard, where you'll need to click Next to proceed.

In the upper-right figure on the facing page, you'll see what should be the next screen. It lists the files which were found in the folder you selected. If there are many files, you may have to scroll down to see the entire listing. If there are any files in the listing that you don't want included in the importation, select them and click the Exclude button. This won't delete the file from your disk; it just removes the filename from the listing in this dialog box so that it won't be imported along with the other files in the listing. When you're satisfied with the list of files to be included, click the Next button.

The next screen is the final one of the Import Web Wizard. Unless you want to hit the Back button to change some of your previous choices, just click the Finish button to wrap things up and get the web imported. Things happen so quickly here compared to downloading files from the World Wide Web that you'll barely have time to blink before the web is completed. There's no dialog box to show the progress of the file importation. If you want to see the files, just go to any view that includes a file listing (like the Folders view) and take a look. Remember that there won't be anything showing in the Page view unless you double-click one of the filenames in the Folders view (or any other view showing filenames).

TAKE NOTE

THERE'S NO UNDO BUTTON HERE

If you exclude a file you didn't mean to, there is no Undo button to reverse the action, but you can click the Refresh button. The drawback to this is that it restores all the files from the selected folder to the list, not just the most recent one you excluded. If you've cleared out several files, this means that you have to start excluding them all over again. In that case, you might be better off to just make a note of the file's name and import it by itself later on (see "Importing Existing Pages" earlier in this chapter).

THAT LITTLE NUMBER

The number to the right of the word "Files" above the file listing shows the number of files currently in the listing. It changes to reflect exclusions and refreshes.

JUMPING FILES

As you use the Exclude button on the filenames in the import file list, the list may, from time to time, jump around a bit, which can be somewhat confusing, since you'd normally expect it to look the same — minus the excluded files. If you find this happening, just use the scroll bar to scroll back up to where you were.

CROSS-REFERENCE
See "Importing Existing Pages" earlier in this chapter.

FIND IT ONLINE
Two Hawks' Trail Guide to Microsoft FrontPage is a charmingly different site found at **http://yukonho. com/brian/frontpage.html.**

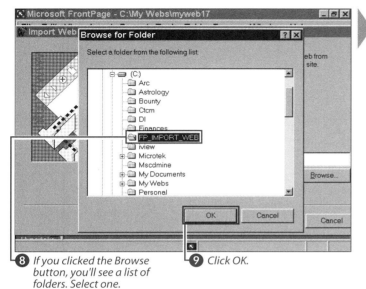

8 If you clicked the Browse button, you'll see a list of folders. Select one.

9 Click OK.

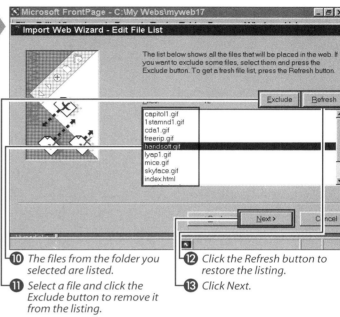

10 The files from the folder you selected are listed.

11 Select a file and click the Exclude button to remove it from the listing.

12 Click the Refresh button to restore the listing.

13 Click Next.

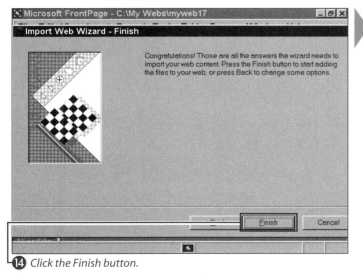

14 Click the Finish button.

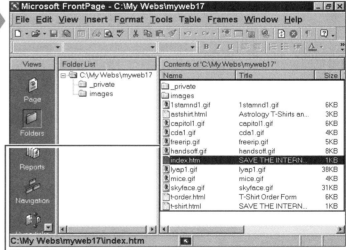

The files are imported into your FrontPage web.

Opening Webs and Pages

To open a FrontPage web, you can use the File ⇨ Open Web option in the main menu, or you can click the down arrow next to the Open button and click Open Web in the drop-down menu (see the upper-left figure, facing page).

With either approach, you'll find yourself looking at the Open Web dialog box, which will be showing the location of the most recent FrontPage web you've worked on. If you want to get to another web, click the Up One Level icon to get to the main web folder and select it from there.

If you want to open a recently used web, then you can access a listing of the last four you worked with by selecting File ⇨ Recent Webs from the main menu. Just click the name of the one you want to use, and it will open.

If you want to work on an individual page instead of an entire web, you can use nearly the same commands to open it. Just click the Open button without bothering with the arrow. You don't have to deal with the arrow and the drop-down menu because the Open button never becomes an Open Web button, no matter what the view; it's always an Open File button. Another way to work on an individual page is to select File ⇨ Open from the main menu. There's also a File ⇨ Recent Files command available there,

which works just like the Recent Webs version, but shows the last pages you worked on. A page opened in this way shows up in Page view; you don't have to go to a file view to get to it. Unlike webs, pages can be closed, and you can open another one without having to exit FrontPage and restart it.

TAKE NOTE

▶ OPENING WEBS DOESN'T OPEN PAGES

When you open a FrontPage web, you may at first be dismayed to not see your index page displayed in the Page view. In order to display any page within the web, you'll have to switch to one of the views that displays filenames and double-click the filename of the page you want to see.

▶ HOW DO I CLOSE A WEB?

Oddly enough, FrontPage doesn't have any way to close a web without shutting the whole program down. If you want to shut down one web and work on another one, you're going to have to exit FrontPage, wait a few seconds, restart it, and then load the other web.

▶ DELETING WEBS

To delete a FrontPage web, choose File ⇨ Delete Web from the menu. You'll be given a choice of whether to remove the files and leave the folder intact or to delete the entire folder.

CROSS-REFERENCE
See "Adding and Deleting Pages" earlier in this chapter.

FIND IT ONLINE
Keith Parnell's FrontPage User Tips Web site is at
http://www.frontpage.to/support/.

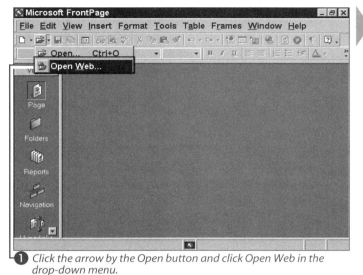

1 Click the arrow by the Open button and click Open Web in the drop-down menu.

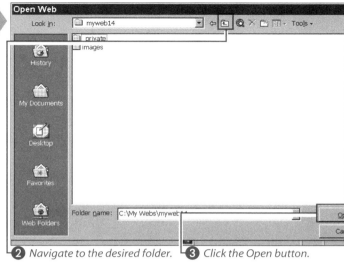

2 Navigate to the desired folder. **3** Click the Open button.

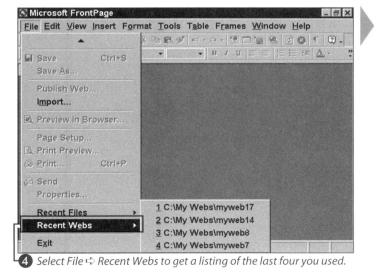

4 Select File ➪ Recent Webs to get a listing of the last four you used.

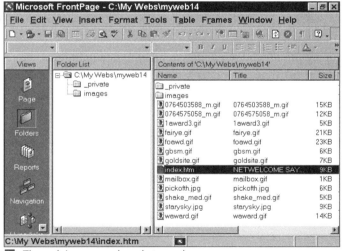

■ The web is open and ready to work on.

Publishing Your Webs

Publishing is the act of uploading your FrontPage web to a Web server. If you've ever worked with Web sites before, you've probably used an FTP (File Transfer Protocol) program to send all the necessary files from your local system to a remote Web server. If so, you're familiar with the slow grind of making sure you've got all the files you need transferred. You're also, without a doubt, familiar with the necessity of making sure that you're using the right method for transferring binary files as opposed to the method for transferring text files.

FrontPage takes all the drudgery out of that task. Uploading — or publishing — is a one-shot process with FrontPage. When you tell it to publish your Web site, it sends all the files in one operation, and it takes care of all the grungy little details for you. All you have to do is tell it where to send them.

To get the ball rolling, you need to have the web opened in FrontPage. Then click the Publish button on the toolbar. This brings up the Publish FrontPage Web dialog box (see the upper-left figure on the facing page). Type the location to which you want to upload the web. If you click the Browse button, you can search for a folder to publish the web to (see the upper-right figure, facing page). You should check the Secure Connection Required (SSL) option if your server requires it.

When you're ready, click the Publish button in the Publish FrontPage Web dialog box (not the one on the toolbar). FrontPage will now point out that it needs to convert the target folder to be compatible with the FrontPage web format (see the lower-left figure). Click Yes to proceed.

After the files have been published, you can click a link to view the newly published web. Otherwise, click the Done button to exit the publishing process.

TAKE NOTE

▶ WHAT DO YOU MEAN, TEXT FILES?

If you think that Web pages aren't just text files, you're mistaken. They're plain vanilla ASCII files. They contain nothing special — the tags, JavaScript programs and so forth in HTML files are just plain old words as far as FrontPage or an FTP program is concerned.

▶ CAN I UPLOAD ANYWHERE?

No. You can only publish to your local system or to a Web server where you have access. If you attempt to publish to one where you don't, the operation will fail before it gets started.

▶ WHAT DOES THE ISP'S BUTTON DO?

If you click the ISP's button in the Publish FrontPage Web dialog box, your Web browser will be launched and you'll go to a Microsoft Web page where there's a listing of ISPs that support the FrontPage 2000 extensions.

CROSS-REFERENCE

See "Creating New Webs," earlier in this chapter.

FIND IT ONLINE

You can find another FrontPage tip-of-the-week site at http://websunlimited.com/mdtips.htm.

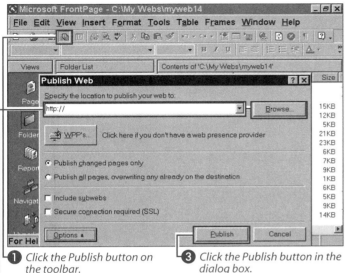

① *Click the Publish button on the toolbar.*

② *Enter the URL you want (or click the Browse button to locate a local folder).*

③ *Click the Publish button in the dialog box.*

④ *If you're browsing, select a folder.*

⑤ *Click the Open button to return to the Publish dialog box.*

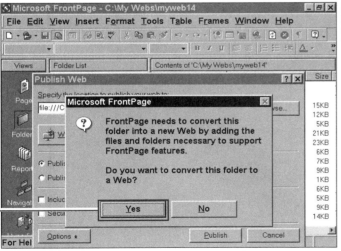

⑥ *When asked if the folder should be converted, click Yes.*

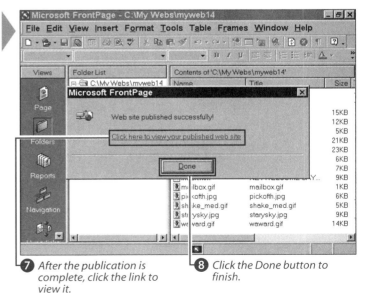

⑦ *After the publication is complete, click the link to view it.*

⑧ *Click the Done button to finish.*

Personal Workbook

Q&A

1 Which view shows link relationships?

_____

_____

_____

2 What does *publishing* mean in FrontPage?

_____

_____

_____

3 How do you save a FrontPage web?

_____

_____

_____

4 What is a *wizard*?

_____

_____

_____

5 What is a *subweb*?

_____

_____

_____

6 What is a *template*?

_____

_____

_____

7 Name the three views in which you can create new pages.

_____

_____

_____

8 What is the name of the default web folder?

_____

_____

_____

ANSWERS: PAGE 321

EXTRA PRACTICE

1 Create several new FrontPage webs from the templates and wizards. Look them over and see which ones you think might be useful to you.

2 Import only a portion of a site on the World Wide Web by setting download limitations in the Import Web Wizard.

3 Publish a small web to a floppy disk, and then reimport it into a folder on your hard drive.

4 Make some webs for the sole purpose of deleting them, so you can get used to the procedure before you really need it.

5 Import an individual Web page into an existing FrontPage web.

REAL-WORLD APPLICATIONS

✔ You've been assigned to revamp a site on the World Wide Web. Your easiest approach to the job would be to just import the whole thing from the Word Wide Web into FrontPage.

✔ You want to dig in to the source code to see what's causing a problem, but the code in the HTML tab isn't easy to read. Why not select View ⇨ Reveal Tags from the menu and look at it in the normal view?

✔ You're going to import a web into FrontPage, but you don't want it to take too long. You might want to set the maximum file size to a lot less than the default 500K. Most Web files are considerably smaller than that, on the order of from 1 to 100K.

Visual Quiz

What is this dialog box? Name two ways to navigate to it.

_____

_____

_____

_____

_____

_____

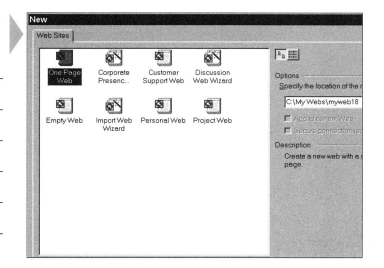

CHAPTER **2**

MASTER THESE SKILLS

▶ **Entering Symbols**

▶ **Using Horizontal Lines**

▶ **Setting Paragraph Styles**

▶ **Creating Lists**

▶ **Spell Checking**

▶ **Viewing, Editing, and Printing HTML Source Code**

Adding Text

You can't escape the facts: although attractive graphics are important to Web pages and can greatly enhance the appearance and beauty of any Web site, the majority of the material on the World Wide Web (and the part that generally carries the greatest meaning) is in the form of words. Text constitutes the largest part of almost every Web page in existence, and mastering its uses and structure can make all the difference in your Web site design efforts.

In this chapter, we'll start off by showing you how to handle those situations where the normal keyboard characters just won't do the trick and what to do if even FrontPage doesn't have the special characters you need. We'll also cover that all-important-but-too-often-neglected step — spell checking — that can make the difference between a well-received Web site and one that's just plain laughable.

There's more to Web text than just typing. Structuring the text on your Web pages so the results are more readable and useful is the key to making them rise above the masses of other Web sites that just pile endless words together. Headings and horizontal lines are two of the easiest and fastest ways to change the appearance and functionality of a Web page. Proper use of these two elements alone can make the difference between readability and failure. We'll also clue you in to the other paragraph styles that FrontPage offers.

We'll be showing you how to use different kinds of lists as another method of presenting information in a more coherent format, and we'll warn you about the pitfalls of the ones you won't want to use. Lists are more versatile in Web design than they've been given credit for, and most Web designers don't even try to get all they can out of them, settling only for simple text. But both bulleted and numbered lists can contain elements besides text, and the design possibilities under those conditions are practically endless.

Finally, we'll get down to the nitty-gritty of how to dive headfirst into the HTML source code behind your Web page. Of course, if you don't want to dive in, you don't have to; FrontPage is fully capable of developing the most complex Web pages without your having to "get your hands dirty," but for those whose interests reach beneath the surface, it's there in all its glory.

Entering Symbols

You type normal text right from the keyboard. What happens, however, if you need some special character that's not found on your keyboard? A financial Web site needs symbols for the yen and pound in addition to the dollar. A weather page can certainly use a handy degree symbol. A food store might want to add the kosher symbol. A different kind of commercial site could use the trademark sign, and every site should have a copyright symbol somewhere on it.

To add a symbol to your Web page, select Insert ➪ Symbol from the main menu. In the Symbol dialog box, click the symbol you want to add, and then click the Insert button. If you need to add more than one symbol in a row, just keep selecting and inserting them. When you're done, click the Close button.

Unfortunately, there's no way to just shove the Symbol dialog box aside and keep it handy; you either insert from it or close it. If you know you're going to need to insert several special symbols on your page, but they don't happen to go neatly one after another, you can use a simple trick to save time and trouble. Before you get started, just fire up the Symbol dialog box and insert each symbol you're going to be needing on a line by itself. Then, when it comes time to use them, they're right there for you to copy or cut and paste.

TAKE NOTE

▶ THE OLD WAY

There are other ways to put symbols into your HTML pages. The code for the copyright symbol is © for example. All the *character entity references*, to use the technical term, require an ampersand to start with and a semicolon to finish. You can also use © which is the older numerical code. It will show up as the copyright symbol instead of the code on the normal screen. It's much nicer, though, and more in keeping with the FrontPage philosophy, to have everything plainly visible right where you're working on it and not have to mess with the actual coding. If you're going to use either the character entity or numerical codes for special characters, you'll have to click the HTML tab and do it on the HTML page; if you just type them onto the normal page, they won't work.

▶ NOT TOTALLY COMPREHENSIVE

As annoying as the old way of adding symbols is, the symbols available in the FrontPage Insert menu aren't the only ones available. If you need something like an ellipsis, you'll have to dig it up from the list at the Web site in the Find It Online below. By the way, there's an interesting quirk you should bear in mind when using these reference codes. While it's true that © will show up on the preview screen and in a Web browser as the copyright symbol, it doesn't show up on the normal screen that way. You have to use lowercase — © — in order for it to be properly displayed on the normal screen. In fact, some of the character entity references won't work at all if you use uppercase to type them in.

CROSS-REFERENCE

See "Viewing, Editing, and Printing HTML Source Code," later in this chapter.

FIND IT ONLINE

You can check out the old way of putting in symbols at **http://www.w3.org/TR/REC-html40/sgml/ entities.html.**

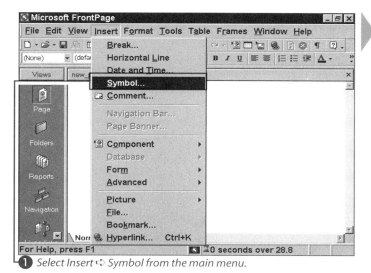

1 Select Insert ⇨ Symbol from the main menu.

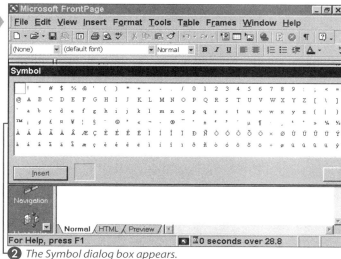

2 The Symbol dialog box appears.

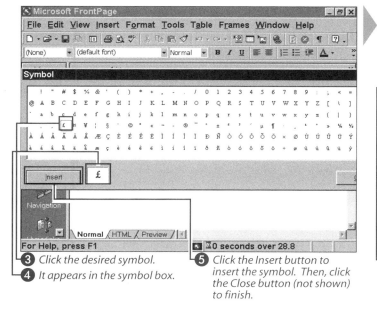

3 Click the desired symbol.

4 It appears in the symbol box.

5 Click the Insert button to insert the symbol. Then, click the Close button (not shown) to finish.

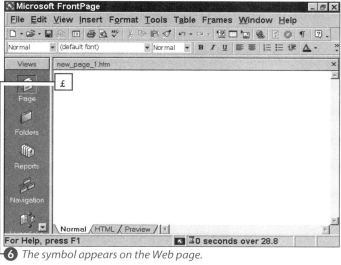

6 The symbol appears on the Web page.

Using Horizontal Lines

Horizontal lines are a common feature of many Web pages. They're usually used to set off one part of a page from the rest of it, and may be used throughout the entire page to divide multiple items.

To set a horizontal line on your page, place the cursor where you want to put the line, and then select Insert ⇨ Horizontal Line from the main menu. The line will show up right where you had placed the cursor.

To change the line settings, right-click it and choose Horizontal Line Properties from the popup menu. The lower-right figure on the facing page shows the default settings in the Horizontal Line Properties dialog box. You must first choose whether you want the width to be a percentage of the window width or to be an absolute size in pixels. Which is best? It depends on your purposes and your audience. If you're creating a page for general users of the World Wide Web, then you've got to take into account that zillions of people are using different computers with varying screen resolutions. If you set an absolute pixel width of 900 pixels, the page won't display well for 640 × 480 or 800 × 600 monitors. For this reason, most people would choose to leave the width as a percentage of the window; after all, 50 percent is half the screen, regardless of what the resolution is. On the other hand, you may have some specific design purpose in mind which requires an absolute size. You may want to have horizontal lines above and below a specific image, for instance, and need them to be the same width as the image.

The default of 2 pixels for line height is fine for a solid line, but doesn't show a shaded line very well. For shaded lines, you might want to up the height to between 4 and 6 pixels. The shaded or hollow line, by the way, is the default. If you want a solid line, you need to select the Solid Line check box at the bottom of the dialog box.

Choosing alignment for the line only has an effect if the line width is less than the screen width. The default version, which is as wide as the entire screen, can't really be said to be aligned to the left, center, or right, regardless of the setting.

If you want to specify a color for the horizontal line, the procedure is identical to that for setting font colors, which is covered in Chapter 3.

TAKE NOTE

RULES OR LINES?

Although FrontPage calls it a horizontal line, the proper term is *actually horizontal rule*, and the HTML code for the element is <HR>. Click the HTML tab to see this in the coding.

CROSS-REFERENCE

See "Changing Text Color" in Chapter 3.

FIND IT ONLINE

You'll find a page of interesting items divided by horizontal lines at **http://munshi.sonoma.edu/jamal/weird.html**.

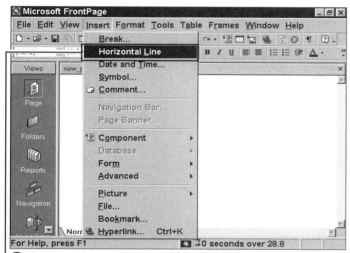

1 Select Insert ➪ Horizontal Line from the main menu.

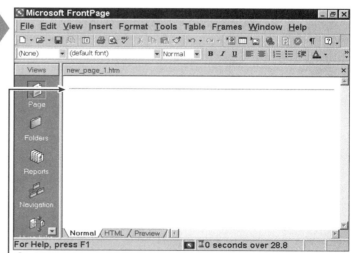

2 The horizontal line appears on your Web page.

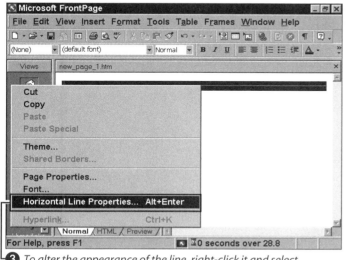

3 To alter the appearance of the line, right-click it and select Horizontal Line Properties from the popup menu.

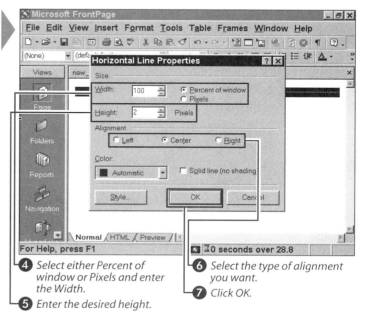

4 Select either Percent of window or Pixels and enter the Width.

5 Enter the desired height.

6 Select the type of alignment you want.

7 Click OK.

Setting Paragraph Styles

Another way to differentiate one part of a Web page from the rest is to use *paragraph styles*. Most often, you do this with various sizes of *heading styles*. A new heading is used to introduce each section of the page. Other styles are more rarely used.

You select paragraph styles by clicking on the drop-down list on the far-left side of the formatting toolbar (see the upper-left figure on the facing page). In this example, we're choosing the Heading 1 style, and you can see the results in the upper-right figure.

The largest heading style in HTML is called H1 and the smallest one is called H6. In FrontPage, these are given the more complete names of Heading 1, Heading 2, and so on. The lower-left figure shows the relative sizes of all six of the heading styles.

Two other paragraph styles see some common usage. One, the *formatted style*, is called the <PRE> element in HTML. If you combine the two — <PRE> and formatted — you get the point. It is for preformatted text. Generally, the text on a Web page is in a variable-width font, and the exact size of a sentence depends on the particular characters in it. The formatted style, with its fixed-width font, uses the exact same size for each and every character. Thus, an *i* is the same size as a *w*. Another peculiarity of formatted text is that white space, which is normally ignored in HTML, is as significant as any other character, so a space or a tab is the same as a letter.

The *address style* was originally meant to give contact information for the author of a Web page but is usually used for the address of the company or organization that owns the page. When applied to a paragraph, it sets that paragraph a little apart from the rest of the text by adding a space above it and making the text small and italic.

The other styles are really part of list making, and are discussed in the following section.

TAKE NOTE

▶ WHAT'S THE DIFFERENCE BETWEEN NORMAL AND NONE?

There isn't any because the "normal" paragraph style (or anything similar) doesn't exist in HTML. However, it's a nice touch to have one in FrontPage, since it makes it easy to remove the real HTML paragraph styles if you change your mind about them. Just put the cursor in any paragraph that has a style applied to it and select the Normal style. That'll remove any other paragraph style. If you check the HTML code before and after, you'll see that the old tags are removed, but nothing replaces them.

▶ PARAGRAPHS

A paragraph in HTML can hold anything from a single character to dozens of sentences. In Normal view, it's defined by paragraph markers, and in the HTML code view, by the <P> and </P> tags.

CROSS-REFERENCE

See "Changing Text Styles" in Chapter 3 for information on how to set font styles.

FIND IT ONLINE

For tech data on heading elements, see **http://www.w3.org/TR/REC-html40/struct/global.html**.

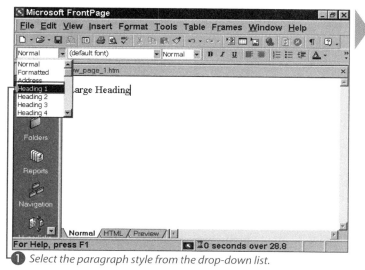

① *Select the paragraph style from the drop-down list.*

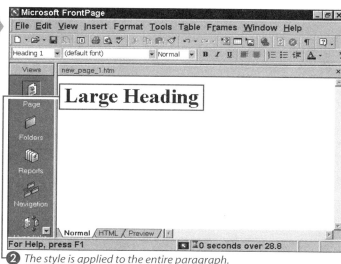

② *The style is applied to the entire paragraph.*

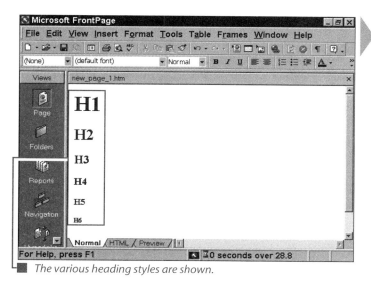

▇ *The various heading styles are shown.*

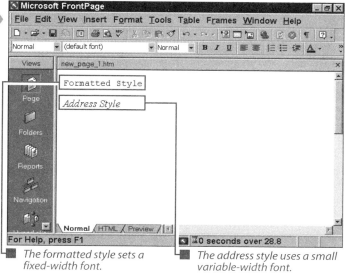

▇ *The formatted style sets a fixed-width font.*

▇ *The address style uses a small variable-width font.*

37

Creating Lists

Lists are a common method of organizing information on Web pages. FrontPage offers five different kinds of lists: bulleted, numbered, definition, directory, and menu lists. Of these five, bulleted lists and numbered lists are often used on a regular basis, while definition lists are very specialized. Directory lists and menu lists are never used at all, and don't work properly in either of the major browsers, anyway.

The two most commonly used lists are bulleted lists and numbered lists (known in HTML parlance as *unordered lists* and *ordered lists*). Both kinds are available in FrontPage by just clicking a button on the toolbar (see the upper-left figure, facing page).

Once you've clicked the numbered list button, the numeral 1 will appear on the Web page. Type an entry and hit the Enter key. The next line will show the numeral 2. Continue to type entries until you're done. When you've made the last entry in the list, just hit the Enter key on the final line without typing an entry. The entries don't have to be text — you can use images or hyperlinks in lists as well.

The bulleted list works the same way, except that the lines show bullets instead of numbers.

Definition lists are meant for dictionaries or glossaries. Place the cursor on the line where you want to put the first term, and then select Defined Term from the Paragraph Styles drop-down list. Type the term you want to define and hit the Enter key. The next line will be automatically indented and set with the Definition style. Type the definition and hit the Enter key again. The next line will be set for the Defined Term style. To end the list, hit the Enter key instead of typing a term.

The remaining two types of lists, the directory list and menu list (both available from the Paragraph Styles drop-down menu), are *deprecated* by the World Wide Web Consortium (W3C). They work identically to bulleted lists and have no real purpose of their own.

TAKE NOTE

WHAT IS DEPRECATION, ANYWAY?

Deprecation is the first step toward discontinuing a feature in HTML. Deprecated features are supposed to be supported by browsers which adhere to the HTML standard, but their usage is officially frowned upon. There's no enforcement capability in the W3C, so Web developers just go on using whatever works, regardless of the official position.

AND WHAT'S THE W3C?

The World Wide Web Consortium is a group composed of any organization with $150,000 to spare ($50,000 dues per year with a three-year commitment). If you're interested in joining as an individual, the cost is "only" one-tenth that of organizational membership. There are no membership requirements other than the dues. The W3C has done a creditable job, nonetheless, of developing a series of standards which attempt to keep the World Wide Web organized.

CROSS-REFERENCE

See the preceding section for more information on paragraph styles.

FIND IT ONLINE

You can view the W3C specs on lists at **http://www.w3.org/TR/REC-html40/struct/lists.html**.

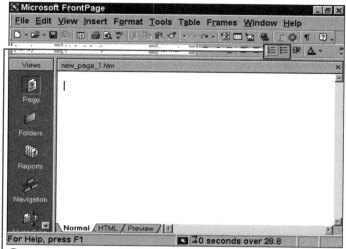

1 *Click the Numbering button to start a numbered list (or click the Bullets button to start a bulleted list).*

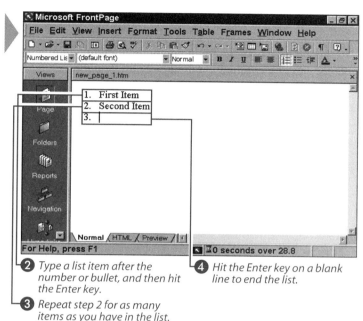

2 *Type a list item after the number or bullet, and then hit the Enter key.*

3 *Repeat step 2 for as many items as you have in the list.*

4 *Hit the Enter key on a blank line to end the list.*

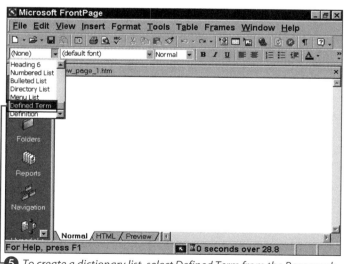

5 *To create a dictionary list, select Defined Term from the Paragraph Styles drop-down list.*

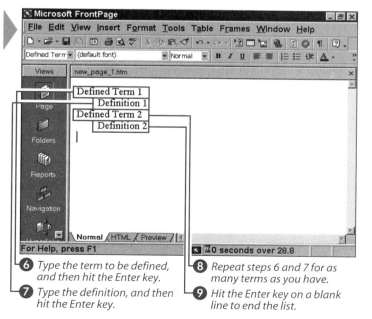

6 *Type the term to be defined, and then hit the Enter key.*

7 *Type the definition, and then hit the Enter key.*

8 *Repeat steps 6 and 7 for as many terms as you have.*

9 *Hit the Enter key on a blank line to end the list.*

Spell Checking

Every Web page should be spell checked before it's shown to the public or your boss. Failure to do so can result in acute embarrassment or, in extremely unlucky cases, job loss.

Launch the spell checker by clicking on the toolbar button with the check mark and the letters ABC on it (see the upper-left figure on the facing page). The Spelling dialog box appears and, when the spell checker finds a word not in its dictionary, the spell checker stops and highlights the unknown word as shown in the upper-right figure. The basic options common to all spell checkers (Ignore, Change, and Add) are represented by the buttons on the right side of the dialog box (the Suggest button is grayed out at this point and will be discussed later). You can correct a misspelling by selecting a term from the list under Suggestions and clicking on the Change button; you can handle a properly spelled term that you don't want to add to the dictionary by clicking on the Ignore button; or you can put the term into the dictionary by clicking on the Add button. The Change and Ignore buttons also have extended versions called Change All and Ignore All. They have the same effect as the Change and Ignore options, but affect all the identical terms in the document, not just this one instance of it.

The Suggest button is useful if you're sure the word is misspelled, but you're equally sure that none of the suggested replacements is the correct word,

either. Select the term under Change To, type the term you think belongs in its place, and then click the Suggest button (it becomes active with the first character you type). The spell checker will search through the dictionary and come up with everything it can find that's similar to the word you typed.

TAKE NOTE

MARKED IN RED

You can spot spelling errors without even running the spell checker since, as with other Microsoft programs, spelling errors are already underlined in red right on the page. Since FrontPage thinks any word that's not in its dictionary is misspelled, that means that any page with unusual terms on it will be full of bogus red marks. In this case, the main use of the spell checker is to educate the dictionary so it won't clutter up your screen with these marks. You might also want to bear in mind that the spell checker will think any word that is in its dictionary is spelled correctly, even if it's actually an error (for example, "field" for "filed").

REPEATED WORDS

The spell checker is a little bit too sensitive in some cases. It picks up the phrase "as well as" and thinks it represents a repeated word. Properly, this should only occur if it were "as as."

CROSS-REFERENCE
See the earlier section, "Entering Symbols," for information on special characters.

FIND IT ONLINE
You'll find a page with numerous spelling links at
http://www.studyweb.com/grammar/punc.htm.

1 *Click the Spelling button to launch the spell checker.*

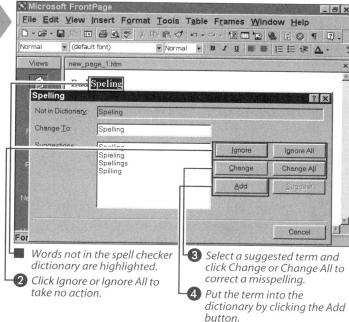

■ *Words not in the spell checker dictionary are highlighted.*

2 *Click Ignore or Ignore All to take no action.*

3 *Select a suggested term and click Change or Change All to correct a misspelling.*

4 *Put the term into the dictionary by clicking the Add button.*

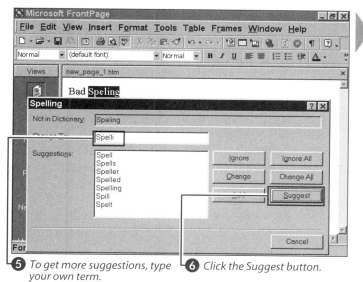

5 *To get more suggestions, type your own term.*

6 *Click the Suggest button.*

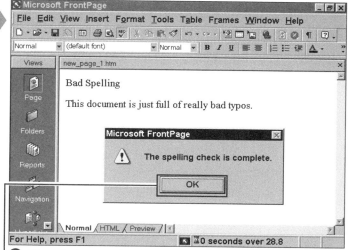

7 *When the last term has been scanned, the spell checker exits. Click OK to finish.*

Viewing, Editing, and Printing HTML Source Code

Although you can use FrontPage without ever once looking at the HTML source code, it's designed to be as versatile a program as possible and to appeal to all levels of Web developers. If you're the kind who likes to get under the hood and monkey directly with the source code, all you've got to do is click the HTML tab and you're off and running.

The upper-left figure on the facing page shows a Web page in FrontPage with the cursor on the heading "E-mail." When you click the HTML tab at the bottom of the page, the source code appears onscreen with that particular line highlighted (see the upper-right figure, facing page).

Once you're in this screen, you have full control over the source code. You can add, delete, and modify it to your heart's content, and anything you do will be reflected in the normal and preview screens.

The final two figures (bottom left and bottom right) show some simple HTML code entered in the HTML screen of a blank Web page and the display that results when you click the Normal tab.

To print HTML source code, just click the Print button while viewing it.

CROSS-REFERENCE

See Chapter 3 for information on modifying text.

FIND IT ONLINE

NetMechanic has an HTML validation service at http://www.netmechanic.com/html_check.htm.

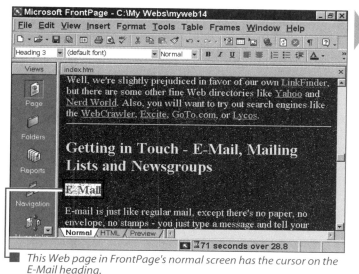

This Web page in FrontPage's normal screen has the cursor on the E-Mail heading.

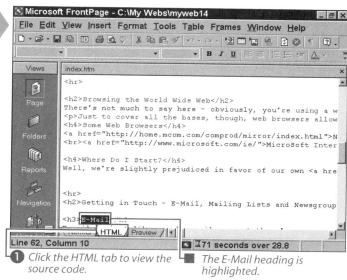

① Click the HTML tab to view the source code.

The E-Mail heading is highlighted.

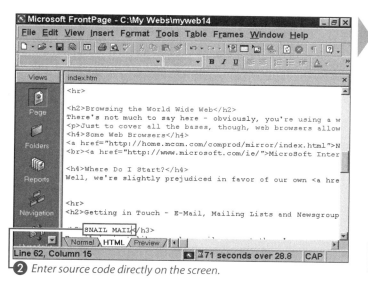

② Enter source code directly on the screen.

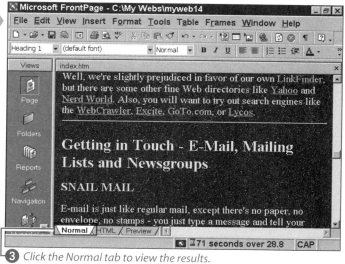

③ Click the Normal tab to view the results.

Personal Workbook

Q&A

1 How do you enter special characters not found on your keyboard?

_____

_____

_____

2 What if special characters are not found in FrontPage either?

_____

_____

_____

3 What is the purpose of horizontal lines?

_____

_____

_____

4 How many sizes of headings are there in HTML?

_____

_____

_____

5 What kind of font does the formatted paragraph style use?

_____

_____

_____

6 What are the two most common kinds of lists?

_____

_____

_____

7 What does red underlining mean on your Web page?

_____

_____

_____

8 What does a validation program do?

_____

_____

_____

ANSWERS: PAGE 322

EXTRA PRACTICE

1. Make a short glossary using paragraph styles.

2. Try various settings for horizontal lines — different heights, widths, and so on. See which you like the look of best.

3. Set up a Web page with deliberate misspellings and see the suggested replacements.

4. Play around with the source code on an unimportant page. Deliberately make errors and see what results.

5. Print out the HTML source code from a Web page and study how it's put together.

6. Make a bulleted list. Put the cursor in it and click the numbered list button to see what happens.

REAL-WORLD APPLICATIONS

✔ You take on a job revising a Web site for a technical firm. You may want to consider running the spell checker over their existing pages so that specialized terms can be entered into the dictionary.

✔ Your boss wants a list on the company Web page. You should probably give some thought to whether it would be better presented as a numbered or bulleted list.

✔ To familiarize yourself with the available special characters, print out the official spec and compare the characters to the ones available in FrontPage. You can mark any you might use which aren't in FrontPage and keep the printout handy.

Visual Quiz

What is this screen? How do you get there? What's wrong with it?

_____

_____

_____

_____

_____

_____

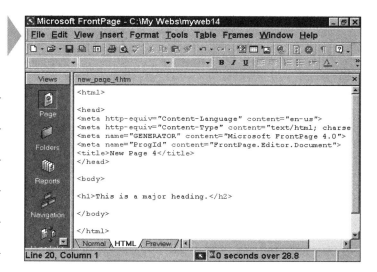

CHAPTER **3**

MASTER
THESE
SKILLS

▶ **Aligning and Indenting Text**

▶ **Changing Font Faces**

▶ **Changing Font Size**

▶ **Changing Text Style**

▶ **Changing Text Color**

▶ **Setting the Background Color**

Modifying Text

Since the bulk of material on the World Wide Web is textual, the ways in which you choose to use and present your words will make a big difference in how your Web pages look and, more importantly, how well they are understood. While the use of language and clarity of verbal presentation are beyond the scope of this book, we'll share a few secrets with you about how to present your gems on the Web.

In addition to the use of paragraph styles, which was covered in the preceding chapter, you have a half dozen ways to use text for the most effective visual appearance. The first, alignment and indentation, affects the actual positioning of the text. *Alignment* places the edges of your sentences at either the left or right margins of the Web page, or it centers the text. *Indentation* alters this placement somewhat in that it moves the edges away from the margins and affects only left or right-aligned text. It does not affect centered text at all.

You're not limited to changing large paragraph blocks, however. You can also change the look of fonts on a small scale — right down to the level of a single character. You can choose a variety of different appearances called *font faces* for your lettering (although we'll tell you why you might want to reconsider using some of the more unusual ones), and you can vary the size of your characters as well.

The style of characters is also open to change. The most commonly used font styles, bold and italic, are available to you at the click of a couple of toolbar buttons, and many other more obscure ones are to be found in FrontPage's dialog boxes. Some of these are relatively useless or duplicative, while others are of interest in only a few specialized situations.

Finally, the use of color for visual effect, both for your textual characters and for the background color of the Web page itself, can make or break the functionality of your Web designs. The two color approaches must work in tandem for the best effect, the background color serving to not only make a page attractive, but also to highlight and properly set off the text color.

Aligning and Indenting Text

Both alignment and indentation affect how a paragraph is placed on a Web page, but they do it in different ways. Alignment determines the starting point of a paragraph and includes three options — left, center, and right. Normally, text is left aligned. (This is the default setting, so a paragraph without a specified alignment is the same as one which has left alignment specified.)

The upper-left figure on the facing page shows three paragraphs before any specific alignment is applied to them. To align them, simply select them one at a time and click the appropriate alignment buttons on the toolbar. The figure in the upper right shows the same paragraphs after they are aligned.

Indentation is slightly different. It moves both the beginning and end of the lines in from the sides of the page. Although the double indentation is not apparent with short pieces of text, it shows up with full paragraphs. The lower-left figure shows two indented paragraphs, one short and the other long.

Indenting a paragraph is as easy as aligning one. Just put the cursor somewhere in it and then click the Increase Indent button to indent it. Repeat that action to indent it more. Use the Decrease Indent button to reverse the effect.

TAKE NOTE

ALIGNMENT AFFECTS INDENTATION

The text alignment that you choose determines how indentation appears. Left-aligned text will be indented from the left side toward the right side, and right-aligned text will be indented from the right side toward the left side. Since indentation of long sentences or full paragraphs shows up on both sides, this effect is only apparent with short bits of text.

WHAT ABOUT CENTERED TEXT?

Centered text will not indent at all. The figure on the lower right shows left, center, and right-aligned paragraphs, each of them with two indentations applied.

HOW DO I INDENT TEXT FROM ONE SIDE ONLY?

You can't indent an entire paragraph from one side, but you can "indent" the beginning of the first sentence by using the Tab key. When you're dealing with very short pieces of text instead of entire paragraphs, this looks just like indentation, but it only works from the left side. Although there really is no Tab in HTML, in which almost all kinds of white space are considered nonexistent, FrontPage will place three nonbreaking spaces into the HTML code when you hit the Tab key. Nonbreaking spaces are one of the very few exceptions to the white space rule in HTML. If you look at the HTML code generated by hitting the Tab key, you'll see the code   is inserted. That's the character code for the nonbreaking space.

CROSS-REFERENCE

See Chapter 2 for more information on character codes.

FIND IT ONLINE

Chris's FrontPage Information Web is located at
http://jazzpiano.com/frontpage/.

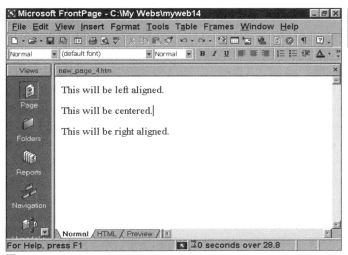

■ The Web page with three unaligned paragraphs.

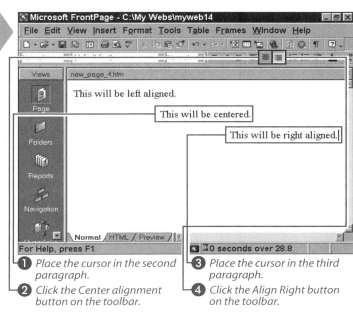

① Place the cursor in the second paragraph.

② Click the Center alignment button on the toolbar.

③ Place the cursor in the third paragraph.

④ Click the Align Right button on the toolbar.

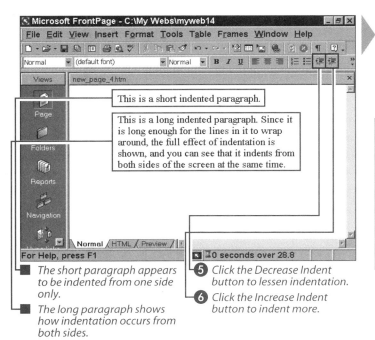

■ The short paragraph appears to be indented from one side only.

■ The long paragraph shows how indentation occurs from both sides.

⑤ Click the Decrease Indent button to lessen indentation.

⑥ Click the Increase Indent button to indent more.

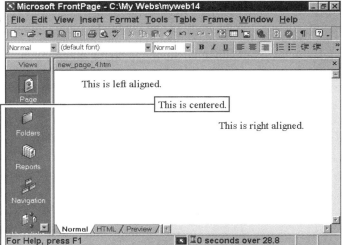

⑦ Center alignment negates indentation.

49

Changing Font Faces

Font faces — the shapes, as opposed to the other aspects of lettering like size, color, and style — come in a wide variety. Even if you haven't gone to the trouble of deliberately collecting several different fonts, you've doubtlessly got a pretty large selection available to you. In addition to the ones that came with your basic operating system, every word processing program includes dozens of them; many graphics editors come with hundreds or even thousands of new fonts.

While you have the technical ability to populate your Web page with any kind of font face ever invented (as long as it's available in digital format, and most of them are), there are compelling reasons to limit your creative expression in this case. The World Wide Web has zillions of people on it who are using an incredible number of differing computer systems, and not all of these systems are fully capable of using all the fonts there are. The fact is, there are three different font faces that are definitely available on nearly all computer systems and, since they'll serve any reasonable design need, you're better off sticking with them. Those three are Arial (also called Helvetica), Times (also called Times Roman or Times New Roman), and Courier (also called Courier New).

To change a font face, select the characters you want to change, and then click the down arrow on the Font list on the toolbar. Scroll down until you find the font you want, and click it.

CROSS-REFERENCE

See Chapter 2 for more information on fonts.

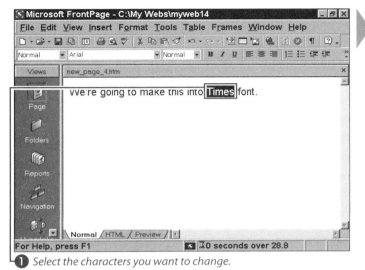

① *Select the characters you want to change.*

② *Click the down arrow on the Font list to get the font listing.*

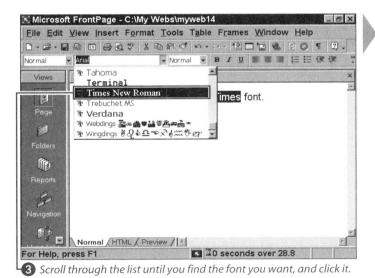

③ *Scroll through the list until you find the font you want, and click it.*

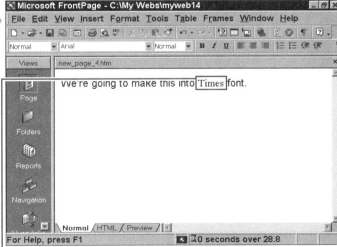

■ *The font face on the Web page now reflects your choice.*

Changing Font Size

You may recall from the section, "Setting Paragraph Styles," in Chapter 2 that some paragraph styles alter the size of the fonts in the paragraph to which they're applied. The six heading styles, for instance, correspond to six different font sizes. The address style changes text not only to italic, but to a small size. Here, however, we're dealing with the capability of changing font size on any scale, not just the full paragraph. You can change it for a single character, or for every character on the entire page.

To change font size, first select the characters you want to enlarge or shrink, and then click the down arrow of the Font Size listing. Scroll down, if necessary, to find the size you want, and click it. The default size of "Normal," by the way, is the same as Size 3, which is nominally 12 points (see the comments on point size in the Take Note section on this page), so changing a "normal" font size to Size 3 will have no effect at all. The lower-right figure on the facing page illustrates the seven font sizes as they appear onscreen.

Bearing in mind that the font size setting can be applied to individual characters, you may want to use it to create a larger initial character in paragraphs. Or, you may want to make each character in a single word a different size for artistic effect.

CROSS-REFERENCE

See Chapter 16 for information on using Cascading Style Sheets.

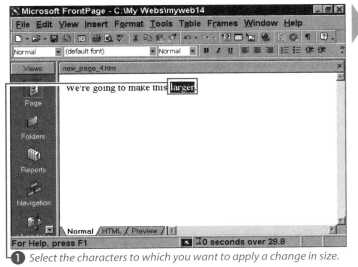

① Select the characters to which you want to apply a change in size.

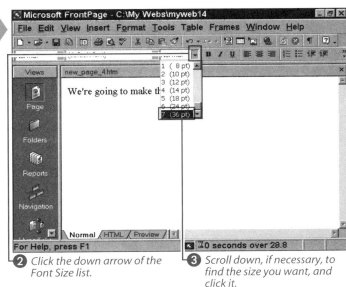

② Click the down arrow of the Font Size list.

③ Scroll down, if necessary, to find the size you want, and click it.

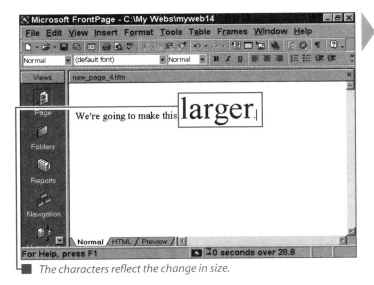

■ The characters reflect the change in size.

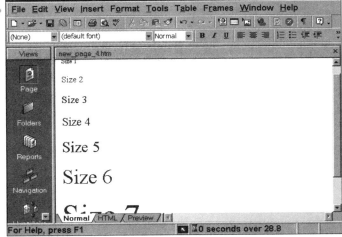

■ This screen shows all seven font sizes.

Changing Text Style

Font styles, as opposed to paragraph styles, can be applied down to the single character level. The "style" of text means, at its simplest, whether it is normal, bold, or italic. Bold and italic styles are commonly used for emphasis. Bold text is darker and thicker than normal, whereas italic text is thinner than normal and slanted to the right. Both types of styles can be combined for greater impact.

To change the style of characters to bold or italic, select the ones you want to emphasize, and then click either the Bold or Italic buttons on the toolbar. To get bold italic text, click both of them (it doesn't matter which one you click first). As you can see in the upper-right figure on the facing page, the buttons change design to show that they are active after you click them. If you want to remove one of the styles from one or all of the characters it has been applied to, simply select the characters and click the appropriate style button again. The button will no longer appear as pushed, and the style will no longer be applied to the characters.

There are, of course, many more font styles than just bold and italic, although those two are the most commonly used on the Web in normal situations. The figures on the bottom left and bottom right show how to access the rest of them if you have a need to. Very few of these are ever used in normal Web design, and some are pretty useless or even annoying. The Strong and Emphasis font styles, for example, simply duplicate bold and italic styles, and will show up that way in a Web browser. The Blink style is something most Web designers would rather lose their modems than use. Try it for five minutes and you'll see why.

TAKE NOTE

WHY NOT TALK ABOUT UNDERLINING?

You've most likely observed that the toolbar has three text style buttons — bold, italic, and underlined. These buttons appear simply because they are standards in word processing and other textual applications, and the FrontPage toolbar, in order to be consistent with other Microsoft Office applications, duplicates their appearance. Underlining terms, however, has no real place on the World Wide Web. You can underline (that is to say, you have the technical ability to do so) but it's a really poor design idea because hyperlinks — the connections between different Web pages that are the heart of the World Wide Web — are recognized by the fact that they are underlined. (You don't have to manually underline hyperlinks; they look that way already.) If you underline other text on your Web pages, you'll confuse your visitors because they'll think that the underlined text represents hyperlinks.

CROSS-REFERENCE

See Chapter 2 for more information on paragraph styles.

FIND IT ONLINE

You can find the FrontPage Awareness Forum at **http://frontpage.netnation.com/HyperNews/get/ frontpage.html**.

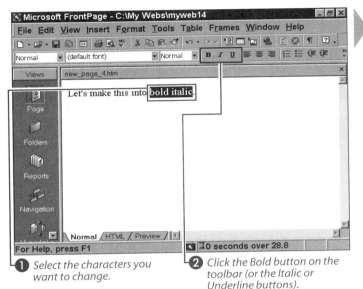

1 Select the characters you want to change.

2 Click the Bold button on the toolbar (or the Italic or Underline buttons).

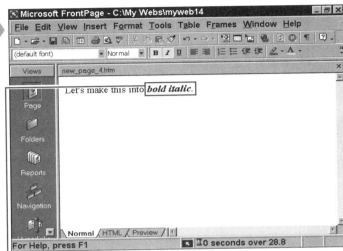

The style or styles will be applied to the selection.

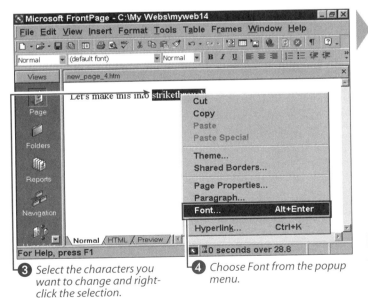

3 Select the characters you want to change and right-click the selection.

4 Choose Font from the popup menu.

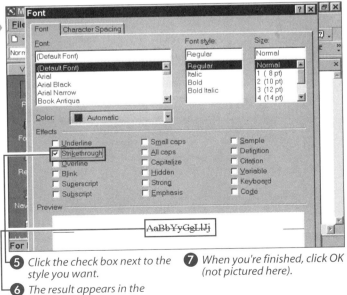

5 Click the check box next to the style you want.

6 The result appears in the Preview window.

7 When you're finished, click OK (not pictured here).

Changing Text Color

Normally, text is black, but you're not stuck with that color. Changing the color of all of your text can result in a more visually attractive Web page. Changing the color of some, but not all, text enables you to selectively add emphasis.

To change text color, first select the characters to which you want to apply a change. If this isn't the first time you've done it, and you want to use the same color you used the last time, all you have to do is click the Font Color button and the selection will change to the color you used before. If you want to choose a new color, you'll need to click the down arrow next to the Font Color button. This brings up (or drops down, rather) a choice of the 16 standard Web colors. Simply click one of the color boxes and you're done.

If you want more color choices, click the More Colors button. This brings up the Color dialog box (shown in the figure on the lower left). You can click any color in the hexagram (or in the gray shaded cells below it). The color you've chosen will appear in the color window along with the currently applied color. Once you've got the color you want, click the OK button.

If none of them will do, you can click the Custom button. (Custom color choices are covered in the next section on background colors.)

CROSS-REFERENCE

See the next section on setting background color for information on using custom colors.

FIND IT ONLINE

Inside Microsoft FrontPage magazine can be found at http://www.zdjournals.com/forms/mfp/cu2001.htm.

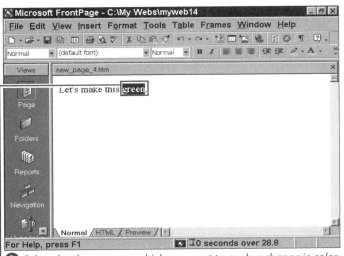

① Select the characters to which you want to apply a change in color.

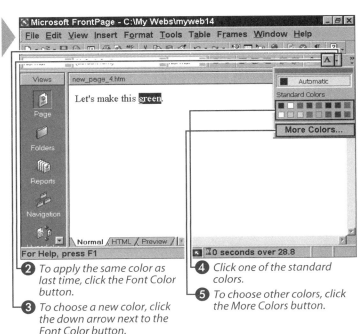

② To apply the same color as last time, click the Font Color button.

③ To choose a new color, click the down arrow next to the Font Color button.

④ Click one of the standard colors.

⑤ To choose other colors, click the More Colors button.

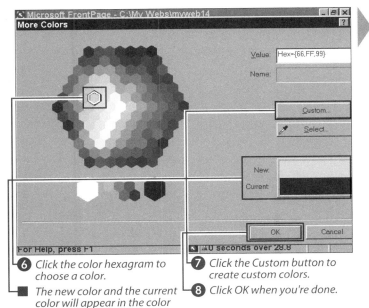

⑥ Click the color hexagram to choose a color.

■ The new color and the current color will appear in the color window.

⑦ Click the Custom button to create custom colors.

⑧ Click OK when you're done.

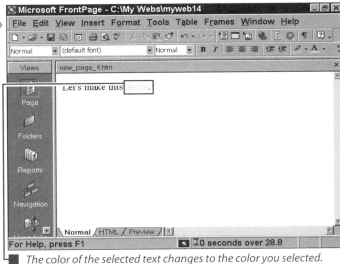

■ The color of the selected text changes to the color you selected.

Setting the Background Color

Just as you're not stuck with black text, you're not required to leave the background color white, either. In fact, you'll probably want to change the two as a single artistic unit, using the foreground text color and the background page color to achieve the total appearance you desire. While most general conceptions of color design call for light text against a dark background and dark text against a light background, there's a bit more to it than that, and you'll need to spend some time experimenting with various color combinations before you find the one that's just right for your particular situation.

To change the background color, you need to choose Format ⇨ Background from the menu. This takes you to the Page Properties dialog box shown in the upper-right figure on the next page. You can also get the same results by right-clicking anywhere on a blank part of the page and select Page Properties from the popup menu, but this adds one more step. You get to the same dialog box, but you'll be on the wrong tab, so you'll have to click the Background tab to get the same dialog.

Once you're there, you click the down arrow next to the word "Background." The resulting dialog box gives you three choices: the Standard colors, Document's colors (the colors currently in use in the Web page), or More Colors. If you make one of the first two choices, simply click the OK button to finish up. If you choose More Colors, you'll end up in the Colors dialog box and your options are identical to the ones already covered in the preceding section on font colors.

Continued

TAKE NOTE

▶ DULL GRAY

The original default background color on the World Wide Web was a medium gray. The new default white background makes the average Web page much more readable, at least when used in tandem with dark text, but it has one drawback — the 3D effect of the horizontal rule doesn't show up properly against a white background. A "shaded" black horizontal rule against a medium gray background appears to be sunk into the surface of the page; on a white background, it simply looks hollow. Although you can change the color of the horizontal rule and experiment with the appearance of shaded horizontal rules of various colors against different background colors, you'll never be able to achieve the same look as that original. The problem occurs because no two monitors or color cards ever reproduce the exact same color, except in the simplest cases — like white, black, and medium gray.

CROSS-REFERENCE
See the preceding section on text colors.

FIND IT ONLINE
The Complete Webmaster has a good FrontPage site at **http://abiglime.com/webmaster/articles/frontpage. htm**.

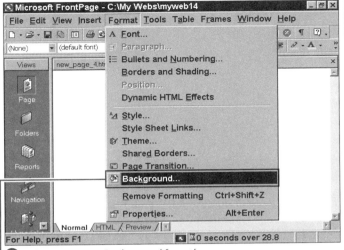

❶ *Select Format* ▷ *Background from the menu.*

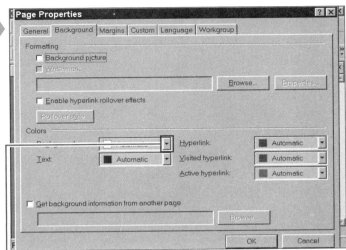

❷ *In the Page Properties dialog box, click the down arrow next to the Background area.*

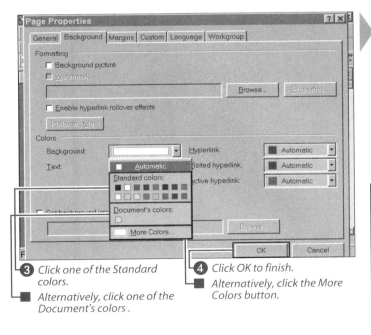

❸ *Click one of the Standard colors.*

■ *Alternatively, click one of the Document's colors.*

❹ *Click OK to finish.*

■ *Alternatively, click the More Colors button.*

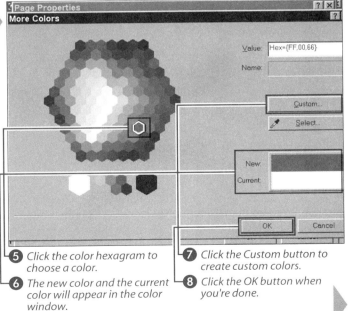

❺ *Click the color hexagram to choose a color.*

❻ *The new color and the current color will appear in the color window.*

❼ *Click the Custom button to create custom colors.*

❽ *Click the OK button when you're done.*

Setting the Background Color
Continued

The creation of custom colors is a matter for either the most sophisticated Web pages, which cater to an exclusive audience, or a situation (such as an intranet) in which you know exactly what hardware and software is going to be used to access your Web pages. The fact is that many people on the World Wide Web are using relatively low-end graphics equipment that cannot properly handle the subtleties of true color shades.

If you clicked on the Custom button in the Colors dialog box, you'll find yourself in the Color dialog box (not much difference in the name, but much in function). Here, you can select every subtle shade of the rainbow for use on your Web pages. Click in one of the Custom colors boxes and then click the multi-color swatch on the right of the dialog box to choose a color. You can place the cursor anywhere in the swatch and then use the slider bar to move up and down in the particular area of the rainbow you're currently exploring. The results appear in the color box underneath it. You can also directly enter numbers in the boxes for hue, saturation, luminance, and so on if you prefer. When you're satisfied with the shade, click the Add to Custom Colors button, and click the OK button to finish.

When you're done making your custom color, you'll need to back out step by step along the path you entered by. Once you click either the OK button to accept the color or the Cancel button to reject it, you find yourself back in the Colors dialog box,

where you once again have to click the OK or Cancel button (make sure you click the OK button all the way along the return path if you want the color, and click the Cancel button all the way along it if you don't). That drops you back into the Page Properties dialog box and — you guessed it — you click either the OK or Cancel button to finish up there, too.

CROSS-REFERENCE
See Chapter 6 for information on how to use background images.

FIND IT ONLINE
Keith Parnell runs a FrontPage discussion forum at http://www.frontpage.to/discussion/index.html.

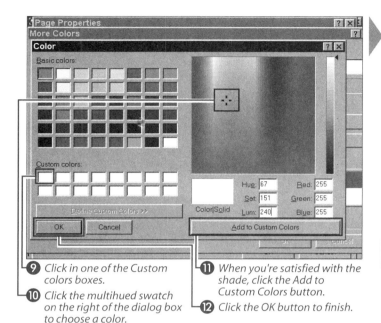

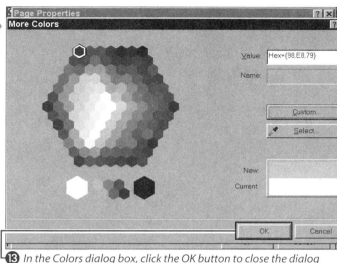

9 Click in one of the Custom colors boxes.

10 Click the multihued swatch on the right of the dialog box to choose a color.

11 When you're satisfied with the shade, click the Add to Custom Colors button.

12 Click the OK button to finish.

13 In the Colors dialog box, click the OK button to close the dialog box.

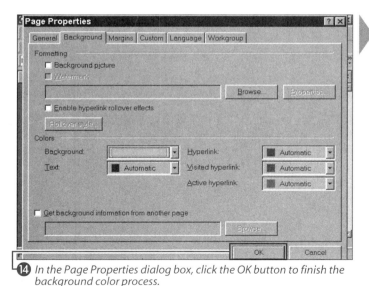

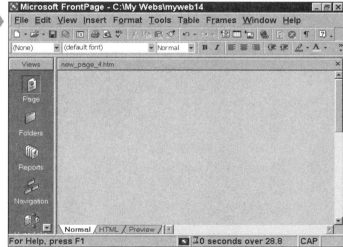

14 In the Page Properties dialog box, click the OK button to finish the background color process.

■ The page now has the background color you've chosen.

Personal Workbook

Q&A

1 How does center alignment affect indentation?

_____

_____

_____

2 How many font sizes are there in HTML?

_____

_____

_____

3 Which font size is the smallest?

_____

_____

4 What size is the "Normal" font size?

_____

_____

_____

5 Why shouldn't you use underlined characters?

_____

_____

_____

6 How many standard colors are there?

_____

_____

_____

7 What is the meaning of _Document's Colors_?

_____

_____

_____

8 What type of text color should be used with a dark background?

_____

_____

_____

ANSWERS: PAGE 322

EXTRA PRACTICE

1 Create a paragraph and repeatedly hit the Increase Indent button.

2 Develop some Web pages with different colored backgrounds; see which text colors look best against them.

3 View a Web page with both Internet Explorer and Netscape Navigator. Do the colors look the same?

4 Experiment with applying various text styles to some paragraphs.

5 If you have access to different computer systems, use some obscure font faces on your Web page and view it with different computers.

6 View a colored Web page in different color depths by changing your system's settings. How do the colors fare at lower settings?

REAL-WORLD APPLICATIONS

✔ You're called in to jazz up a dull Web page. You may decide to add a bit of color to it.

✔ You're using a sans serif font for your Web text. You could improve the readability by using a serif font for most of the text and saving the sans serif for special situations.

✔ You want to create a really artistic look for a logo, but you don't want to increase download time by using an image file for it. You could create a rainbow effect by varying the color of each letter in it.

✔ You like the look of your rainbow logo but want something just a bit more interesting. You could change the size of each individual character to create a visually appealing shape.

Visual Quiz

What does this drop-down list do? Why are the point listings not necessarily accurate?

_____

_____

_____

_____

_____

_____

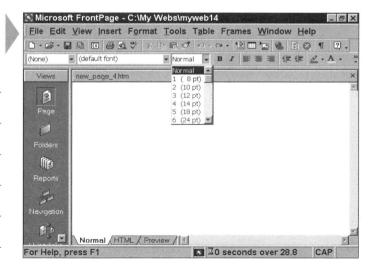

CHAPTER 4

MASTER
THESE
SKILLS

▶ **Creating Text and Image Links**

▶ **Modifying Links**

▶ **Adding Parameters**

▶ **Creating Bookmarks**

▶ **Linking to Bookmarks**

▶ **Following Links**

▶ **Using the Hyperlinks View**

▶ **Using Link Reports**

Adding Hyperlinks

The connecting strands of the World Wide Web are called *hyperlinks* (or just *links,* for short). What do they link? Resources. A *resource* is anything that's connected to the Internet. Just as your home or office is located by a unique description we call a street address, each Web resource has its own unique address that's called a Uniform Resource Locator (or URL).

The official standards for describing URLs are called *schemes,* and although there are a vast number of them, only a few are in common use today. Some of them refer to older systems that have largely faded out of usage, like WAIS (Wide Area Information Service), a forerunner of the World Wide Web. Others are planned for future usage, such as the TV URL scheme, which will enable Web users to access different television stations via their computers.

The most common resources on the Web are, of course, Web pages. The URL scheme, which handles Web page addressing is called HTTP, which stands for Hypertext Transfer Protocol. This is why Web addresses are in the form **http://www.somethingorother.com/index.html**. The **http://** part at the beginning specifies that

it's a Web page you're trying to connect to, and the remainder is the specific location on the Internet where the file is found.

Web browsers use the URL to find the linked file so they can display it. When a Web page is found on a site other than the one the originating hyperlink is on, then you need to provide the entire Web address in the originating link. This is called an *absolute* URL. If the page is on the same site as the page the link originates from, then you can use a shortened version called a *relative* URL. The Web browser first has to find the Web site that holds the page before it can locate the page; so if it's already at that site, then it doesn't need to locate it again, just find another page.

Most hyperlinks are in text form, and they stand out on a Web page because they're in color (usually blue) and underlined. However, you can also use images as a hyperlink source. Hyperlink images are normally outlined in the same color used for text links, but FrontPage creates a bit of a problem with this, and you'll learn how to solve it in the section, "Creating Text and Image Links."

Creating Text and Image Links

Hyperlinks can be based in either text or images. Whenever visitors to your Web page click on the text or image link, their Web browsers take them to the location you specified when you created the link. The procedure is the same for both text and images, except that, due to a peculiarity of FrontPage, you'll need to take one extra step for images after creating the link (see "Image Links and Borders" in the Take Note section on this page).

The first step in creating a hyperlink is to select the link source on your Web page. For text, this means highlighting the word or words you want to base the link on. For an image, you simply click it.

Next, click the hyperlink button on the toolbar. This brings up the Create Hyperlink dialog box shown in the upper-right figure on the facing page. You can type the Web address in the URL edit box. If you don't know the address to type, you have a great deal of assistance from FrontPage.

If you're making a link to a URL you've used before, you can access it from a drop-down list by clicking the down arrow at the right side of the URL edit box. If it's a new URL, the four URL locator buttons to the right will take care of it for you. Their uses are discussed throughout this chapter. The first one launches your default Web browser (FrontPage, even though it's from Microsoft, can work with Netscape Navigator). Whatever URL you browse to is automatically imported into FrontPage. The second button brings up a standard Select File dialog box, which enables you to find files on your local system.

Continued

Continued

TAKE NOTE

IMAGE LINKS AND BORDERS

In standard HTML, image links are recognizable by the fact that they're outlined in the same color used for text links. This is the default behavior, and FrontPage violates this convention by overriding the border in images. By default in FrontPage, border size in images, instead of being unspecified, which works properly with image links, is specifically set to 0, which means that no border at all is allowed to show. You have to go into the image properties and manually set the border in order for image links to be properly displayed. See Chapter 6 for the border-setting procedure.

YOU MIGHT NOT WANT TO TYPE IT

Even if you know the Web address by heart, you might want to use FrontPage's URL locator buttons anyway. A simple typographical error will mess up your link, making it lead to either limbo or the wrong location. This is especially likely if the URL is a long and complex one. Browsing to the correct URL is a sure way to avoid typos.

CROSS-REFERENCE
See Chapter 6 for more information on image borders.

FIND IT ONLINE
There's a FrontPage discussion forum at
http://www.akorn.net/frontpage/forum.htm.

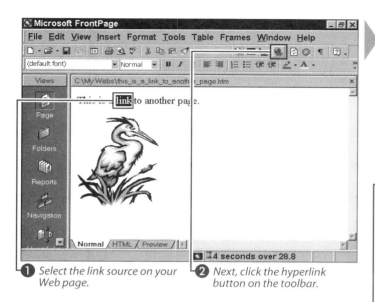

1 Select the link source on your Web page.

2 Next, click the hyperlink button on the toolbar.

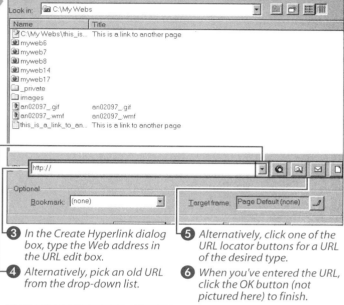

3 In the Create Hyperlink dialog box, type the Web address in the URL edit box.

4 Alternatively, pick an old URL from the drop-down list.

5 Alternatively, click one of the URL locator buttons for a URL of the desired type.

6 When you've entered the URL, click the OK button (not pictured here) to finish.

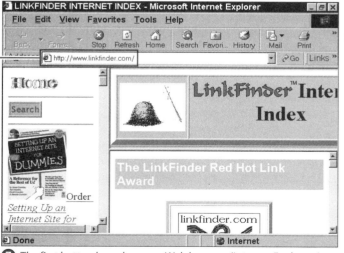

7 The first button launches your Web browser (Internet Explorer, in this case). The URL you browse to is automatically imported into FrontPage.

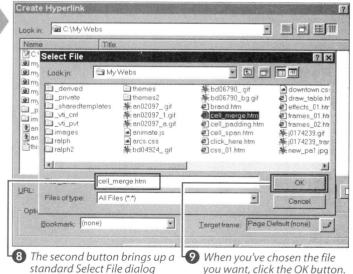

8 The second button brings up a standard Select File dialog box, which enables you to find files on your local system.

9 When you've chosen the file you want, click the OK button.

Creating Text and Image Links
Continued

The third button is for a specialized type of URL called a *mailto* link. This link gives an e-mail address and, when accessed, launches the Web browser's associated e-mail client program with a blank message already addressed to the recipient you specified in the link.

The fourth button actually creates the page you're going to link to. When you click it, the New page dialog box appears just as if you had selected File ⇨ New ⇨ Page from FrontPage's main menu. Picking a page from this dialog box under these circumstances both creates the page and establishes the link to it. The newly created page, rather than the page you linked to it from, will be displayed, and you'll need to hit the back arrow on the toolbar to return to your link page.

Whichever technique you use, the page you linked from will reflect the change you've made. The link will show as blue underlined words or a blue outlined image as shown in the figure on the lower right.

You should note, however, that although a blue-bordered image is the normal way to show a hyperlink on a Web page, FrontPage automatically sets image borders to a zero thickness. This means, of course, that no border will show at all, and there's no way to see if the image is normal or an image link. You'll have to manually set the border to a non-zero value in order for the link cue to show up (see Chapter 6).

TAKE NOTE

ANOTHER WAY TO SET LINKS

If you prefer using menus to toolbar buttons, you can right-click the link source after it's selected and get a popup menu that includes the command, Hyperlink. Just select the Hyperlink option from the popup menu and the Create Hyperlink dialog box appears. You can save yourself a step when you're making an image link. With text, you need to select the link source, and then right-click to bring up the popup menu. With an image, skip the first step and just right-click it. That both selects it and brings up the popup menu in one move.

MULTIPLE LINKS IN A SINGLE IMAGE

Just as you can only have one link in a word, you can't put more than one link in an image. However, you can use a technique called *image mapping*, which requires a different approach entirely. It divides an image into zones, each of which has its own separate link. Image mapping is described in detail in Chapter 8.

WHY BOTH HTTP AND WWW?

Actually, in most cases you don't need both of them in a Web address. Early on in the development of the Web, someone realized that since the URL already starts with http://, the www part is a useless redundancy, and most Web addresses don't really need it anymore. Thus, you can usually skip the www part of a Web address, even if it's officially listed that way. If you have trouble connecting to a site when you leave it out, put it back in and try again, or just play it conservatively and use the full form to begin with.

CROSS-REFERENCE
See Chapter 1 for more information on creating new pages.

FIND IT ONLINE
DPA Software has add-ons for FrontPage at
http://www.dpasoftware.com/.

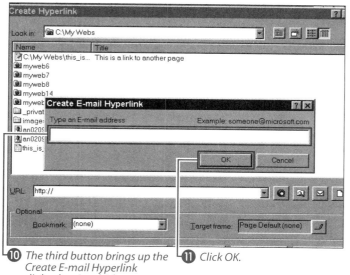

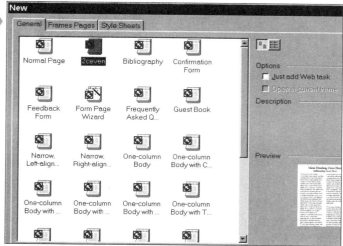

10 The third button brings up the Create E-mail Hyperlink dialog box in which you enter the e-mail address you want to link to.

11 Click OK.

■ The fourth button brings up the New Page dialog box.

12 When you've picked your new page, click OK (not pictured here).

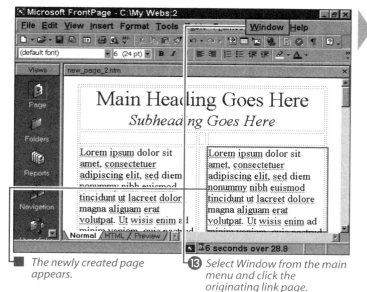

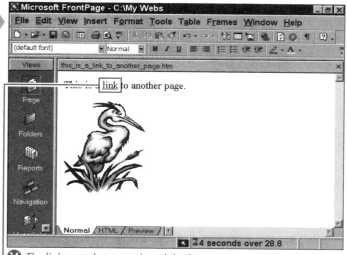

■ The newly created page appears.

13 Select Window from the main menu and click the originating link page.

14 The link now shows on the original page.

Modifying Links

Once a link has been established, you can change it at any time. Links can be edited or even deleted entirely. To edit a link, you can use virtually the same procedure as for creating one or you can use a popup menu approach. For text, click anywhere within the link and then click the Hyperlink button on the toolbar. For an image, click it and then click the Hyperlink button. With either text or images, you can also right-click the link and then select Hyperlink Properties from the popup menu.

Regardless of the approach you prefer, you'll find yourself at the Hyperlink Properties dialog box, which is identical to the Create Hyperlink dialog box, except that it already has the link information filled in. To remove the link, delete the Web address in the URL edit box. To correct a typographical error in the address, you can place the cursor in the URL and manually correct it. Alternatively, you can use the Browser or File URL locator buttons to go to the URL and enter it. When you're done, click the OK button and the link is fixed.

CROSS-REFERENCE
See Chapter 16 for information on using Cascading Style Sheets.

FIND IT ONLINE
You can find Brad Berson's FrontPage Tips 'n Tricks at **http://www.rectaltronics.com/frontpage.htm**.

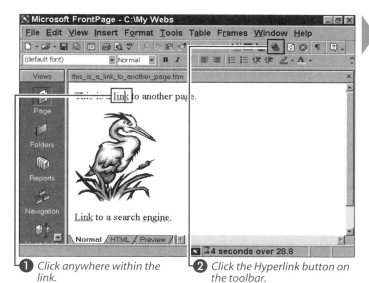

1 Click anywhere within the link.

2 Click the Hyperlink button on the toolbar.

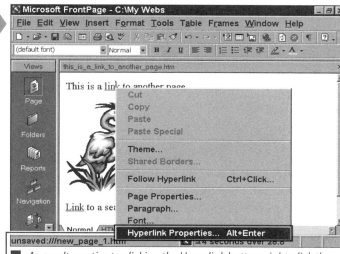

■ As an alternative to clicking the Hyperlink button, right-click the link and select Hyperlink Properties from the popup menu.

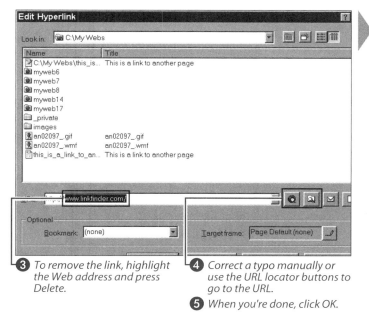

3 To remove the link, highlight the Web address and press Delete.

4 Correct a typo manually or use the URL locator buttons to go to the URL.

5 When you're done, click OK.

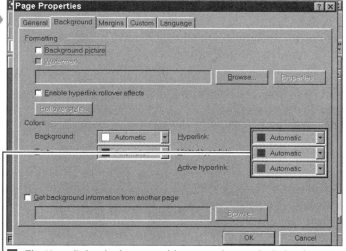

■ The Hyperlink color boxes enable you to change the link colors.

Adding Parameters

Beyond the basic URL that takes you to a particular Web page, you sometimes need to feed information of one kind or another to a program that's accessed from that page. These pieces of information are known as *parameters*. If you've ever visited a search engine, for instance, you've used parameters whether you realize it or not. To see them in action, go to Webcrawler, HotBot, Excite, or any other search engine and enter some search terms. When you click the Search button (or whatever equivalent the site you choose uses), watch what happens to the URL in the Address Bar of your Web browser. Suddenly, in addition to the basic address information, you'll find a question mark, maybe some arcane codes, and your search terms. (The query will probably also be referred to as a program in the cgi-bin directory as well; see the Take Note section on this page.)

If, for instance, you wanted to set up a link to Webcrawler, you could just link to their main page at **http://www.webcrawler.com/** and let it go at that. On the other hand, if you wanted to let your Web site visitors perform fresh searches on Webcrawler on a variety of subjects, you could code your hyperlinks so that a simple click would do the trick. A link to **http://www.webcrawler.com/cgi-bin/WebQuery/ ?searchText=war+1812** would perform a fresh search on the War of 1812 every time it was clicked. A minor variation on it, **http://www.webcrawler. com/cgi-bin/WebQuery/?searchText=war+civil**, would do the same for the Civil War.

You can add parameters to your Web links in three ways. You can just type them in manually as a part of the basic URL in the Create Hyperlink or Edit Hyperlink dialog boxes. You can also surf to the site via the Web browser button, perform a search (or use whatever other program on the site requires parameters), and let FrontPage insert the URL, complete with parameters.

The third possibility is to click the Parameters button. The Hyperlink Parameters dialog box shows the URL path to the file at the top and the query string (the parameters themselves) at the bottom. The parameters are broken into name/value pairs, and you can add new ones, modify existing ones (the add and modify dialog boxes are identical), or delete them individually or en masse. You can also move a particular name/value pair up or down in the listing, thus changing its position in the URL.

TAKE NOTE

WHAT'S CGI-BIN?

CGI stands for Common Gateway Interface, the usual method by which information is passed from Web pages to programs (on a Web server) that are designed to interface with Web forms. Although it's not an absolute requirement, such programs are usually found in a directory called cgi-bin.

CROSS-REFERENCE

See the earlier section, "Creating Text and Image Links."

FIND IT ONLINE

Techweb has FrontPage tips at **http://www.techweb. com/tools/tipsSubCat?majorCat=5&mjCatDesc= Web+Management**.

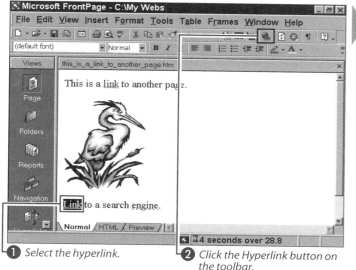

❶ Select the hyperlink.

❷ Click the Hyperlink button on the toolbar.

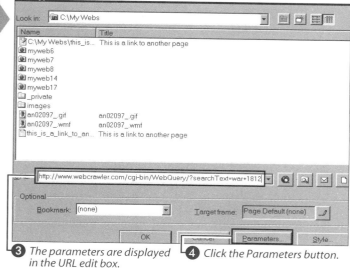

❸ The parameters are displayed in the URL edit box.

❹ Click the Parameters button.

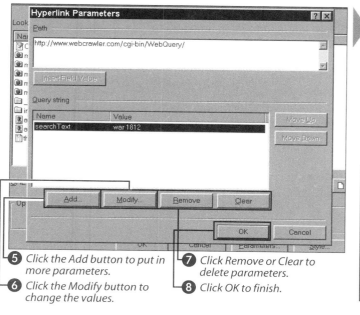

❺ Click the Add button to put in more parameters.

❻ Click the Modify button to change the values.

❼ Click Remove or Clear to delete parameters.

❽ Click OK to finish.

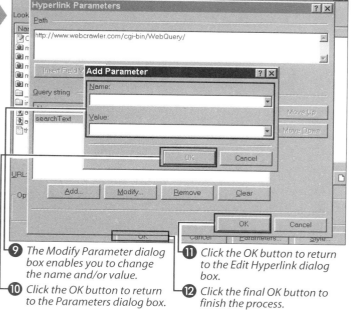

❾ The Modify Parameter dialog box enables you to change the name and/or value.

❿ Click the OK button to return to the Parameters dialog box.

⓫ Click the OK button to return to the Edit Hyperlink dialog box.

⓬ Click the final OK button to finish the process.

Creating Bookmarks

A URL that points to a Web page, of course, always leads to the beginning of that page. It's not something that anyone even gives any thought to; it's just the way it works. There's an unofficial variation, however, that enables you to set up links so that visitors enter your Web pages anywhere you want them to. It's called a *fragment* URL or, in common parlance, a *bookmark*.

Bookmarks can be placed just like links, by highlighting text or selecting images. They can also be placed anywhere else on a Web page. Unlike links, they don't have to be bound to any other element. This means that you can place a bookmark at the beginning of a sentence or in the middle of a word, before or after an image, or, for that matter, anywhere else you want. Depending on which of these approaches you take, the visual cues in FrontPage will vary. If you place a bookmark by itself, unassociated with any element, the bookmark appears as a flag icon. If you place a bookmark by highlighting text, the text is shown underlined, much like with a link but the underlining is a series of dashes instead of a solid line. Placing a bookmark by selecting an image results in no visual cue whatsoever.

Whichever way you decide to use, the next step is about as simple as it can get. Just select Insert Bookmark from the menu, give the bookmark an identifying name in the Bookmark dialog box, and click the OK button. To change it later, right-click it and select Bookmark Properties from the popup menu (see the lower-right figure).

CROSS-REFERENCE

See the next section on linking to bookmarks.

FIND IT ONLINE

You can get daily e-mail tips on FrontPage and other programs from **http://www.dummiesdaily.com/**.

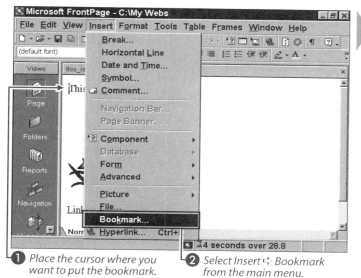

❶ *Place the cursor where you want to put the bookmark.*

❷ *Select Insert ➪ Bookmark from the main menu.*

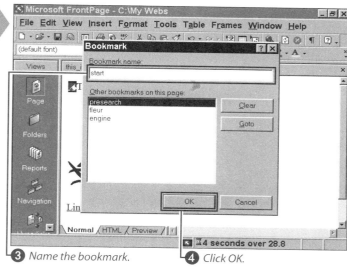

❸ *Name the bookmark.*

❹ *Click OK.*

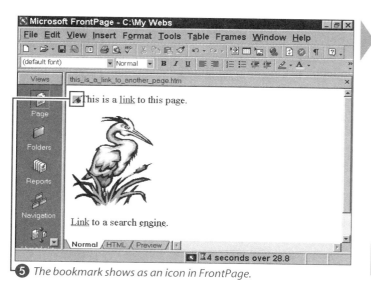

❺ *The bookmark shows as an icon in FrontPage.*

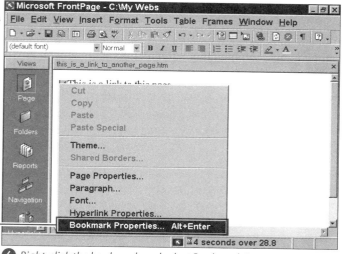

❻ *Right-click the bookmark and select Bookmark Properties to edit it.*

Linking to Bookmarks

Linking to a bookmark is a bit different from setting up a regular hyperlink. You first need to link to the page it's on (unless, of course, the bookmark is on the same page you're linking from), and then specify which bookmark you want to jump to when that link is followed. In the beginning, you just start off as though you were going to create a regular link.

You should note the "Optional" panel at the bottom of the Create Hyperlink dialog box. The first entry in it is the Bookmarks listing. At first, it simply says "None" since no bookmark is selected. If you click the down arrow, the drop-down list of bookmarks appears. This list shows all the bookmarks on a given page, depending on whether or not you've selected a page in the URL edit box. If you haven't selected any page, then the bookmarks shown will be the ones on the same page that the link is on. If you have specified a different page, then the bookmarks from that page will be shown in the drop-down list. Of course, if the page doesn't have any bookmarks on it, then the only selection available to you in the drop-down list will be "None."

Select the desired bookmark from the listing and the name of the bookmark is appended to the Web address, following a hash mark (#). Thus, if the URL is **http://www.aeiouandy.com/index.html** and the bookmark is named "middle," the URL edit box will show the URL as **http://www.aeiouandy.com/index.html#middle**. If you're linking to a bookmark on the same page as the link itself is on, then the only thing in the URL edit box will be the hash mark and the name of the bookmark. From here, just click the OK button and the link to the bookmark is set.

TAKE NOTE

TABLES OF CONTENTS

Bookmarks are commonly used to create a table of contents at the top of a Web page with links to various parts of the page. In turn, a bookmark is usually placed at the beginning of the page and linked back to the other parts of the page so that a visitor to the page can jump from the top to the middle and back again without having to bother with the scroll bar.

UNOFFICIAL SUPPORT

The fragment URL (or "bookmark") isn't an official part of any URL scheme or, indeed, any official standard at all (although it rates a mention in a few of them), but is nonetheless accepted and acted upon by every Web browser. You can use it without worrying about browser compatibility.

CROSS-REFERENCE

See the preceding section on creating bookmarks.

FIND IT ONLINE

The Online Help Desk at **http://help.inlinenet.net/** has good FrontPage material.

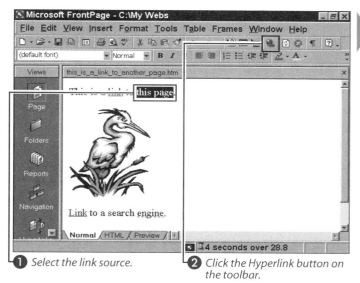

① *Select the link source.*

② *Click the Hyperlink button on the toolbar.*

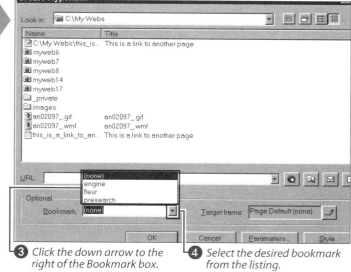

③ *Click the down arrow to the right of the Bookmark box.*

④ *Select the desired bookmark from the listing.*

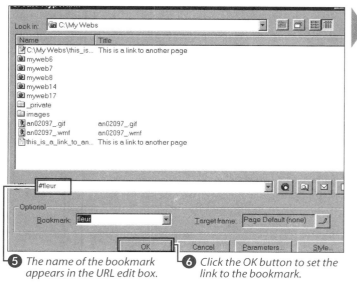

⑤ *The name of the bookmark appears in the URL edit box.*

⑥ *Click the OK button to set the link to the bookmark.*

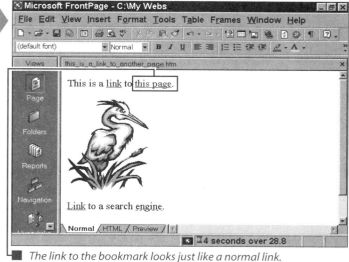

■ *The link to the bookmark looks just like a normal link.*

Following Links

For a rough rehearsal of your Web page, you can right-click the link in Page view and select Follow Link from the popup menu. Alternatively, you can use the keyboard and mouse shortcut by simply holding down the Ctrl key and clicking the mouse while the pointer is over the link. At this point, FrontPage retrieves the linked page. If the link is to a local page, the retrieval is instantaneous. If the link is to a remote page, it may appear as though nothing is happening, but you can see a message in the status bar and the Stop button on the toolbar suddenly becomes active. After a few moments, the page will appear. To return to the link page, click the Back button on the toolbar.

It's a really good idea to personally visit any links to pages that aren't on your own Web site. Since these are not under your control, they can change unexpectedly or even disappear entirely without any warning. Make sure that you check them out yourself at three stages — during the design phase, just before you launch your final version of your Web site, and periodically afterward.

You can also get a sort of dress rehearsal by switching into Preview mode and just proceeding as though the whole thing were happening in a Web browser. To get there, simply click the Preview tab. In Preview mode, you can just click the link to follow it.

Of course, you can also click the "Preview in Browser" button and actually make sure that the thing is ready for opening night.

TAKE NOTE

MAKE SURE YOU'RE CONNECTED

If you're offline and trying to follow a link to an online source, you're going to get a rude surprise. All of your links to the World Wide Web will fail unless you're hooked up to the Internet, and FrontPage will dutifully inform you that a link to the Web is bad, even though it is, in fact, good. This isn't any fault of the program; it's just that it's getting bad information because it doesn't get the feedback it expects. It's a classic case of GIGO — Garbage In, Garbage Out.

DIFFERENT RESULTS

You might find that some links will give you problems if you follow them in Page view, but work fine in Preview mode or in a Web browser. For example, if you attempt to access a CGI Perl script via a link in Page view, you'll be informed that FrontPage can't handle files that end in ".pl" and you'll be asked if you want to save the file (which won't solve the problem). The same URL, accessed in Preview mode, works fine and, of course, Web browsers have no problems with such things (unless the filename or address is bad, of course).

GETTING UNDER THE HOOD

If you want to see the code behind all the links (and indeed behind everything else on your Web page), just select View ➪ Reveal Tags from the menu. You can see the results in the lower-right figure on the next page.

CROSS-REFERENCE

See the first section in this chapter, "Creating Text and Image Links" for more information about links.

FIND IT ONLINE

Netc.'s FrontPage FAQ is located at **http://www.inetc. net/services/Technology/FrontPage/fpfaq.htm**.

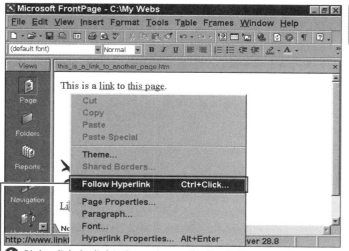

① Right-click the link in Page view and select Follow Hyperlink from the popup menu.

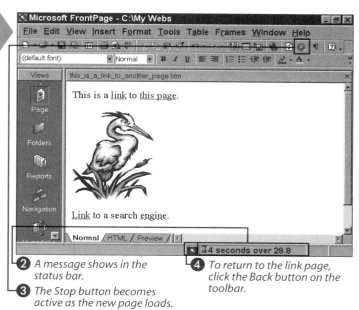

② A message shows in the status bar.

③ The Stop button becomes active as the new page loads.

④ To return to the link page, click the Back button on the toolbar.

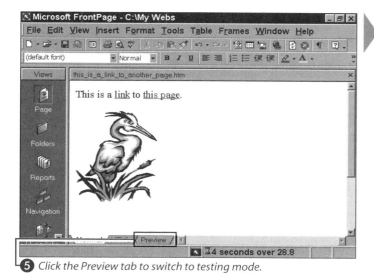

⑤ Click the Preview tab to switch to testing mode.

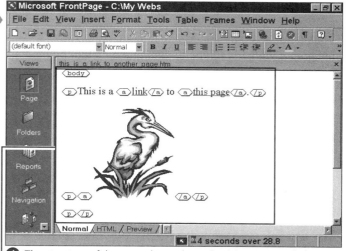

⑥ The structure of the page shows through with tags revealed.

Using the Hyperlinks View

Although the other views are handled in detail in the section on managing your FrontPage webs, it's best to introduce you to the Hyperlinks view here. It can be of inestimable value to you in understanding the interconnections among your own Web pages and those on the World Wide Web as well.

In addition to Web pages there are other types of files, such as image files, which you may have hyperlinks to. The Hyperlinks view shows them all, enabling you to keep track of what is happening on your site.

To get into Hyperlinks view, click the Hyperlinks icon in the Views bar (or select View ➪ Hyperlinks from the main menu). You'll see a graphical representation, a sort of hyperlinks map, of the links in your FrontPage web. The page you were working on in Page view will appear as an icon in the center of the right-hand window, with arrows going to icons of each of the pages (or other files) that it's linked to. The page icons with blue globes refer to external links. The plain page icons refer to links within your own FrontPage web. To change the hyperlinks map so that another page is shown as the focus, right-click that page's icon and select Move to Center from the popup menu.

TAKE NOTE

VERIFIED AND UNVERIFIED LINKS

When you pass your mouse cursor over one of the links in the Hyperlinks view, hold it there a moment and you'll get a popup message that tells you the URL and, if it has not been verified, it will say "Not Verified." To change the status of the link, right-click it and select Verify Hyperlink from the popup menu (see the lower-right figure on the facing page). FrontPage checks to make sure the page or other file (such as an image file) is there. This does not mean that you are totally freed from ever checking a link manually. The fact that a Web server confirms to FrontPage that there's a file when it accesses that URL doesn't necessarily mean that it's the right one. You should still manually check external files you link to, at least after a period of time has passed. This is especially true if the file is at an online community like GeoCities, where the same address may be used by different people for different purposes over a period of time.

EXPANDING THE SCOPE

The plus and minus signs next to some of the pages in the graphical display enable you to expand and contract the display of links in the same manner as you're familiar with in folder displays.

CROSS-REFERENCE

See Chapter 6 for more information on images.

FIND IT ONLINE

There's a good overview of how to use FrontPage with virtual hosting at **http://frontpage.iserv.net/ fp-demonstrations.htm**.

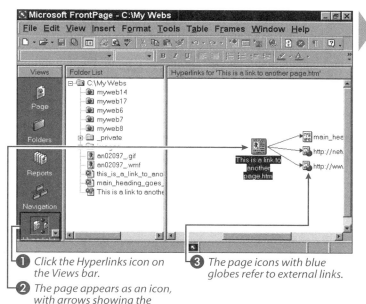

1 Click the Hyperlinks icon on the Views bar.

2 The page appears as an icon, with arrows showing the pages it's linked to.

3 The page icons with blue globes refer to external links.

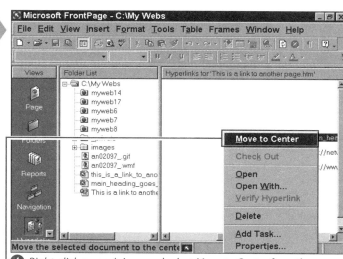

4 Right-click a page's icon and select Move to Center from the popup menu.

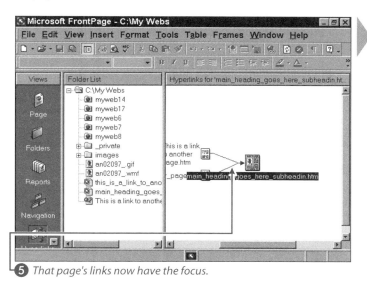

5 That page's links now have the focus.

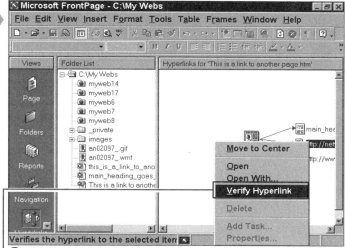

6 Right-click a link and select Verify Hyperlink from the popup menu.

Using Link Reports

It's a good idea, even though you've exercised diligent care in assembling your hyperlinks, to test them when you're done creating the page they're on. And not only at the time of creation, but afterward as well. This is especially true, considering the ever changing nature of the World Wide Web, if the links point to pages not on your own site. Since you have no control over what other Webmasters do with their sites, you will constantly find that the site you thought was going to be there forever has moved, changed, or is just plain gone. This can happen overnight, without warning, and the very least prudent Webmasters should do is to run a test on all the links on their sites on a regular basis. Little is more frustrating to the average Web visitor than following a link with high expectations only to find that it's a dead end. Too many such experiences and your regular users will quickly learn to turn elsewhere and find more reliable sites.

The Site Summary, which is the default screen for the Reports view, includes five separate sets of information about the hyperlinks on your site. The first of these is a count of all the hyperlinks. This information is then broken down into smaller segments showing those links which have not yet been verified, those which have been tested and are definitely broken, and finally, external links and internal links. Double-clicking on any of these listings will bring up the Broken Hyperlinks report as shown in the lower-right figure on the next page. This report will show you, not just the number of broken links, but the URL of the link's target, the filename for the origin page of the link, and the title of the originating Web page. If you are in a multiauthor environment, the data on who modified the page will also be useful. Despite the title of the report, it will also show unverified links in addition to just the broken ones. Thus, it's a good idea to run a link verification before taking the results of the report too seriously.

TAKE NOTE

SAVE THOSE CHANGES!

When you check for broken hyperlinks or, for that matter, anything involving them, FrontPage uses the saved version of the pages to check against, not the onscreen version. So, if you've made a change and it doesn't show up in the link reports (or the Hyperlinks view), make sure you've saved the affected page or pages.

RECALCULATING HYPERLINKS

If you're in a multi-author Web development environment and you're getting unexpected results when running checks on the links, you may want to have FrontPage recalculate the hyperlinks to incorporate any changes other developers may have made. To do so, select Tools ⇨ Recalculate Hyperlinks from the menu.

CROSS-REFERENCE

See "Modifying Links" earlier in this chapter.

FIND IT ONLINE

You can find SpeeHost's FrontPage Resources at **http://www.speedhost.net/frontpage.htm**.

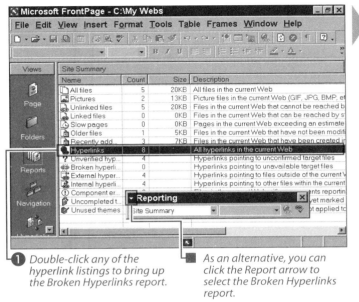

① Double-click any of the hyperlink listings to bring up the Broken Hyperlinks report.

■ As an alternative, you can click the Report arrow to select the Broken Hyperlinks report.

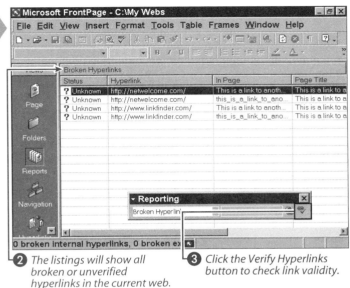

② The listings will show all broken or unverified hyperlinks in the current web.

③ Click the Verify Hyperlinks button to check link validity.

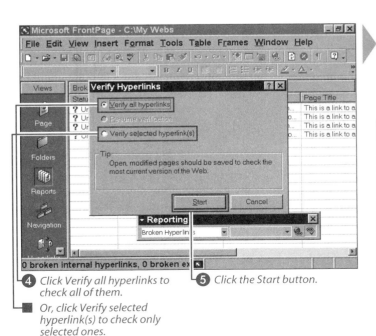

④ Click Verify all hyperlinks to check all of them.

■ Or, click Verify selected hyperlink(s) to check only selected ones.

⑤ Click the Start button.

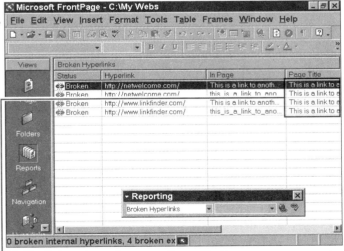

■ The listings shows the status after verification.

Personal Workbook

Q&A

1 What does *URL* stand for?

_____

_____

_____

2 What does a *mailto* link do?

_____

_____

_____

3 How do you delete a link without deleting the text or image it's based in?

_____

_____

_____

4 What does *HTTP* stand for?

_____

_____

_____

5 What is a *bookmark?*

_____

_____

_____

6 Do you have to use the "www" prefix in a Web address? Is so, why? If not, why not?

_____

_____

_____

7 What are the usual colors for hyperlinks on a Web page?

_____

_____

_____

8 What HTML element is common to both links and bookmarks?

_____

_____

_____

ANSWERS: PAGE 323

EXTRA PRACTICE

① On a single page, create a series of bookmarks and links to them that enable you to jump from one area of the page to another and back again.

② Do the same with two separate pages so you can jump from one page to an area of the other and back again.

③ Create a page with links to other pages and to an image file. View that page in Hyperlinks view.

④ Follow the same link in Page view, Preview mode, and in a Web browser.

⑤ Use the Reports view to assess the status of the hyperlinks in a series of Web pages.

⑥ Create a URL with parameters for use in a popular search engine.

REAL-WORLD APPLICATIONS

✔ If you have a very long Web page with several different headings, you may want to create a series of bookmarks to access them with.

✔ You're part of a team using FrontPage to develop a large Web site. Since someone else may have made changes you're unaware of, you may want to periodically recalculate hyperlinks.

✔ You might want to make sure that each of your Web pages has a mailto link on it so that visitors to your site can report problems to you.

✔ If you have a large number of image links, you may want to consider combining them into a single image that utilizes an image map instead.

Visual Quiz

What do you use the four buttons to the right of the URL text box for? How do you get to this dialog box?

_____

_____

_____

_____

_____

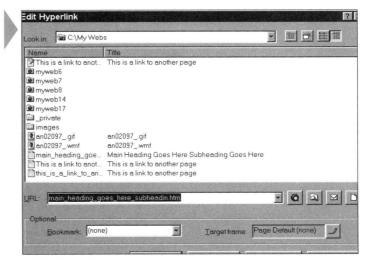

PART

II

FrontPage 2000 and Graphic Images

The chapters in this section cover the use of graphics in FrontPage webs. Chapter 5, "Applying Graphical Themes," demonstrates how to use predesigned layouts for either entire webs or individual pages. These graphical themes include background colors and images, button graphics, text settings, and so on that have been created by professional designers for your use.

In the sixth chapter, "Adding Images," you learn how to insert image files into your Web pages from local sources, the Clip Art Gallery, and the World Wide Web. You'll also find a few more advanced topics such as converting image file types.

The seventh chapter, "Modifying Images," offers greater detail on using images in your designs, including such topics as resizing, adding text, creating thumbnail images, absolute positioning, and rotating and flipping images.

The eighth chapter, "Using Image Maps," covers a specialized kind of image link that enables you to set multiple links from a single image.

CHAPTER 5

MASTER
THESE
SKILLS

▶ **Choosing a Theme**

▶ **Installing Additional Themes**

▶ **Using Theme Variations**

▶ **Modifying Colors**

▶ **Modifying Graphics**

▶ **Modifying Text**

Applying Graphical Themes

FrontPage *graphical themes* enable you to quickly and easily set a common look to your Web site. A graphical theme applies a predesigned artistic appearance to several elements on your Web pages. For example, a particular theme may set all the H1 heading elements to be red, make all the bullets diamond shaped, and use a fancy horizontal line. You can choose whether to use a background image, whether to use normal or vivid colors, and whether to have "active graphics" — animated elements instead of plain elements. For instance, active graphics display hover buttons instead of regular buttons. FrontPage themes were first introduced in FrontPage 98 and they were one of the earliest commercial applications of the concept of Cascading Style Sheets (discussed in Chapter 16). Themes are still the easiest way to use CSS in your Web page design.

The basic FrontPage installation comes with 13 principal themes, by default, and you can choose to load an additional 54 themes from the CD-ROM after you install the program, for a total of 67 themes. (If you're a power user and choose a custom installation, you can load all the themes initially, although simply clicking the Install Additional Themes option later is a lot easier than doing a custom installation.) Although the core idea of themes is to give every page in your site the same appearance, for the sake of overall consistency, you can also apply different themes to various parts of your site on a page-by-page basis. This ability can be especially useful if your particular Web site design consists of distinctly separate sections, or *subwebs*, thus extending the concept of consistency to individual segments rather than tying the entire Web site into one overall design.

Each theme also includes some variations of itself — changes of color, graphics, and backgrounds — that are available at the click of a mouse. If none of the supplied themes or their variations suit you, then you can still use the FrontPage theme facilities. You can modify any and all elements in any theme and save it as a new custom theme of your own. Feel free to change colors, fonts, background images, or graphics to suit yourself. Thanks to the ease of use inherent in FrontPage themes, CSS functionality is no longer the sole domain of the power user.

Choosing a Theme

You can apply a theme deliberately, page by page, or set a default theme that is automatically applied to every page in your web. The basic themes and how to select them are described in this section.

The Basic Graphical Themes

▶ **Artsy.** A black background with brighter text in varying shades of yellow, mustard, and orange. The font for text is Arial. Banners and buttons are reminiscent of torn paper or canvas that is painted in smears of medium-dark colors. Bullets, horizontal lines, and navigation buttons are in medium blues and greens.

▶ **Blank.** A background of white with light-gray squares. The text is black Arial. Banners are solid gray with black outlines on top and bottom, and have blue Arial text. Both regular buttons and navigation buttons are white with gray outlines and blue Arial text. Bullets are solid-black geometrical figures, and horizontal lines are plain and black.

▶ **Blueprint.** A white background with blue and black Arial text. Banners and buttons are white, outlined in light blue with curves and tick marks. Bullets are crosshairs, and horizontal lines are black with tick marks. Navigation buttons are solid light blue with a white box on the left side that contains the arrows.

▶ **Bold Stripes.** Basic black, gray, and white design. The background is white with black Arial text. Banners and buttons are solid light gray with a gray border surrounding a thin strip of white. Bullets and horizontal lines are solid black.

▶ **Capsules.** A white background with blue and black Arial text. Banners are solid blue rimmed in green. Regular buttons and navigation buttons are green, except that the regular buttons have a white interior. Banners, buttons, and navigation buttons mix straight edges and curves. Bullets are solid blue, and horizontal lines are green and blue.

▶ **Citrus Punch.** The background is plain white, and the body text is black, but the heading text is orange and the banner is a blazing blend of orange and green with a smattering of other colors. Buttons are orange balls, bullets are green squares, and horizontal lines are a potpourri of shades. Navigation buttons are white with a thin green outline and orange arrows.

Continued

TAKE NOTE

▶ BEYOND THE THEME PREVIEW

The elements shown in the theme preview aren't the only ones affected by themes. Default settings also exist for other elements, such as table borders, that are not shown in the preview. If you want to see these, you have to apply the theme and insert the element on your page.

CROSS-REFERENCE

See the following section for directions on how to add more themes.

FIND IT ONLINE

Custom themes are available at
http://www.stetsonspalace.com/.

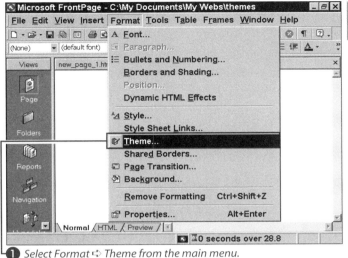

① Select Format ➪ Theme from the main menu.

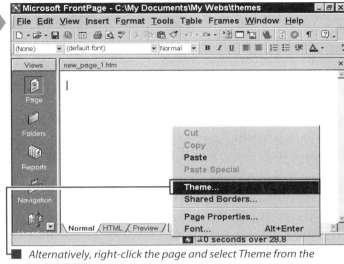

Alternatively, right-click the page and select Theme from the popup menu.

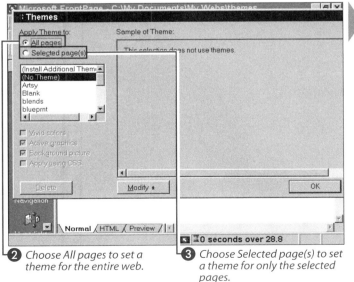

② Choose All pages to set a theme for the entire web.

③ Choose Selected page(s) to set a theme for only the selected pages.

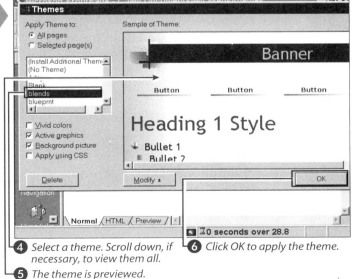

④ Select a theme. Scroll down, if necessary, to view them all.

⑤ The theme is previewed.

⑥ Click OK to apply the theme.

The Basic Graphical Themes

▶ **Expedition**. A white background with black Times text. Banners and buttons are a nice blend of black and gold. Bullets are black and brown X shapes, horizontal lines are a series of brown dashes, and navigation buttons are an attractive design in black, gold, and silver.

▶ **Industrial**. A white background with black and blue Arial text. Banners and buttons are gray with diagonal slashes of black and blue for a steel-like effect. Bullets are solid black, brown, or blue circles; horizontal lines are a series of black dots; and navigation buttons are blue, gradually fading into white, with white circles outlining the arrows.

▶ **Rice Paper**. A white background with black Times text. Banners are white with black underlining. Buttons, bullets, horizontal lines, and navigation buttons all are black.

▶ **Romanesque**. A very stylish theme with light-olive background. Text is light-brown Times. Banners are vaguely Grecian, with a silvery-gray color. Buttons are solid rectangles in the same color. Bullets are 3D diamonds, horizontal lines are a series of squares, and navigation buttons are silver-gray rectangles whose arrows have the same 3D appearance as the bullets.

▶ **Straight Edge**. A white background with black Arial text, black bullets, and horizontal lines. Banners, buttons, and navigation buttons are light-olive rectangles with black edging.

▶ **Sumi Painting**. A white background with black Arial text. Banners and buttons are a purplish gray, with undulating edges. Bullets are purple and maroon, horizontal lines are a meandering purple line, and navigation buttons are purple ovoids with ragged edges.

TAKE NOTE

▶ "ALL PAGES" DOESN'T MEAN YOU HAVE NO OPTIONS

Selecting the All pages option under "Apply Theme to" does not prevent you from later applying a different theme to an individual page or several pages. To override the overall theme, simply select a page and then apply the theme to it. After you do that, the new theme overrides the main theme for the page or pages to which you applied the new theme. Also, the All pages option is grayed out if you don't have a web open.

▶ CHANGING YOUR MIND — REMOVING THEMES

You can apply a different theme simply by following the same procedure that you used to apply the first one. Your latest choice overrides any previous choice. This is also the procedure for removing a theme totally, either from individual pages or the entire web. Instead of selecting a particular theme to replace the old one with, you choose "(No Theme)." After you click OK, the old theme is removed and, because no theme has been chosen to replace it, no theme is applied.

CROSS-REFERENCE
See Chapter 2 for more information on text.

FIND IT ONLINE
The Pixel Mill has custom themes at
http://www.pixelmill.net/catalog.asp.

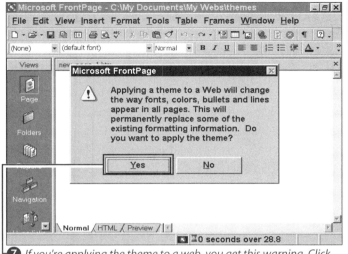

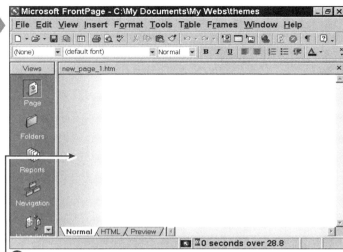

⑦ If you're applying the theme to a web, you get this warning. Click the Yes button to continue.

⑧ After some time, the theme is applied. At first, unless you already have elements in place, only the background shows.

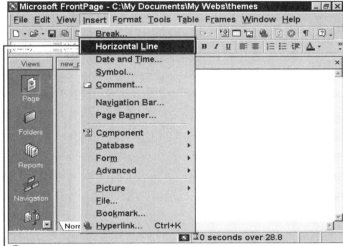

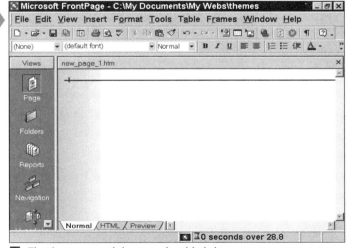

⑨ To see more effects of the theme, add elements (in this case, a horizontal line).

■ The theme controls how newly added elements appear onscreen.

Installing Additional Themes

When you install FrontPage, only the basic 13 graphical themes are copied onto your hard drive. However, that's only about one-fifth of the themes that come with FrontPage. If you want to use all the available themes, you need to add the other 54 of them. As explained in the introduction to this chapter, you may not need to perform this step. Power users who selected a custom installation may have chosen at that time to install all the themes. This section applies only to those who either chose the typical installation or chose to do a custom installation but did not select the option to install all themes.

If you're not sure what installation options were chosen regarding graphical themes, either because you didn't note them at the time or because someone else installed the program for you, you can find out by looking at the Themes listing in the Themes dialog box. The upper-right figure on the facing page shows this dialog box. If the first item listed is "(Install Additional Themes)," then you need to follow the process described in this section. If the first item listed is "(No Theme)," then all the themes have already been installed. Don't let the phrase "No Theme" confuse you, because it has nothing to do with how many themes are available to you, but simply means that the current web has no theme applied to it yet.

You're not limited to even the 67 total themes that FrontPage is supplied with. You can also create your own themes by modifying the colors, graphics, and text, as explained in the last three sections of this chapter. After you find the look that you want, you simply save the new theme under a different name, and it is available to you for instant use from then on. You can also get themes that other people have created. Some sources for such themes are listed in some of the Find It Online segments in this chapter.

TAKE NOTE

▶ **YOU CAN ALSO USE THE MAIN MENU**
If you don't like popup menus and prefer to use the menu bar, you can also get to the Themes dialog box by selecting Format ⇨ Theme from the main menu.

▶ **THE FULL INSTALLATION PROCESS**
The lower-left figure on the facing page represents only the first screen in the whole installation process. As the Windows installer goes through the process, you will see several more screens, but the options remain the same — wait for the process to complete, or click the Cancel button to abort it.

CROSS-REFERENCE
See the next section, "Using Theme Variations," for more information on applying themes.

FIND IT ONLINE
More themes are available from the Theme Mart at http://www.thememart.com/.

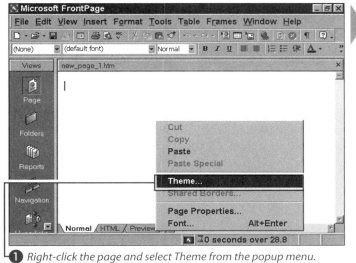

① *Right-click the page and select Theme from the popup menu.*

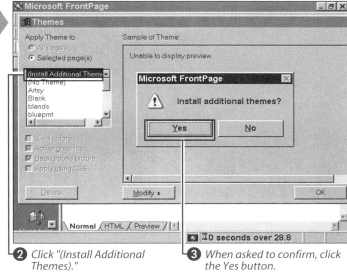

② *Click "(Install Additional Themes)."*

③ *When asked to confirm, click the Yes button.*

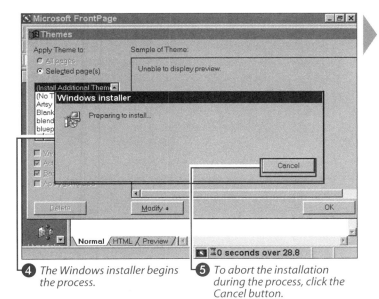

④ *The Windows installer begins the process.*

⑤ *To abort the installation during the process, click the Cancel button.*

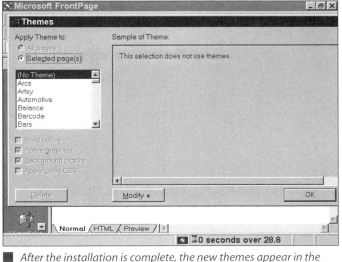

■ *After the installation is complete, the new themes appear in the listing.*

Using Theme Variations

I n addition to the normal look, each theme has a few variations available. Choices include two different sets of colors, two different sets of graphical elements, and the option to have either a background image or just a background color.

By default, the normal colors are used (meaning, in terms of the Themes dialog box, that the Vivid Colors check box is not selected). Active graphics are also the norm, as is the presence of a background image (which FrontPage calls a "background picture" in this case). "Active graphics" are animated elements, such as hover buttons, instead of static elements, such as normal buttons. Generally, active graphics are preferable, because they have a much nicer appearance than the relatively dull normal graphics.

Every theme, in theory, has a choice of either a normal set of colors or an alternative "vivid" set of colors that you may apply to the page elements (such as text colors, hyperlink colors, and so forth). In many cases, however, selecting the vivid colors over the normal colors doesn't change the appearance very much. Generally, you get more of an impact from the vivid set of colors if you don't use a background image. Using vivid colors causes the background color to change, but this change can't be seen if you have a background image is in place, because the background image covers the background color.

Your most basic choice is whether to use a background image. Although this may seem like a choice between using a background color or a background image, technically, when you choose to use a background image, the background color is still present — it's simply hidden behind the image.

TAKE NOTE

▶ NOT ALL THEMES HAVE BACKGROUND IMAGES

While the vast majority of the graphical themes do have background images, some don't, such as the Artsy and Safari themes, which have a plain black background color instead.

▶ YOU CAN USE THE MAIN MENU

If you prefer to use the menu bar, you can get to the Themes dialog box by selecting Format ⇨ Theme from the main menu.

▶ WHAT IS THAT CSS CHECK BOX FOR?

Although it's grouped together with the three check boxes for altering theme colors and graphics, the check box labeled "Apply using CSS" isn't really related to them at all. Selecting that check box generates an external Cascading Style Sheet file that serves the same purpose as a FrontPage theme. The difference between the two approaches is, as they say, "transparent to the user," and you don't need to concern yourself with the file even if you take the CSS approach. Any changes that you make to the theme will be recorded in the external CSS file if you're using one.

CROSS-REFERENCE
See Chapter 6 for more information on background images.

FIND IT ONLINE
You can also get custom themes from http://www.themepak.com/.

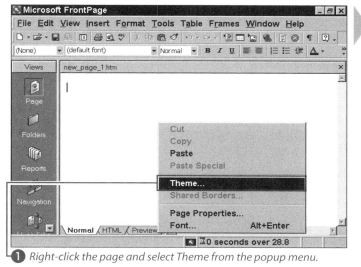

1 *Right-click the page and select Theme from the popup menu.*

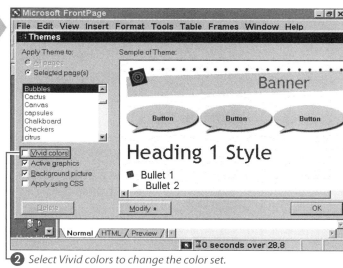

2 *Select Vivid colors to change the color set.*

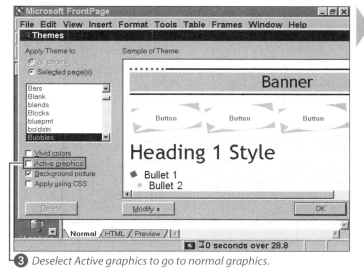

3 *Deselect Active graphics to go to normal graphics.*

4 *Deselect Background picture to remove the background image.*

5 *Click OK to complete the process.*

Modifying Colors

If none of the themes supplied with FrontPage is exactly what you need, you can use any of them as the basis for creating your own custom themes. This section, the first of three in this chapter that deal with custom themes, explains how to alter the colors in a theme.

Every theme has two color sets available to it, which are supposed to be radically different from each other. The normal color set is the default, and the vivid color set is the alternative. In many themes, however, the vivid colors don't vary too much from the normal colors, and the term "vivid" is singularly inappropriate for some of these colors. You simply have to try both sets for any particular theme that you're interested in using, to see how much difference exists between them. As noted in the preceding section, the vivid color set often looks its best when no background image is in place. By using the program's color modification dialog boxes, you can alter the colors in either the normal or the vivid set (or both, but you still have to do them one set at a time).

When using FrontPage themes, you can use any one of three different methods to modify the colors of your Web pages' elements. In the first method, illustrated in the lower-right figure on the facing page, all the current themes are listed, along with a color bar showing the principal colors in each theme.

You can click any theme name or its associated color bar to make that entire color scheme available for your custom theme. Thus, you can replace the colors in one theme with the colors in another theme. This is a really useful technique if you find that you like the graphics in one theme but prefer the colors from another one. By using the other theme's color scheme, you can create your own custom third theme that has the best features of both the others.

Continued

TAKE NOTE

▶ YOU CAN ALSO USE THE MAIN MENU

If you don't like popup menus and prefer to use the menu bar, you can also get to the Themes dialog box by selecting Format ⇨ Theme from the main menu.

▶ DON'T MAKE IT HIDEOUS

The wise Web page designer realizes that the ability to alter colors doesn't automatically confer artistic taste. Good Web artists tailor their output for the audience they intend to appeal to. Before you commit to using color changes, take a good, long, dispassionate look at them to be sure that they are going to be pleasing to your audience. If you're looking for a cyberpunk audience, glaring colors with high contrast are fine. If, on the other hand, you're dealing with a more conservative viewership, you may want to tone it down a bit.

CROSS-REFERENCE

See the preceding section, "Using Theme Variations."

FIND IT ONLINE

Check out FrontLook at **http://www.dpasoftware. com/flproddesc.htm**.

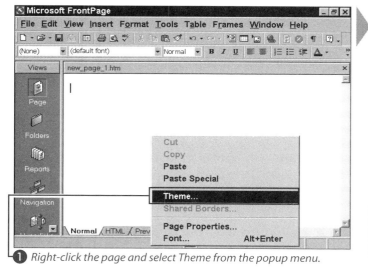

① *Right-click the page and select Theme from the popup menu.*

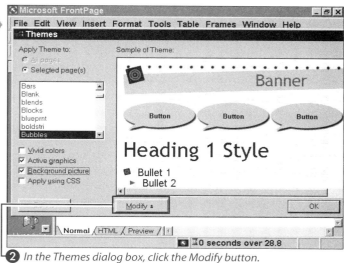

② *In the Themes dialog box, click the Modify button.*

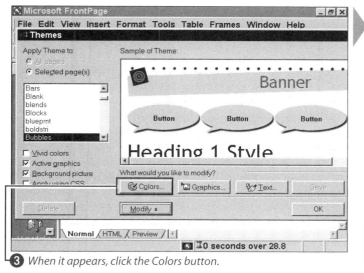

③ *When it appears, click the Colors button.*

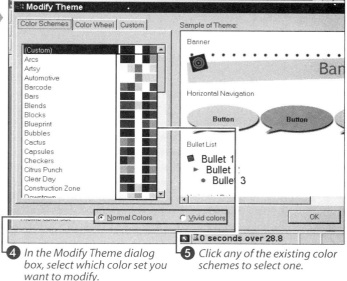

④ *In the Modify Theme dialog box, select which color set you want to modify.*

⑤ *Click any of the existing color schemes to select one.*

Modifying Colors
Continued

The second color-modification method is to use the color wheel, a tool for automatically selecting an entire set of colors simultaneously. The upper-left figure on the facing page shows the color wheel.

When you want to use the color wheel or select a color scheme from one of the existing themes, remember that the five colors shown in the color bar are not all the colors in the entire theme. That display actually is limited. The colors that are shown only represent, in this order, Heading 2, Heading 1, Background, Regular Text, and Regular Hyperlink. However, because those five elements represent the majority of items on a typical Web page, the color bar does give a pretty good thumbnail sketch of how the finished page will look.

The third color-modification method, shown in the upper-right figure on the facing page, skips the color scheme approach entirely and presents a more detailed means of altering colors. With this approach, you modify the colors of individual elements, in much the same way that you change a font color or background color in Page view. In fact, the actual process of color selection is totally identical.

The items whose color you can alter in this manner are Background, Banner Text, Body, Headings 1 through 6, Hyperlinks, Hyperlinks (Active), Hyperlinks (Followed), Navigation Text, and Table Border.

TAKE NOTE

USING "MORE COLORS"

A fully detailed description of the process for choosing colors is provided in the "Changing Text Color" and "Setting the Background Color" sections of Chapter 3.

YOU CAN'T SAVE OVER A MICROSOFT THEME

The only graphical theme files you can save over by using the Save button, or delete by using the Delete button, are your own custom themes. The original themes from Microsoft are impossible to save over or delete, at least from within FrontPage. If you modify an original theme file and want to save your changes, you have to use the Save As button to rename the file as a new file. If you're familiar with Windows file management, you can use Windows Explorer to alter the names and locations of the theme files just as you can with any other type of file. You also can alter the original theme files by utilizing any decent text editor and saving over them.

FINDING THE THEME FILES

Although the original theme files are located in C:\Program Files\Common Files\Microsoft Shared\Themes, the custom ones are found in C:\WINDOWS\Application Data\Microsoft\Themes (assuming that you have done a normal installation on your C drive).

CROSS-REFERENCE

See Chapter 3 for detailed information on setting colors.

FIND IT ONLINE

Try the Captivations Theme Mall at http://www.captivations.com/theme/designers/adr.htm.

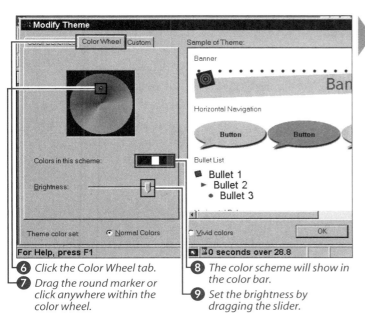

6 *Click the Color Wheel tab.*

7 *Drag the round marker or click anywhere within the color wheel.*

8 *The color scheme will show in the color bar.*

9 *Set the brightness by dragging the slider.*

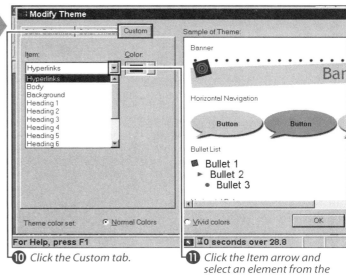

10 *Click the Custom tab.*

11 *Click the Item arrow and select an element from the list.*

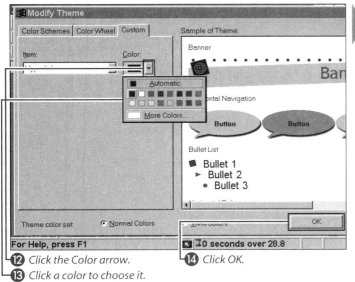

12 *Click the Color arrow.*

13 *Click a color to choose it.*

14 *Click OK.*

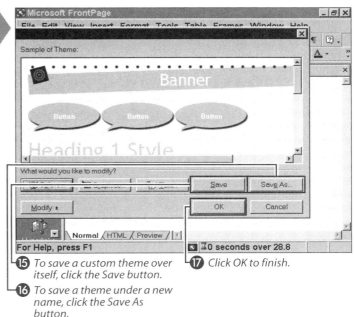

15 *To save a custom theme over itself, click the Save button.*

16 *To save a theme under a new name, click the Save As button.*

17 *Click OK to finish.*

Modifying Graphics

FrontPage themes include several graphical elements, such as bullets and buttons, that you can modify to suit yourself. The following items can be altered via the Graphics modification screen: Background Picture, Banner, Bullet List, Global Navigation Buttons, Horizontal Navigation, Horizontal Rule, Quick Back Button, Quick Home Button, Quick Next Button, Quick Up Button, and Vertical Navigation.

As with the color settings, you can choose either of two graphics sets — Normal and Active. When the graphics modification screen first appears, you aren't given the option to choose between the normal graphics set and the active graphics set. These radio buttons are grayed out at this point for one simple reason: the first item in the listing is the Background Picture, for which both graphics sets use the same background image. When you select a different item from the drop-down list that has a different file for each of the two separate graphics sets, the radio buttons become active, and you can then choose between graphics sets. (Incidentally, the same thing occurs with the Global Navigation Buttons setting, for the same reason.)

If you decide to change the graphics file associated with a particular element in one of the graphics sets, you should consider all the other elements before you even begin to design the replacement graphic. The themes supplied with FrontPage were, after all, developed by some very talented Web page designers, and all the elements in them were carefully chosen to work together in creating an overall appearance that is both pleasant and workable. Altering any one element without giving due consideration to that alteration's impact on the other elements may well leave you with a look to your Web pages that is other than what you desire.

Continued

TAKE NOTE

▶ YOU CAN ALSO USE THE MAIN MENU

If you don't like popup menus and prefer to use the menu bar, you can also get to the Themes dialog box by selecting Format ⇨ Theme from the main menu.

▶ YOU CAN CHOOSE SETS AHEAD OF TIME

If you select the graphics set (normal or active graphics) by setting or clearing the Active Graphics check box in the Themes dialog box before you begin the modification, then you don't need to make a selection later. FrontPage remembers which set you chose and automatically selects the appropriate radio button. Of course, you can also use the radio buttons to change your mind, if desired.

CROSS-REFERENCE
See Chapter 6 for additional information on images.

FIND IT ONLINE
Alysta FrontPage Themes is located at http://www.alysta.com/fpthemes/resource.htm.

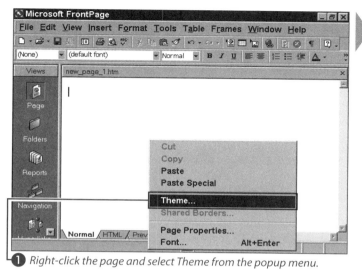

❶ Right-click the page and select Theme from the popup menu.

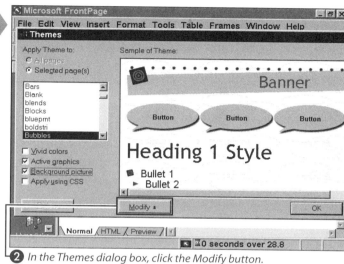

❷ In the Themes dialog box, click the Modify button.

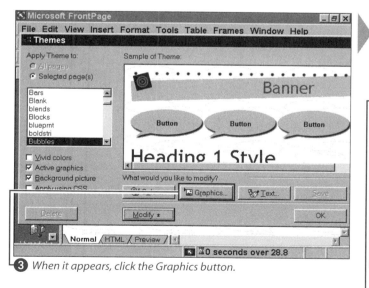

❸ When it appears, click the Graphics button.

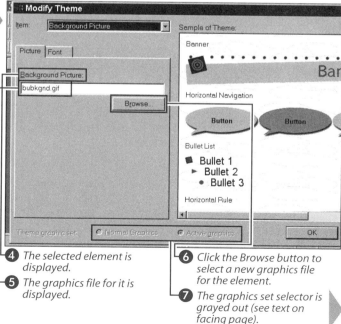

❹ The selected element is displayed.

❺ The graphics file for it is displayed.

❻ Click the Browse button to select a new graphics file for the element.

❼ The graphics set selector is grayed out (see text on facing page).

Modifying Graphics

Continued

Changing Fonts, Styles, and Sizes

In addition to simply changing the base file from which graphical elements are built, you also need to consider the fonts and styles that are used for those elements that use fonts — and the majority of graphical elements in FrontPage themes do use fonts.

The only items that do not have associated fonts are the Background Picture, Bullet List, and the Horizontal Rule. All the other graphical elements do have fonts, and you can select which fonts they use, or alter the settings for the existing fonts. For instance, you may want to keep a particular font but change its size. Perhaps you like everything about the font except for its vertical or horizontal alignment. Whatever your desires, FrontPage themes are very accommodating to even the most demanding Web designer.

A word of advice about font sizes. The listed font sizes, 1 through 7, include specified point sizes (8 points through 36 points) and these are not really accurate. Many factors can affect the way in which fonts are displayed on the screen of a visitor to your Web site. If you haven't read Chapter 3, "Modifying Text," then you should be aware that you can't set a precise point size for your fonts by selecting these sizes. The point sizes listed are merely those that appear if the user of a Microsoft Web browser has accepted the default settings and has never customized their browser or used the font magnification capabilities that all the major browsers have. If you want total control over the size of the fonts as they are viewed in a visitor's Web browser, then you'll have to master the intricacies of Cascading Style Sheets (see Chapter 16); CSS gives you complete control over this issue — to the degree the viewer's Web browser conforms with CSS standards.

The fonts can be horizontally aligned to the left, center, or right, and vertically aligned to the top, middle, or bottom.

TAKE NOTE

FONT STYLES ARE LIMITED

FrontPage themes don't give you the full range of possible font styles. You can't, for instance, make a font strikethrough or blinking. You are limited in this instance to setting the fonts to regular, bold, italic, or a combination of the last two styles, bold italic.

WHAT'S NORMAL, ANYWAY?

The "Normal" font setting doesn't really exist. It's just a kind of shorthand for the default font size setting of 3.

WHAT'S THE POINT?

A "point" is $1/72$ of an inch. Thus, a 36-point font (size 7) is $1/2$ inch in height, an 18-point font (size 5) is $1/4$ inch in height, and a 12-point font (size 3) is $1/6$ of an inch in height.

CROSS-REFERENCE

See Chapter 3, "Modifying Text" for more information on font styles.

FIND IT ONLINE

The Graphics Depot has FrontPage themes at http://www.graficadesign.com/.

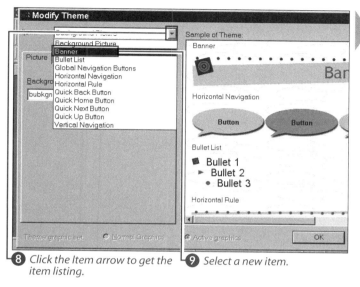

8 Click the Item arrow to get the item listing.

9 Select a new item.

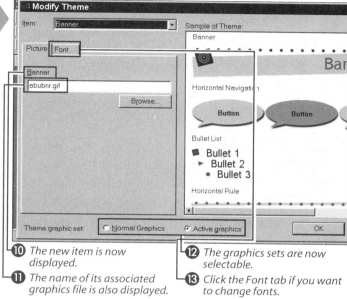

10 The new item is now displayed.

11 The name of its associated graphics file is also displayed.

12 The graphics sets are now selectable.

13 Click the Font tab if you want to change fonts.

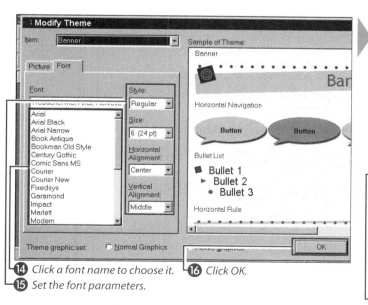

14 Click a font name to choose it.

15 Set the font parameters.

16 Click OK.

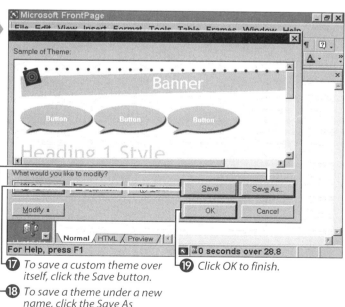

17 To save a custom theme over itself, click the Save button.

18 To save a theme under a new name, click the Save As button.

19 Click OK to finish.

Modifying Text

The term "text modification" doesn't refer to the same thing for FrontPage themes as it does for the fonts on graphical items, such as banners and navigation buttons. For FrontPage themes, text modification refers strictly to the body text and the heading levels 1 through 6 (or, in HTML parlance, H1 through H6). If you want to change the fonts on any other items on your Web page, you need to refer to the instructions in the preceding section, "Modifying Graphics."

Unlike text modification on graphical items, the selected item in a theme isn't listed in a separate label in the dialog box (see the lower-right figure on the facing page), but only shows up as the selected element in the Item list box. Another, very important, difference to consider between graphics modification and color modification is that the fonts and styles on all of your Web pages are exactly the same, regardless of which graphics or color set is chosen. With color, you have normal and vivid colors. With graphics, you have normal and active graphics. Text in FrontPage themes makes no distinction between normal and anything else; text is text, regardless of what other options you choose. Whatever choices you do make for the text affects all the pages in your Web, regardless of what other options you select for graphical or color displays. What this means, in practical terms, is that you have to settle on one font that you will be happy with for both normal and vivid colors, and both active and normal graphics.

Continued

TAKE NOTE

YOU CAN ALSO USE THE MAIN MENU

If you don't like popup menus and prefer to use the menu bar, you can also get to the Themes dialog box by selecting Format ⇨ Theme from the main menu.

WHY ARE MULTIPLE FONTS LISTED?

You probably noticed that some items have multiple different fonts listed. The body font, for instance, lists "Arial, Arial, Helvetica" for the font (see the lower-right figure on the facing page). The reason is that the Web page might be viewed on various major computer systems, each of which may have different fonts available. Say, for instance, that one visitor is using a UNIX system and another visitor is using a Windows system. A very similar font may exist on one system that is not found on the other. Unfortunately, FrontPage is not advanced enough to take this phenomenon into account when dealing with its themes. No way exists to list multiple fonts in FrontPage themes; the listing is derived from those fonts that are available on your own particular system, and selecting one eliminates another.

KEEP IT SIMPLE

It's best not to yield to the temptation to use really fancy fonts for these settings. The body text and headings are critical to the look of your Web page. Try to keep them easily readable.

CROSS-REFERENCE

See the preceding section, "Modifying Graphics."

FIND IT ONLINE

Take a look at Rich's FrontPage Themes at
http://server5.hypermart.net/rsnider2/.

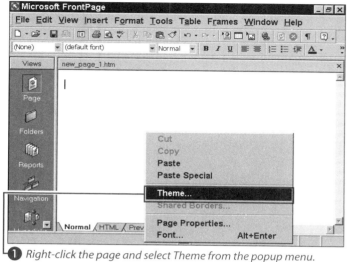

1 Right-click the page and select Theme from the popup menu.

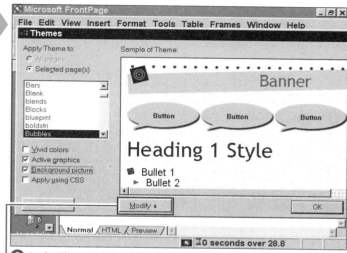

2 In the Themes dialog box, click the Modify button.

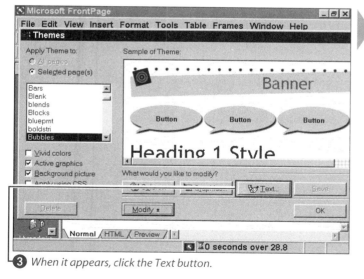

3 When it appears, click the Text button.

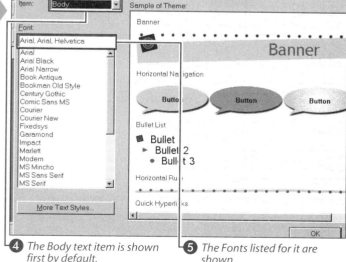

4 The Body text item is shown first by default.

5 The Fonts listed for it are shown.

Modifying Text

Continued

When you are dealing with fonts in FrontPage themes, remember that you can change font settings only for the body text (the text that is the bulk of your Web page, including all hyperlinks, whether Normal, Followed, or Active) and the six heading levels (H1 through H6).

Any changes that you make are displayed for your attention in the preview window at the right of the dialog box. (See the upper-right figure on the facing page for details.) If you don't like the look of the changes you have made, feel free to experiment further with the font for that element.

Also remember that, unlike when you use pure HTML, you can't specify multiple fonts in a FrontPage theme. Unfortunately, FrontPage limits the fonts you can use to articulate your ideas to those modes of expression established by Microsoft's programmers.

TAKE NOTE

▶ BODY TEXT IS IN HYPERLINKS, TOO

The body text setting affects not only the font associated with the general text on a Web page, but also the text in which hyperlinks are displayed. You'll notice in the preview window that, when you change the font for the Regular Text Sample, the same font is applied to the Regular Hyperlink, Followed Hyperlink, and Active Hyperlink examples in the preview window. You cannot, unfortunately, set a separate font for hyperlinks only.

▶ TAKE CARE WHICH FONTS YOU USE

Only three fonts are in common usage on all the major computer systems: Arial (also called Helvetica), Times (also called Times Roman or Times New Roman), and Courier (also called Courier New). If you choose other fonts that are available on your computer, your pages may not display the same way on other people's systems. As a default measure, a visitor's Web browser will try its best to accommodate your font settings by displaying the font that it believes to be the closest to the one that you have specified.

▶ FEEL FREE TO ABORT

As long as you haven't saved the changes yet, any time that you want to cancel the changes that you have made to the fonts in your FrontPage theme, just hit the Escape (Esc) key. If you want to ditch the whole operation instead of just retracting the latest changes, continue to press the Esc key until you get all the way back to the original Web page.

CROSS-REFERENCE

See Chapter 3 for more information on font size and style.

FIND IT ONLINE

The EB Themeshop is at http://www.ebthemeshop.com/.

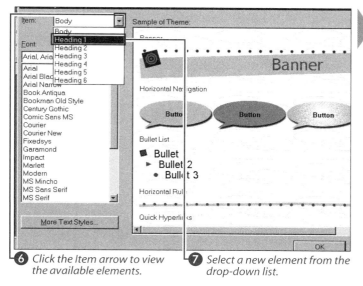

6 Click the Item arrow to view the available elements.

7 Select a new element from the drop-down list.

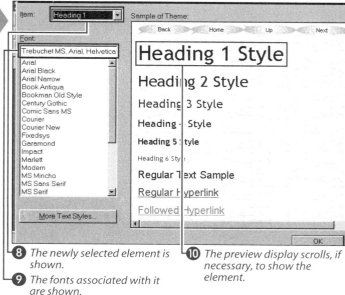

8 The newly selected element is shown.

9 The fonts associated with it are shown.

10 The preview display scrolls, if necessary, to show the element.

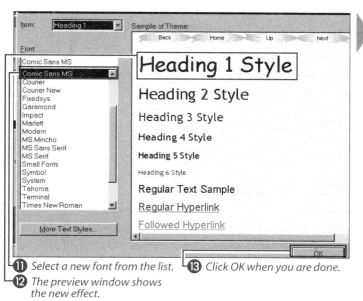

11 Select a new font from the list.

12 The preview window shows the new effect.

13 Click OK when you are done.

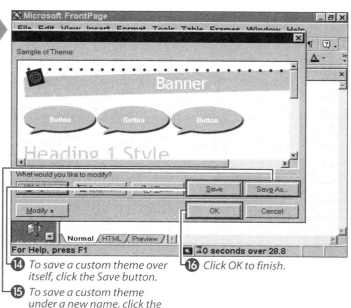

14 To save a custom theme over itself, click the Save button.

15 To save a custom theme under a new name, click the Save As button.

16 Click OK to finish.

Personal Workbook

Q&A

1 What is the purpose of a FrontPage graphical theme?

_____

_____

_____

2 How many basic themes are there? How many additional?

_____

_____

_____

3 How do you create a custom theme?

_____

_____

_____

4 How do you remove a theme from a page or web that has one?

_____

_____

_____

5 How do you delete a theme from the listing?

_____

_____

_____

6 How many color sets does each theme have? How many graphics sets?

_____

_____

_____

7 Does each graphics set have its own background image?

_____

_____

_____

8 Which sets are affected by font modifications?

_____

_____

_____

ANSWERS: PAGE 324

EXTRA PRACTICE

1 Create a Web page that uses several elements and then try out different themes on it.

2 Use one of the FrontPage themes to base your own custom theme on.

3 Experiment with changing the graphical elements in a theme.

4 Try out different background colors with a theme.

5 Change the heading elements in a theme so that they use Arial font instead of Times.

6 If you're comfortable with Windows files, take a look at the actual themes and see how they're constructed.

REAL-WORLD APPLICATIONS

✔ You're faced with designing an entire Web site for a client or your company. Rather than start from scratch, you might want to try out the graphical themes to see whether one of them will suit your needs.

✔ You're almost satisfied with a particular graphical theme, but it doesn't quite work for your needs. Perhaps altering some of the elements, such as by adding your own graphics, would do the trick.

✔ You like some of the elements from one theme and some from another. If you created your own custom theme, you could blend the elements.

✔ If you're not comfortable with creating your own themes, you might want to check out some of the ones other people have made.

Visual Quiz

How do you get to this dialog box? What do the five-color bars represent?

_____

_____

_____

_____

_____

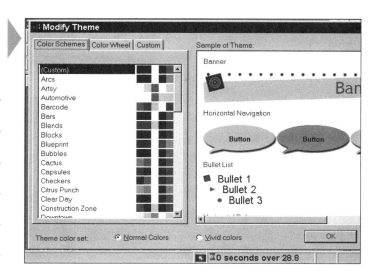

CHAPTER 6

Adding Images

Images are an important part of most Web sites today. They add color and visual appeal to a Web page and, when properly chosen and applied, can vastly increase the viability and understandability of your presentation.

Many sources of images in computerized formats are available. One such source is the *Clip Art Gallery*, which comes with FrontPage and is designed to work from within it. The images that come with the Clip Art Gallery vary widely in both topic and quality, and many more are available at Microsoft's support Web site; these images can be imported directly into the Clip Art Gallery. Other sources include CD-ROMs that come with popular graphics programs (or are available for separate purchase at office supply, art, and computer stores), artists' sites on the World Wide Web, and image archives on the Web.

After you place images on your Web pages, you can use FrontPage to convert them from a variety of popular file formats into one of the three formats that are common on the Web. These formats — GIF, JPEG, and PNG — are the only ones that work with all common Web browsers.

You can also use FrontPage to manipulate the images on your Web pages. Although many of the program's graphics capabilities are covered in the next chapter, a few of them are examined here, such as the capability to set the text alignment and word wrap characteristics, which determine how words that accompany your images are displayed on your Web pages.

This chapter also shows you how to use image spacing to control the spacing between your images and other elements on your page, how to use borders, and how to set up your graphics programs to work seamlessly with FrontPage so that you can edit images without interrupting your Web page design process. You'll also discover different ways to keep visitors to your Web site happy while they wait for images to download, such as by using alternate text to describe the images before they appear, or by loading lower-resolution copies first. Then, you'll learn why you should use alternate text to help visitors with certain handicaps feel at home on your Web site.

Finally, you'll see how to choose and use the right kind of background images for your Web pages, picking the right size and color depth for your intended audience.

Inserting Images from the Clip Art Gallery

The Clip Art Gallery (the "Gallery") is a separate program from FrontPage, but it's fully integrated with it and can be used from within FrontPage. As its name implies, the Clip Art Gallery is a collection of clip art, and you can use the clips on your Web pages. However, it is more than just a bunch of images — it is actually a database program that is specifically geared to handle computerized clip art.

The Gallery's images are classified by various categories, such as Animals, Food & Dining, Weather, and so forth. In addition to the Gallery's categories, you can create your own and assign any of the images to them. The same image can be in more than one category; for instance, a simple, colored square may be found under both the Bullets & Icons category and the Web Bullets category. The various categories of images that the Gallery provides are searchable by keywords.

Although the majority of the images available in the Clip Art Gallery are fairly simplistic (ranging from color cartoons to line drawings that are more in the nature of iconic symbols than accurate artistic representations), a decent amount of worthwhile artwork can be found among the selections. In addition to the artwork itself, the Gallery includes several photographs.

The Clip Art Gallery is designed for the purpose of inserting a single image, and it shuts itself down at the time that you make the insertion. This feature might pose problems in some applications, but it's fine for Web design, where most images are standalones.

Continued

TAKE NOTE

WINDOWS METAFILE FORMAT

The images that come with the Clip Art Gallery are all in Windows Metafile format (WMF). If you're already familiar with using images on the Web, this may cause you to wonder a bit, because this isn't one of the few commonly accepted image file formats in use on the Web. The reason for this is that the Clip Art Gallery isn't really designed for use specifically with FrontPage and the Web, but is designed for the general Microsoft Office suite of programs. Because FrontPage is now an integral part of Office, Microsoft apparently decided simply to use its existing program and clip art rather than develop ones that were specifically geared toward Web developers. Although WMF images work with Microsoft Internet Explorer, they won't work with any other Web browser, so it's best to convert any images that you insert from the Clip Art Gallery into one of the more acceptable image file formats, as described later in this chapter.

CROSS-REFERENCE

See "Converting Image Types" later in this chapter.

FIND IT ONLINE

Brandi Jasmine's Gallery is at http://www.twostar.com/gallery/.

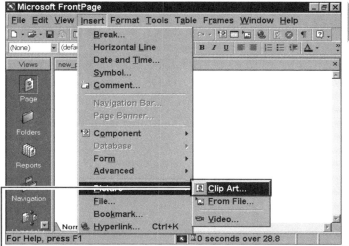

1 Select Insert ⇨ Picture ⇨ Clip Art from the main menu.

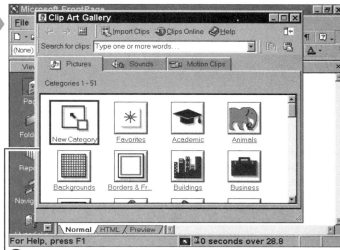

2 Click one of the categories to browse the clip art.

■ Alternatively, type keywords into the search box and press the Enter key.

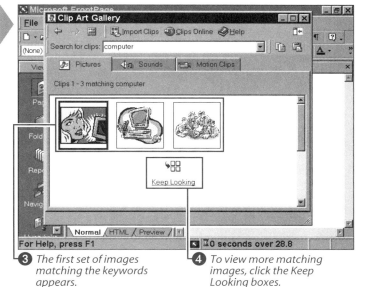

3 The first set of images matching the keywords appears.

4 To view more matching images, click the Keep Looking boxes.

Inserting Images from the Clip Art Gallery *Continued*

To find out an image's file format, size, and the first several keywords in its listing, rest the mouse pointer on it for a moment and read the data from the popup help bubble. When you're selecting images in the Clip Art Gallery, the set of options that you are given depends on whether you click the left-mouse button or the right-mouse button. When you click the left-mouse button, you get an iconic popup menu that offers four options — Insert clip, Preview clip, Add clip to Favorites or other category, and Find similar clips. When you click the right-mouse button, you get a standard popup menu with these options: Insert, Copy, Paste, Delete, Select All, Recover, and Clip Properties.

You can use the Clip Art Gallery to store all of your images, regardless of their format. The fact that it comes with all of its clip art in WMF format doesn't mean a thing — that's just the format that Microsoft chose to use for its Office-related clip art. Likewise, you don't really need to store your images in the Gallery, because you can insert images from disk or the Web without ever using the Gallery. However, storing your images in the Gallery does offer one major advantage: you can categorize all of your clip art and assign keywords to each of your images.

TAKE NOTE

▶ THE SMALL WINDOW BUTTON

If the Clip Art Gallery dialog box is too large for your tastes, you can use it in a much thinner form by clicking the Change to Small Window button in the upper-right corner. You can restore it to its normal size by clicking the same button (now renamed the Change to Full Window button). If you prefer the complex keyboard alternatives, you can minimize the dialog box by using Ctrl+Shift+< and maximize it by pressing Ctrl+Shift+>.

▶ FILE MANAGEMENT BONUS

If you prefer, you can use the Clip Art Gallery to manage your image files, but still keep them separately available. Just copy them into the Gallery instead of moving them into it.

▶ THE RECOVER OPTION

The Recover option in the right-click popup menu is used to manage the Clip Art Gallery's database. Like any other database, it can develop holes and wasted space due to a series of deletions and insertions. The Recover option enables you to either compact the database or restore images whose information has been deleted from the database. Note that you can't use it to restore a deleted image, just the deleted information for an existing image.

CROSS-REFERENCE
See Chapter 7 for more information on modifying images.

FIND IT ONLINE
Take a look at FrontPage Frenzy at http://www.411law.com/ff/index.htm.

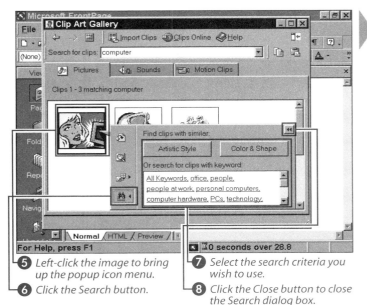

5 Left-click the image to bring up the popup icon menu.

6 Click the Search button.

7 Select the search criteria you wish to use.

8 Click the Close button to close the Search dialog box.

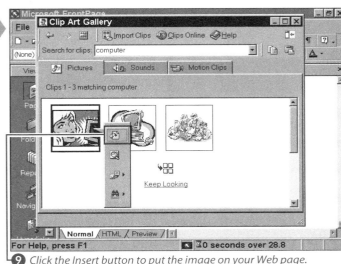

9 Click the Insert button to put the image on your Web page.

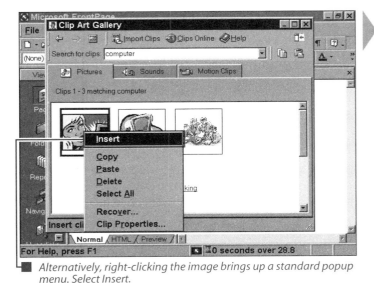

■ Alternatively, right-clicking the image brings up a standard popup menu. Select Insert.

■ The image appears on your Web page.

Inserting Images from Files

You don't have to limit your graphical work with FrontPage to using only the images found in the Clip Art Gallery. You can also insert images from files, whether they're on your local hard drive, floppy disk, CD-ROM, other mass-storage device, or another node in a network that your computer is a part of.

FrontPage can handle a large variety of image file types in addition to the normal GIF, JPEG, and PNG types that are commonly used for Web sites. The preceding section regarding the Clip Art Gallery already mentioned the WMF format (.wmf extension), but FrontPage goes much farther than that, enabling you to insert images in the following formats: Windows Bitmap (.bmp), Tagged Image Format Files, or TIFF (.tif), Sun Raster (.ras), Postscript (.eps), PCX (.pcx), Kodak PhotoCD (.pcd), and Targa (.tga). As previously stated, though, these image file formats normally aren't encountered on the Web, and they won't work in their original state in Web browsers. However, when you save a page that includes file formats that aren't Web-compatible, FrontPage automatically converts those images into GIFs, by default. This process also converts the images to 256-color images, because that's the most colors that can be displayed in a GIF image. If you want to preserve an image that has a greater color depth than a GIF file can support, you can avoid this color-depth conversion by converting the image to a JPEG image before you save the page that contains it. Because a JPEG file is already Web-compatible, FrontPage won't perform its automatic file format conversion on it. The same is also true of the newer PNG file format. Which format should you use? Most graphics people agree that a PNG is better for images with straight lines and solid colors, whereas a JPEG is better for images with subtle changes and color shadings, such as nature shots or portraits.

TAKE NOTE

▶ CD-ROM CLIP ART COLLECTIONS

The vast majority of computer graphics programs include a variety of clip art as a part of their basic package. Sometimes, this amounts to tens of thousands of professionally drawn illustrations or stock photographs that you can include in your Web page designs. Even if you don't do any of your own graphic development and don't own a professional graphics program, several CD-ROM clip art collections should be available at any good computer or office supply store.

▶ CHECK THAT FORMAT!

If you do purchase a clip art collection that you intend to use with FrontPage, make sure that the images are in one of the formats that FrontPage can handle. Although it can cope with most of the available formats, it doesn't work with all of them.

CROSS-REFERENCE
See the following section for instructions on how to insert images from the Web.

FIND IT ONLINE
The Webpedia Animation Archive is at http://animations.webpedia.com/.

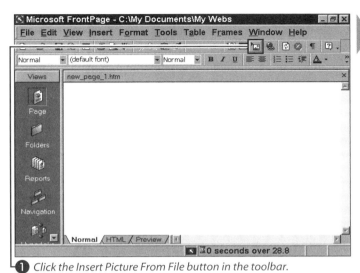

1 Click the Insert Picture From File button in the toolbar.

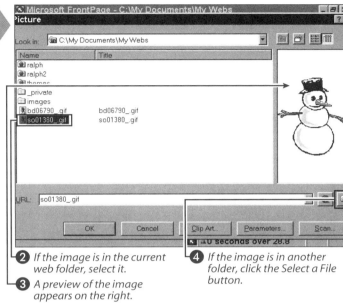

2 If the image is in the current web folder, select it.

3 A preview of the image appears on the right.

4 If the image is in another folder, click the Select a File button.

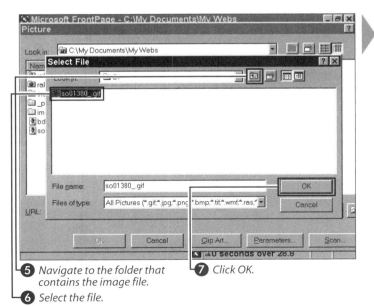

5 Navigate to the folder that contains the image file.

6 Select the file.

7 Click OK.

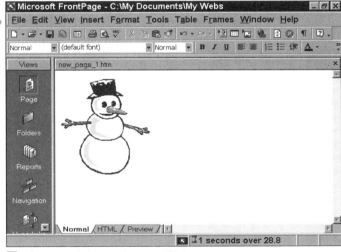

■ The image is inserted on your Web page.

119

Inserting Images from the Web

Most people who've been around the Web for any amount of time have found many striking bits of art that they've downloaded and stored in folders on their hard drives. Some folks even have carefully catalogued sets of floppies or Zip disks filled with them. When it's time to add one of these images to a Web page, you have to locate it and go through the image-insertion procedure outlined in the previous section. This has been the time-honored and invariable process if you find an image that you want to use on a Web site.

FrontPage offers an interesting alternative approach to this procedure, however. Whereas the traditional procedure is to Web surf, download a Web image file, add it to your file collection, and then open FrontPage and insert the image onto your Web page in an entirely separate operation, FrontPage lets you grab the image from the Web and insert it directly into your own Web page in a single process. You simply start just like you were going to insert an image from a local file, but instead of choosing to search your files, you switch to your Web browser and go picture hunting. After you find an image that you want, FrontPage will zing it directly to your own Web page.

Continued

TAKE NOTE

COPYRIGHT PROBLEMS

The *ability* to copy an image and the *right* to copy an image are two different things. Generally, the right to publish an image resides with the creator of that image. Although very little possibility exists that you would get in any trouble if you keep a copy of a copyrighted image for your own enjoyment, using it on your Web page presents an entirely different situation, because you're *publishing* it, which requires the copyright holder's permission. In many cases, you can get such permission simply by asking for it; in other cases, you have to pay a fee. Usually, some sort of policy statement is posted on the Web site; if in doubt, e-mail the Webmaster. Some images are in the *public domain*, which means that nobody holds the copyright to them. However, determining whether an image lying around the Web is in the public domain is difficult. Collections of images that come with graphics programs generally are available for your use as a part of the program's software license.

WORKING A TRADE

Many artists who display their work on the Web are happy to make a variety of trades with you. They'll often let you publish their images in exchange for nothing more than a credit and a link back to their own home page. Others might be happy to accept an offer of exchanging your services as a Web page developer for some of their images. It never hurts to ask.

CROSS-REFERENCE

See the preceding section for directions on how to insert images from files.

FIND IT ONLINE

Drop in to Free GIFs and Animations at http://fg-a.com/gifs.html.

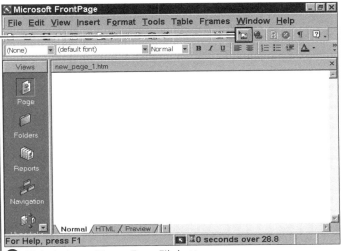

❶ *Click the Insert Picture From File button.*

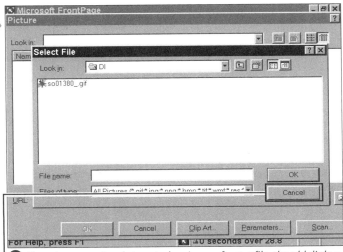

❷ *If you have previously inserted an image from a file, the old dialog box will still show. Click the Cancel button.*

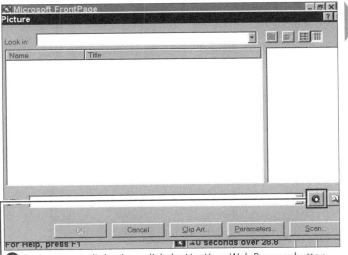

❸ *In the Picture dialog box, click the Use Your Web Browser button.*

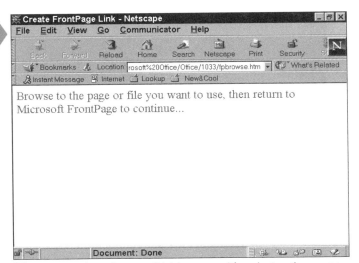

■ *FrontPage launches your Web browser with an instructions page showing.*

Almost incredibly, Microsoft has created a capability in FrontPage that you can't use with Microsoft's own Web browser, Internet Explorer. Well, you can use it a little bit, under perfect circumstances (if they happen to come along), but it's really not very functional. When you go Web surfing to look for an image to insert into FrontPage, the program keeps track of the current URL and uses it as the basis for downloading the image that you decide you want. This is where the problem comes in. You have to be able to use the *image's* URL, not the URL of the Web page that you find the image on.

Internet Explorer won't let you get an image's URL unless it's at the end of a link. However, Netscape Navigator will let you get an image's URL even if the image is embedded on a Web page. The distinction between the two types of image URLs is fairly simple. An image that is separately linked to a Web page via a hyperlink is displayed all by itself in a Web browser, and thus the URL displayed in the Location window is the URL of the image. However, when an image is embedded as part of a Web page — not displayed as a separate file — its URL is merely part of the HTML source code for that Web page, and the URL that shows in the Location window is the URL of the Web page, not the image. So, unless the designer of the Web page that you like has provided a separate link leading to the display of the image, you're out of luck with Internet Explorer.

In practical terms, this means that if you want to download an image from the Web into FrontPage, you'd better put Netscape Navigator (part of the Netscape Communicator suite of programs) on your computer and make it your default Web browser. Then, when you find an image that you want, you simply ask Navigator to display it separately, and you can then download it right into FrontPage.

TAKE NOTE

▶ DEFAULT CAN BE TEMPORARY

If you need to insert images from the Web, but still want to keep Internet Explorer as your default Web browser, you can just keep switching back and forth between them. You can set both browsers so that each asks every time it starts whether you want to make it the default browser. Just start Navigator before you start FrontPage and accept it as the default browser. When you're done, shut down both programs, fire up Internet Explorer, and accept it as your default browser. You have to shut down FrontPage, because it checks to see which is the default browser only when it starts. FrontPage won't know that you've made a change until you shut it down and restart it.

CROSS-REFERENCE

See the following section for instructions on how to use the Web to update your clip art.

FIND IT ONLINE

K. Jordan Web Design has free images at
http://www.web.matters.com/freegifs.htm.

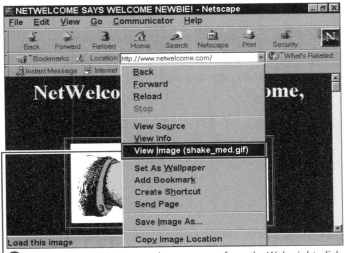

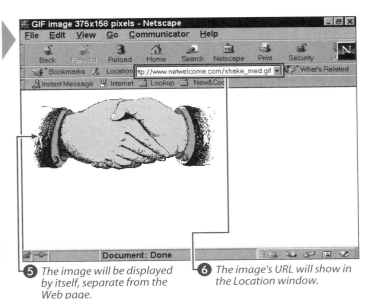

4 After you locate the image that you want from the Web, right-click it and select View Image from the popup menu.

5 The image will be displayed by itself, separate from the Web page.

6 The image's URL will show in the Location window.

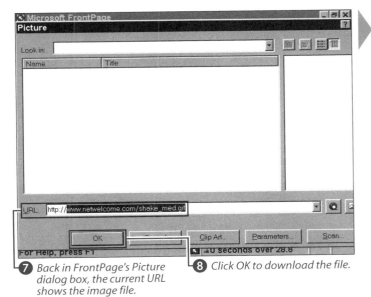

7 Back in FrontPage's Picture dialog box, the current URL shows the image file.

8 Click OK to download the file.

■ The image will appear on your Web page in FrontPage.

Updating the Clip Art Gallery from the Web

One of the really nice things about the Clip Art Gallery is that you can go to Microsoft's support Web site and download brand new images at no extra cost. This is not the same thing as inserting images onto your pages from the Web as covered in the preceding section. Instead, it is strictly for adding more clip art images to the ones available from within the Clip Art Gallery. The Clip Gallery Live Web site has tons of new images that you can browse and download, and the good news is that the downloads go right into the Clip Art Gallery itself.

Fortunately, updating the Clip Art Gallery is really easy, because it was designed from the beginning with exactly this capability in mind. Just bring up the Gallery and click the Clips Online button, which automatically launches your Web browser and connects it to the Clip Gallery Live Web site. From there, you simply look at the pictures and decide which ones you want. It's a plain old graphical shopping spree. Grab everything you want; it won't cost you a dime.

The files are uniformly small in size, so the downloads don't take long, even with a relatively slow modem connection. And they don't take up much space on your hard drive, either. Also, like the clip art images that come with the Clip Art Gallery, these clips vary widely in both style and quality. Some of the pictures are colorful, some are dull. Some are relatively complex while others are childishly simplistic.

You won't find much of the world's most stunning art here, but the variety of types and styles of images from which you can select is one of the strongest points of this site.

Continued

TAKE NOTE

THEY'RE NOT WEB-COMPATIBLE

The images that are available from the Clip Gallery Live Web site are WMF files, like the ones that come with the Clip Art Gallery. These files can't be used directly on the Web, because only three graphics file formats are commonly accepted on the Web: GIF, JPEG, and PNG (WMF files display in Internet Explorer, but not in other browsers). However, if you use the Clip Art Gallery to insert these images into FrontPage, they are automatically converted to GIF format when you save the page that they're on.

A BIT OF BACKGROUND

The Clip Gallery Live Web site is a good source for background images for your Web pages. Make sure you take a moment to browse through the many images in the Background category while you're there.

CROSS-REFERENCE

See Chapter 7 for more information on image file types.

FIND IT ONLINE

The Clip Art Gallery Web site home page is at http://cgl.microsoft.com/clipgallerylive/eula.asp.

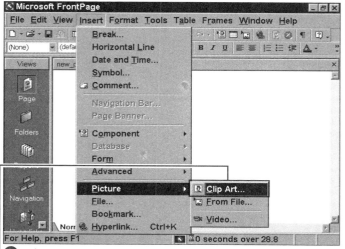

① Select Insert ➪ Picture ➪ Clip Art from the main menu.

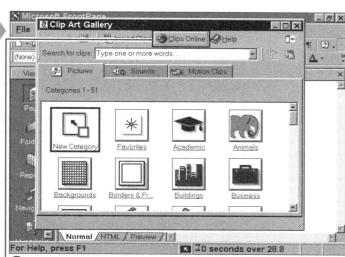

② In the Clip Art Gallery, click the Clips Online button.

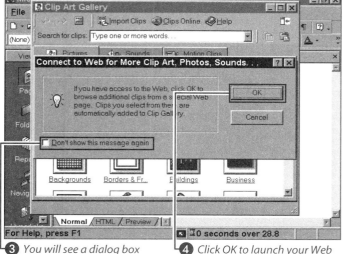

③ You will see a dialog box explaining the process. Click the "Don't show this message again" check box.

④ Click OK to launch your Web browser.

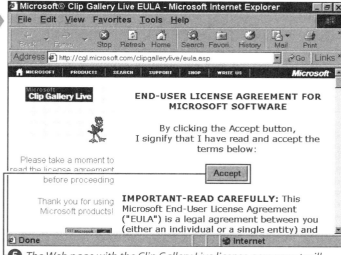

⑤ The Web page with the Clip Gallery Live license agreement will appear. Click the Accept button to agree to the terms of the license agreement.

125

Updating the Clip Art Gallery from the Web *Continued*

You don't have to do anything further to make the clip art that you downloaded from the Clip Gallery Live Web site available to you. You'll find that the clips are automatically added to the ones in the Clip Art Gallery. They're placed, appropriately enough, in the Downloaded Clips category, and they come complete with keywords and categories all ready for inclusion in the Clip Art Gallery's database — again, with no effort on your part.

The ease of use and the abundant variety of art available make the Clip Art Gallery and the Clip Gallery Live Web site a combination that adds immeasurably to the functionality of FrontPage as a Web design program. The artwork itself also offers a quick and easy way to add beauty, whimsy, and meaning to all of your own Web pages. After all, a properly chosen image can add greatly to the understandability of your site, and the Clip Art Gallery offers you a wide spectrum of graphical options. Also, if you are using FrontPage as part of Microsoft Office instead of as a stand-alone program, don't forget that you can also use the Clip Art Gallery images in other Office programs.

You should note, however, that you can't use Netscape Navigator to update the Clip Art Gallery. The whole process — from Clip Art Gallery to the Clip Gallery Live Web site to the final update — involves Microsoft products and so it has to be done with Microsoft's Internet Explorer as the Web browser.

TAKE NOTE

DROP IN ANY OLD TIME

You might want to get into the habit of browsing through the Microsoft Clip Gallery Live Web site even when you don't have a specific need for an image. Microsoft updates the artwork periodically, and you'll be much more aware of what's available if you look over its offerings at leisure rather than wait for an emergency need to arise. In fact, downloading anything that strikes your fancy while you're there might be a good idea, because you never know when it might come in handy.

YOU CAN REASSIGN CATEGORIES

All the clip art on the Clip Gallery Live site is assigned to one or more categories in the program's associated database. Although downloaded clips have their own categories assigned (such as Industry, Music, People, and so forth), they're also all put in the Downloaded Clips category. You don't, however, have to leave a downloaded clip in that category. That's just the place it automatically lands. If you want to, you can right-click the image in the Clip Art Gallery, select Clip Properties from the popup menu, and use the check boxes in the resultant dialog box to assign it to other categories instead. Just make sure to deselect the check box labeled Downloaded Clips to remove it from that category after you assign it to another one (or ones), unless you also wish to still keep it there.

CROSS-REFERENCE

See the preceding section for directions on how to add images directly to your pages from the Web.

FIND IT ONLINE

Try the Free GIFs Index at http://www.mexia.com/dan-shan/gifindex.htm.

6 To search the clips by keywords, enter the terms and click the Go button.

Alternatively, click the links on the right to see selected clips.

7 To browse by category, click the down arrow.

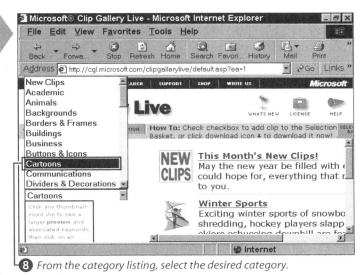

8 From the category listing, select the desired category.

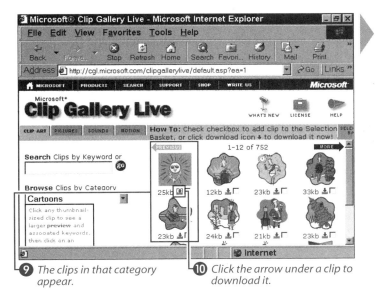

9 The clips in that category appear.

10 Click the arrow under a clip to download it.

■ Downloaded clips are available right away in the Clip Art Gallery.

Configuring an Image Editor

If you want to edit the exact appearance of images that you're going to use on your Web pages, you should be aware that FrontPage doesn't offer too much in the way of sophisticated image editing. True, you can crop, resize, rotate and flip, play around with contrast, and so forth, but FrontPage doesn't offer tools for tasks such as HSV (hue, saturation, and value) adjustments, gamma correction, or color switching. Unfortunately, FrontPage also lacks the capacity to perform color-depth conversion (the ability to change an image from truecolor to 256 color or from 256 color to black and white, for instance). So, for full image editing capabilities — especially if you want to create your own images from scratch — you have to turn to an outside editor.

Microsoft Image Composer is included with the stand-alone version of FrontPage, but you may already have an image editor that you like and are comfortable using. If so, you don't need to learn the ins and outs of a new one; FrontPage easily accommodates the addition of any image editor to your set of tools for Web page development. You can go with a full professional program, such as Photoshop, or one of the popular shareware paint programs, such as PaintShop Pro. If you don't want to make your own artwork, but still want more sophisticated image manipulation capabilities than FrontPage has to offer, you might try the shareware image editor LView Pro or the fine freeware program called IrfanView.

Whatever your choice of image editor programs, they all work well with FrontPage. This is definitely one place where Microsoft has gone out of its way to be totally accommodating to the Web page designer. Anything goes when it comes to picking which image editor you feel comfortable with using.

TAKE NOTE

▶ MICROSOFT IMAGE COMPOSER

Microsoft Image Composer is a very good, full-featured image editor, and some people buy FrontPage solely for the purpose of getting their hands on it. Other graphics programs with similar features cost hundreds of dollars more than the entire FrontPage package, so you can easily understand why they jump at the chance to get a comparable program for much less.

▶ CONFIGURE IT FIRST

To open an image for editing in FrontPage, you simply double-click it. However, if you haven't specified an image editor and try to edit an image, all that you get is an error message telling you that you need to take care of the configuration first.

CROSS-REFERENCE

See Chapter 7 for more information on FrontPage's image editing features.

FIND IT ONLINE

You can find IrfanView at **http://stud1.tuwien. ac.at/~e9227474/**.

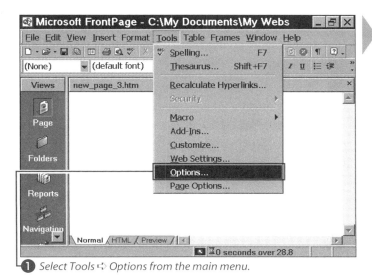

❶ Select Tools ➪ Options from the main menu.

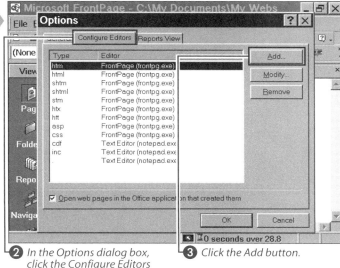

❷ In the Options dialog box, click the Configure Editors tab.

❸ Click the Add button.

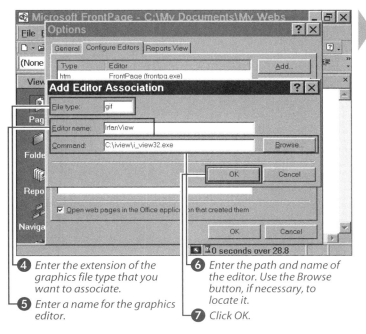

❹ Enter the extension of the graphics file type that you want to associate.

❺ Enter a name for the graphics editor.

❻ Enter the path and name of the editor. Use the Browse button, if necessary, to locate it.

❼ Click OK.

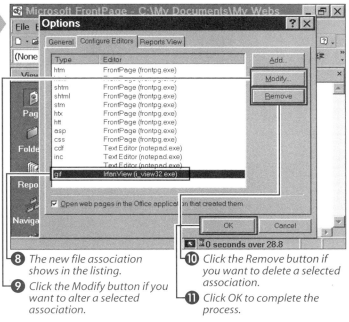

❽ The new file association shows in the listing.

❾ Click the Modify button if you want to alter a selected association.

❿ Click the Remove button if you want to delete a selected association.

⓫ Click OK to complete the process.

Converting Image Types

FrontPage supports the three image file formats that are commonly used on the Web — GIF (Graphics Interchange Format), JPEG (Joint Photographic Experts Group), and PNG (Portable Network Graphics).

GIF files were for years the main choice for online use because they had, in the late 1980s, the best compression method for images. They were the standard on CompuServe. JPEG files began to edge out GIFs in many cases for a couple of reasons, the main one being that — in most cases — a JPEG file of an image is a smaller file size than a GIF file of the same image. The other reason is that CompuServe, which didn't own the rights to the LZW compression algorithm used in GIF, but licensed it from Unisys Corporation, found itself caught in the middle between its users and Unisys when the latter announced that, after years of not charging people for the use of the algorithm, it was changing its policy. After much anger and confusion abated, Unisys clarified its position and stated that it would charge only the people and companies who developed graphics programs by using the algorithm, not the end users.

By that time, though, public outrage had sparked a movement to find a viable free replacement for the GIF algorithm, which ultimately resulted in the PNG file format. Why bother with a new format when JPEGs are usually good enough? Well, GIFs and PNGs have some capabilities that are lacking in JPEG files, such as transparency and progressive display. GIFs also have the ability to produce animated images by combining several images into a single file. More importantly, JPEG files are not exact representations of the original image, but an extremely close approximation. While this is more than good enough in the case of graphical images that have subtle shadings from one part to the other — such as in facial portraits — the representation falls short of what you would expect of an exact duplication of a strictly separated band of colors.

Continued

TAKE NOTE

OTHER FILE FORMATS

FrontPage does support some other file formats, such as WMF (Windows Metafile), but WMF files display only in Internet Explorer, and not in any other Web browser. Sticking with the norms is far better in this case. Because the images from the Clip Art Gallery are all in WMF format, you need to convert them to a normal Web format before you can use them on your Web site.

CROSS-REFERENCE

See the section "Setting Transparency" in Chapter 7 for more information on GIFs.

FIND IT ONLINE

The GIF Galaxy is located at **http://freemarketing. com/gifs/front.htm**.

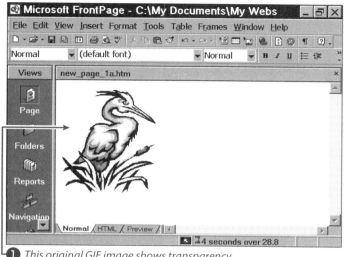

① *This original GIF image shows transparency.*

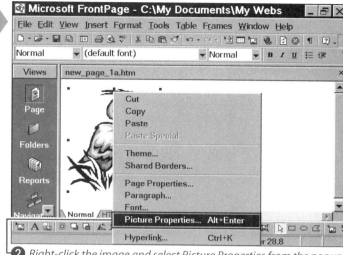

② *Right-click the image and select Picture Properties from the popup menu.*

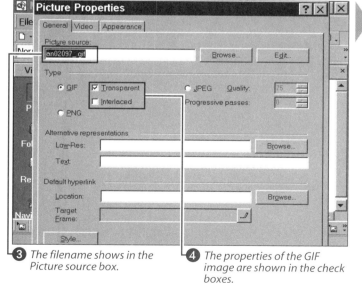

③ *The filename shows in the Picture source box.*

④ *The properties of the GIF image are shown in the check boxes.*

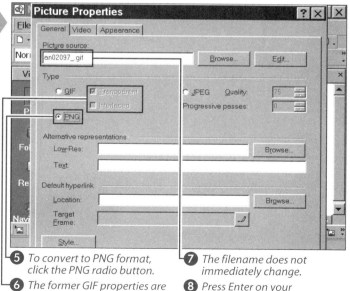

⑤ *To convert to PNG format, click the PNG radio button.*

⑥ *The former GIF properties are now grayed out.*

⑦ *The filename does not immediately change.*

⑧ *Press Enter on your keyboard or click the OK button (not pictured here).*

Converting Image Types
Continued

Each different file format has its own peculiarities. GIF and PNG files, for instance, always produce an exact copy of the image, right down to the last pixel. JPEG files, on the other hand, aren't quite the same. In fact, if you want to get technical about it, JPEG isn't even a file format, but instead is a compression method. The exact manner in which the JPEG image compression information is stored can vary from program to program and still technically follow the JPEG format. The other two formats are absolutely rigid in the way that they store image data.

Because of this difference in storage methods, JPEGs are best used for photographs, whereas GIF and PNG files are best used for line drawings and images in which the exact color of particular pixels is critical to image reliability. All three of the formats support *interlacing*, which is a method of progressively displaying varying lines of the image so that a low resolution version of the image appears rather quickly while the rest of the image is filled in bit by bit (no pun intended). However, FrontPage supports interlacing only for GIF and JPEG files. With GIFs, it's called interlacing, and with JPEGs, it's called *progressive passes*.

JPEG image quality can also vary greatly, depending upon the degree of compression involved. The higher the compression, the lower the quality of the image, and vice versa. So, remember that when you select the "quality" setting for a JPEG image, you affect the file size, too. Generally, go for the lowest quality setting that still gives you a useable image.

TAKE NOTE

INTERLACING ISN'T LOW RES

Using an interlaced image isn't the same approach as providing a separate, low-resolution image that is displayed while the main image is downloading, even though the terminology is similar. With interlacing, only one image file is involved, and it's a full-resolution image, but the lines initially are displayed with small gaps between them, which are progressively filled in as the image finishes downloading.

THIS MING ISN'T A VASE

PNG files don't have all the capabilities that GIF files do. For one thing, only GIF files can hold multiple images that are displayed in sequence to produce animation from a single file. The same people who developed the PNG file format are currently working on the MNG file format to solve this problem. MNG is pronounced "ming," by the way, and PNG is pronounced "ping." MNG is short for *Multiple Network Graphics*, and will add animation to the PNG file's capabilities.

JPEG QUALITY VALUES

Most people agree that a quality setting of somewhere between 70 and 90 is about right for most JPEG images. However, it's a matter of personal opinion and purely a value judgment. You might even be willing to go as low as, say, 50 and still consider the results acceptable. Anywhere near 100 is a waste of time since you won't get any appreciable improvement over the low 90s, and it will cost you more disk space. If you're looking to create a low-res version, explore the area under 50; otherwise, forget the lower settings.

CROSS-REFERENCE
See "Adding Text to Images" in Chapter 7 for more information on GIF images.

FIND IT ONLINE
The Amazing Clip Joint is located at http://www.virtualpublications.com/acj/xj/ac.html.

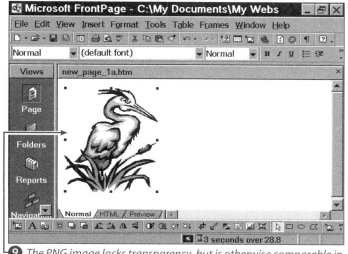

9 *The PNG image lacks transparency, but is otherwise comparable in quality to the GIF.*

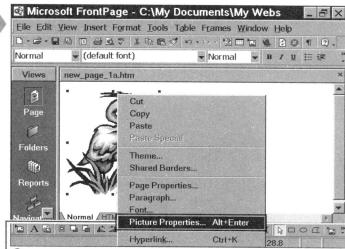

10 *Right-click the image and select Picture Properties from the popup menu.*

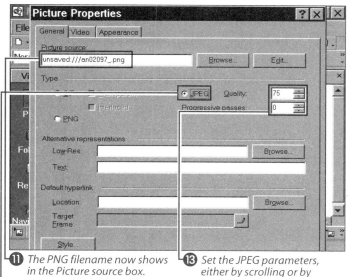

11 *The PNG filename now shows in the Picture source box.*

12 *To convert to JPEG format, click the JPEG radio button.*

13 *Set the JPEG parameters, either by scrolling or by typing.*

14 *Press Enter on your keyboard or click the OK button (not pictured here).*

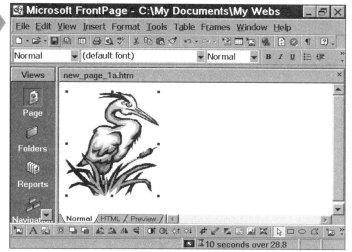

■ *The JPEG image is less sharp than the GIF or PNG for this type of art.*

Setting Text Alignment and Word Wrap

Text alignment, in relation to images, sets the beginning point of a sentence that follows an image (the text must not be separated from the image by a carriage return or anything else, but must come right after it on the same line). Text alignment presents three basic choices — top, middle, and bottom — and each has minor variations; bottom is the default alignment. The top and texttop settings are identical. The middle and center settings are identical, placing the baseline of the text at the midlevel of the image. Absmiddle places the center line of the text in line with the image's center line. The bottom and absbottom settings are identical. The baseline setting is almost the same as bottom, but handles the text relative to *descenders,* those little bits of some letters (such as g, j, and p) that hang below the line; baseline drops the letters so that the descenders fall below the baseline of the image.

Although you indicate settings for word wrap by using the same dialog box as you use for normal text alignment with images, the function is distinctly different. The left and right settings are the only ones that will cause a proper word wrap (when you're choosing left and right here, the reference is to the position of the image, not the text). All the other settings — top, middle, bottom, and their minor variants — are useful only with a short group of words. If used with a full paragraph, you'll find that (with the exception of the bottom settings) the paragraph's

first line starts either at the top or the middle of the image, and the remainder of it continues at the bottom, causing a gap in the word flow. With left and right settings, the text flows smoothly around the image, following its outline, until it passes underneath it.

TAKE NOTE

WORD WRAP AND CSS

Word wrap is dependent upon using normal HTML procedures, and doesn't work if you place the image by using absolute positioning with Cascading Style Sheets (CSS). If an image is absolutely positioned in the same location as a bit of text, it simply lies on top of or under the text, depending upon your z-order choices, but the text itself will have no relationship to the image.

THIS IS NOT PLAIN TEXT ALIGNMENT

In the case of standard text alignment, the choices are the left side of the Web page, the center, and the right side of the page, with no relationship at all to any image on the page. In the case of aligning text with an image, alignment is a property of the image, not the text, and defines how text is displayed in relation to the image.

CROSS-REFERENCE

See Chapter 3 for more information on standard text alignment.

FIND IT ONLINE

Spot's GIF Archive is found at
http://sanfords.net/Spot/photo.htm.

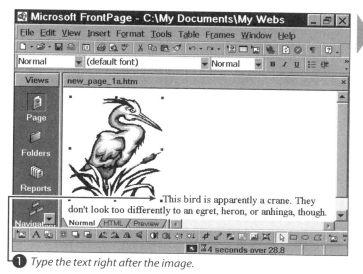

1 *Type the text right after the image.*

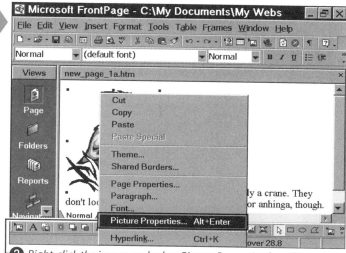

2 *Right-click the image and select Picture Properties from the popup menu.*

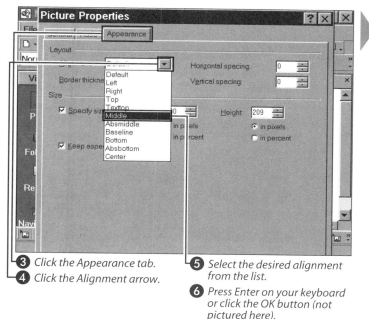

3 *Click the Appearance tab.*
4 *Click the Alignment arrow.*

5 *Select the desired alignment from the list.*

6 *Press Enter on your keyboard or click the OK button (not pictured here).*

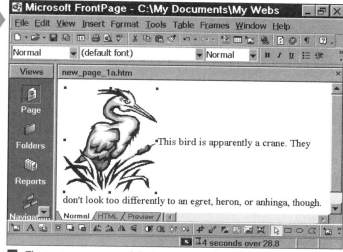

■ *The text wraps around the image according to the setting that you chose.*

Using Spacing and Borders

You can control the amount of space between an image and the other elements around it. Unfortunately, you cannot independently specify the amount of space on all four sides of an image. The only options are for vertical spacing, which sets the same amount of space above and below the image, and for horizontal spacing, which sets the same amount of space to the right and left of the image. Thus, if you set a 50-pixel horizontal space, anything that comes before the image on the same line is kept 50 pixels away from it, and is anything that comes after the image.

With vertical spacing, the element preceding the image, but not on the same line, is kept 50 pixels above it, and any element coming after it is kept 50 pixels below it. An oddity occurs if text precedes an image on the same line. That text is also kept 50 pixels below the image, just as if it had come after it.

Borders are a purely decorative element, and the decision whether to include a border is strictly one of design. They are best used with images that have a distinctly rectangular appearance; images that use transparency to achieve a nonrectangular appearance often suffer when bordered.

TAKE NOTE

THE SKY IS THE LIMIT

If you run the up arrow button to its limit on the settings for spacing and border width, you'll find that the upper limit is 10,000 pixels. Imagining any situation in which you would need to come anywhere near this "limit" is extremely difficult. The optimal size for a border is always in the single-digit to low double-digit range, and the low double digits are usually fine for both horizontal and vertical spacing, too. On the opposite side, the lower limit is zero; you can't specify negative numbers for either spacing or borders.

NORMAL BORDER COLORS

The default color of an image border is the same as that for the fonts in regular text. However, if that image is used as a hyperlink, then the default border color is the same as that for a text link. Thus, in the normal course of events, the default image border is black, as is normal text, and the default border color for an image link is blue, as it is for a normal (textual) hyperlink. You cannot set the color of an individual border the way you can for, say, an individual textual character.

WORD WRAP DEFEATS SPACING

If you use the left or right settings to cause word wrap, the text following the image is unaffected by the vertical spacing settings. It is, however, still subject to the horizontal spacing settings.

CROSS-REFERENCE

See Chapter 4 for more information on image links and borders.

FIND IT ONLINE

You can get free animated GIFs at http://www.rougeau.com/html/freegifs.html.

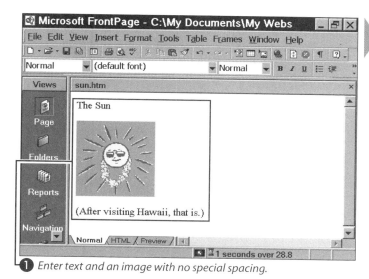

① *Enter text and an image with no special spacing.*

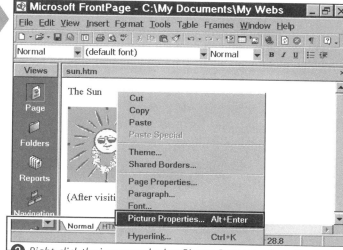

② *Right-click the image and select Picture Properties from the popup menu.*

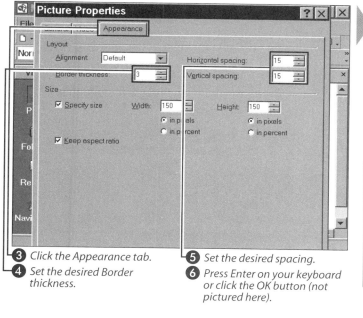

③ *Click the Appearance tab.*
④ *Set the desired Border thickness.*

⑤ *Set the desired spacing.*
⑥ *Press Enter on your keyboard or click the OK button (not pictured here).*

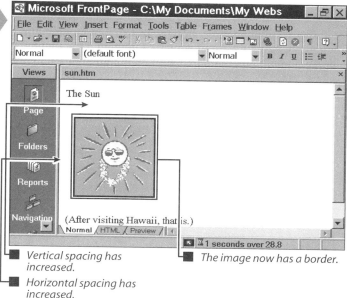

■ *Vertical spacing has increased.*

■ *Horizontal spacing has increased.*

■ *The image now has a border.*

Using Alternate Text or Low-Res Images

One of the things that slows down Web page viewing is waiting for images to download. Other than using fewer graphics, a few tried and true techniques can be used to ease the pain of this situation for your Web site visitors. While an image is downloading, you can clue visitors in to the nature of the image that they're waiting for by using alternate text (called *alt* because that's the HTML abbreviation for it) or a lower-resolution version of the image that will display quickly while your visitors are waiting for the fuller version to show up.

Why should you care if a visitor has an idea about an image in advance? Unless your site is utterly dependent upon the images that it contains, such as an artist's Web site, then a visitor may be much more interested in the other contents than in the beauty of your graphics. If they have to wait until all the graphics are downloaded only to find out that they waited for no really good reason, they won't be happy. Our LinkFinder site, for example, has several graphics on it, but not all of them are essential to the functionality of the site. When you first log on to it, you're apprised right away via alt text that you're waiting for images of a needle in a haystack, the company logo, and the Search button, for instance. Although we're happy with the design of the first two images, they're hardly essential to the average visitor, who may quite rightly move on to the links without bothering to wait for those images to download, saving themselves

an unnecessary delay. If visitors want to use the search feature, though, they know from the alt text that they have to wait for the Search button's image link to appear.

TAKE NOTE

► HELPING THE HANDICAPPED

Alt text is also of great value to sight-impaired people who are surfing the Web. As mentioned elsewhere, the majority of the material on the Web is text, and the special equipment used by blind people to explore the Web can handle text quite well, reading the words and speaking them out loud. For images, however, the only thing that enables these people to be aware of the contents is alt text, which their programs can speak aloud just as for normal text. Without alt text, the only thing that a blind person knows about an image is that it's a picture they can't see. Not many Web designers consider this situation when developing their sites, but a few moments taken to add some descriptive terms to the alt text for an image can make quite a difference for those who cannot see it.

CROSS-REFERENCE

See the following section, "Adding Background Images."

FIND IT ONLINE

You can see LinkFinder at
http://www.linkfinder.com/index.html.

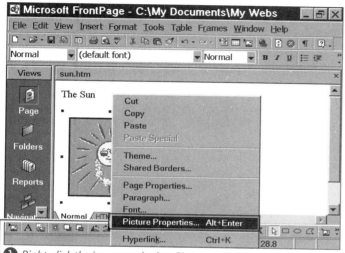

1 Right-click the image and select Picture Properties from the popup menu.

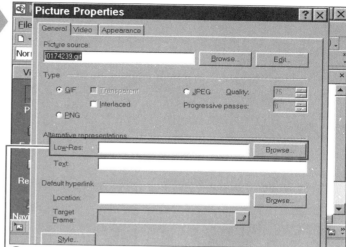

2 Enter the location/filename of the low-resolution image, or click the Browse button to locate the file.

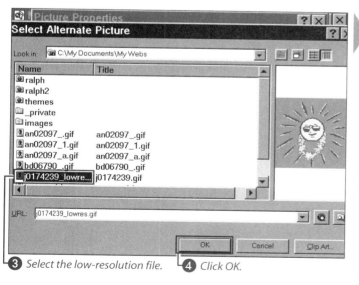

3 Select the low-resolution file.　**4** Click OK.

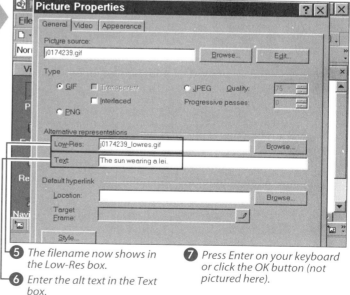

5 The filename now shows in the Low-Res box.

6 Enter the alt text in the Text box.

7 Press Enter on your keyboard or click the OK button (not pictured here).

Adding Background Images

Although most of the pages on the Web use a plain background, and many don't even use a colored background, you can use a background image for your Web pages. You might think that a background image would be the size of the whole page, but background images usually are very small, and Web browsers automatically *tile* them — create repeated copies of the image until it covers the entire page.

The ideal size for a background image depends on the screen resolution you're targeting. If you're creating a Web page for a corporate intranet, you may know the specific screen size that users will use to view your Web pages. The entire company, for instance, may use monitors with a resolution of 640 × 480 or 800 × 600. On the other hand, if you're creating for the Web in general, then you have to deal with the fact that lots of people with lots of different resolutions will be viewing your page. Although many possible resolutions exist, the most common ones won't be under 640 × 480 or over 1024 × 768 (though more and more people are going to 1280 × 1024 as the cost of sophisticated color cards and monitors continues to drop).

The width, not the height, of the image used for the background is what matters for even tiling. Web pages have no limit on their height (being, for all practical purposes, infinitely tall), but are limited in their width (technically, you can use a couple of tricks to make a Web page wider than the screen, but this is rarely done and it's a poor design decision in any case). If you know the screen width that your users will have, then it's a simple matter of picking a fraction of that width for the ideal tiling effect. If the width is 640 pixels, then an image that's 32 pixels wide will tile 20 times evenly; one that's 64 pixels wide will tile 10 times evenly; and so on. If it's not evenly divisible, then part of the last image in each row of images will be cut off. The only viable image width that tiles evenly for all popular resolutions is 32 pixels, which divides evenly into 640, 800, 1024, and 1280. The next best width is 64 pixels, which divides evenly into 640, 1024, and 1280. Of course, if you're willing to let the background image simply get cut off in the middle, you can do so and not worry about the dimensions.

Continued

TAKE NOTE

CLIP ART GALLERY BACKGROUNDS

The Clip Art Gallery includes various clips specifically designed for use as background images on Web pages.

CROSS-REFERENCE
See Chapter 3 for information on background color.

FIND IT ONLINE
The FrontPage Tips and Techniques Home Page is at http://www.ce.utk.edu/frontpage/.

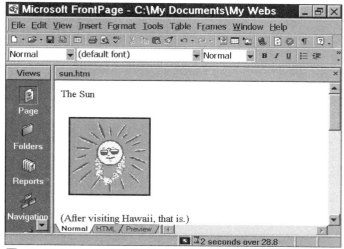

■ *The Web page with no background image.*

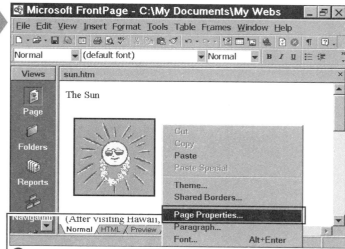

1 *Right-click a blank area of the page and select Page Properties from the popup menu.*

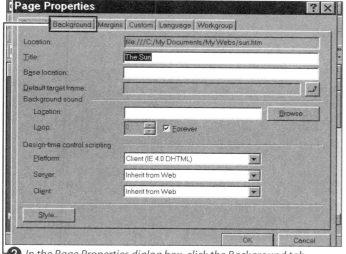

2 *In the Page Properties dialog box, click the Background tab.*

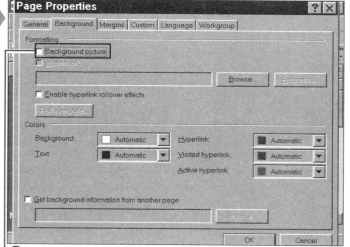

3 *Click the Background picture check box.*

141

Adding Background Images
Continued

You also need to take color depth — the number of colors that can be displayed — into account. An image that looks great while viewed in hicolor or truecolor may look pretty bad in 256 colors. Unless you're aiming at a high-end color market, stick with 256 colors. The simplest way to do this is to make your background image a GIF file, because GIF files can support only 256 colors to begin with, whereas JPEGs and PNGs can support 16.7 million colors. You can also use the Black and White button to create a grayscale image; grayscale images display well in every color resolution.

You should also consider the image itself. Not the file size or format, but the actual picture. Not all images work as backgrounds, no matter how attractive they are. A really good background image, while pleasant, shouldn't attract too much attention to itself. It's like the role of a supporting actor. It should bolster the page it's on, but not overwhelm it. If a background image detracts from the content or clashes with the design of the rest of the page, it's a bad one. You might want to consider just using a background color instead. And the background image, like any other image, increases the download time for the page. If you're already overloaded regarding download time, you may want to get rid of all extraneous images, including the background image.

TAKE NOTE

▶ NOT JUST FOR BACKGROUNDS

The advice on checking the appearance of an image in 256-color settings isn't just for background images. It's true for all the images that you'll be using in your Web pages. Some images look fine at all different color depths, while others look good only in the more sophisticated color depths. This doesn't mean that you have to use GIFs for all of your images or shouldn't ever use photorealistic pictures, just that it's a good idea to check their viewability at different settings.

▶ NOTEBOOKS AND SUCH

If you've ever been to a Web page that looks like it's a spiral notebook, you may have wondered how that effect is achieved. In fact, it's simply a normal background image. The trick is that the image is very short and very wide. The image contains a single line of the notebook with a blue line running from side to side and, on the left, a single loop of wire. As long as the image is wide enough to reach across the entire page, the second wire loop and blue line give the illusion of vertical tiling. This also explains why some Web pages have a vertical image on the left that's repeated somewhere toward the right side of the page — the designer didn't make it long enough.

CROSS-REFERENCE
See Chapter 5 for more information on background images.

FIND IT ONLINE
Check out the Animation Gallery at http://www.animationcreations.com/main/index2.htm.

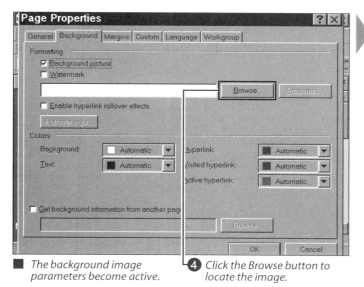

■ *The background image parameters become active.*

④ *Click the Browse button to locate the image.*

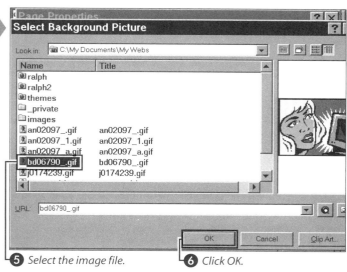

⑤ *Select the image file.*

⑥ *Click OK.*

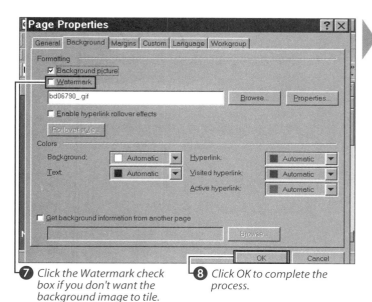

⑦ *Click the Watermark check box if you don't want the background image to tile.*

⑧ *Click OK to complete the process.*

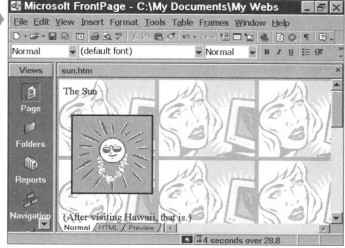

■ *The Web page now has a background image.*

Personal Workbook

Q&A

1 What is the *Clip Art Gallery*?

_____

_____

_____

2 What is the file format of the images in the Gallery?

_____

_____

_____

3 Name at least two image file formats FrontPage can import.

_____

_____

_____

4 What are the three image file formats commonly used on the World Wide Web?

_____

_____

_____

5 What are the two image alignment settings that work properly with word wrap?

_____

_____

_____

6 What is the upper limit for spacing an image?

_____

_____

_____

7 What is the purpose of alternate text?

_____

_____

_____

_____

8 What are some characteristics of good background images?

_____

_____

_____

ANSWERS: PAGE 325

EXTRA PRACTICE

1 Explore the Clip Art Gallery and familiarize yourself with the available images.

2 Practice inserting images from various sources.

3 Go to the Microsoft Clip Gallery Live Web site and download some images.

4 Experiment with the different settings for text alignment.

5 Try different border widths on some images to see what setting you prefer.

6 Check the images on your Web pages and make sure they all have alt text.

REAL-WORLD APPLICATIONS

✔ You need an image on a particular theme in a hurry. Perhaps you could use the keyword search feature of the Clip Art Gallery to find a suitable one.

✔ You know of a good Web site that has copyright-free images available. You might want to use the Web importation capabilities of FrontPage to place them directly on your Web page.

✔ Your boss wants you to use a particular graphics program that's standard in the company. You could integrate it with FrontPage by configuring it as FrontPage's default image editor.

✔ A new federal regulation requires you to make your Web site accessible to people with disabilities. You probably need to go through and add alternate text to all of your images.

Visual Quiz

How do you get to this dialog box? What is the purpose of the selected entry?

_____

_____

_____

_____

_____

_____

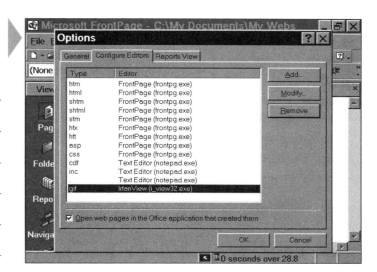

CHAPTER **7**

MASTER
THESE
SKILLS

▶ **Resizing Images**

▶ **Adding Text to Images**

▶ **Using Auto Thumbnail**

▶ **Designing with Absolute Positioning**

▶ **Using Z-Order**

▶ **Rotating and Flipping Images**

▶ **Changing Contrast and Brightness**

▶ **Cropping Images**

▶ **Setting Transparency**

▶ **Black and White and Wash Out**

Modifying Images

FrontPage does much more than just let you plug images into your Web pages. It gives you a great deal of assistance in handling images after they're in place. In keeping with the FrontPage tradition of never having to really get "under the hood" and monkey with the HTML source code, you can do all of your image manipulation with a few mouse clicks.

This chapter follows up on the previous chapter, covering all the things that you can do with your images after you insert them into your Web pages. We start off with the topic of resizing images to make them fit into your design concept. This is the only image manipulation technique that isn't handled via the Picture toolbar.

From there, you'll be taken on a guided tour of the Picture toolbar, exploring each of its buttons from left to right (except for the hotspot buttons, which are covered in Chapter 8 on image mapping techniques). As you practice the various image alterations, feel free to relax and play around with them. As long as you don't save the page, you can click the Restore button (the one on the far right of the Picture toolbar) to undo anything that you do and return the image to its original state. Still, it's a good idea to do your practice sessions on an image that you don't care about, and on a Web page that doesn't matter to you, just in case.

You'll see how to add text to your images and how to create in one simple step a thumbnail image that links to a full-size version of itself. Next, you'll delve into one of the most exciting new developments in Web page design — absolute positioning — which enables you to choose the exact placement of the elements on your pages, instead of leaving the placement up to a Web browser. Absolute positioning gives you control over the elements' horizontal and vertical placement, and even allows you to overlap images.

Later, you'll take a look at some simple but effective alterations that you can make to your images, such as rotation and flipping, controlling contrast and brightness, and cropping for emphasis. You'll also explore the uses of transparency, grayscale conversion, and wash out, and learn about a problem that you need to be aware of when you use them.

Finally, this chapter shows you how to solve the problem of blocky, resized images by using the Resample button.

Resizing Images

Not often will an image just happen to be the absolutely perfect size to fit in perfectly with all the other elements on a Web page. Either because of design considerations or space requirements, you'll occasionally need to adjust the size of at least some of your images. Actually, when you resize an image on a Web page, you're not affecting the original image at all, just the display characteristics of it in a Web browser. Resizing simply adds instructions to the browser and doesn't do anything to the image file.

When it comes to resizing normal Web graphics, shrinking them usually is better than enlarging them. GIF, JPEG, and PNG images that are resized to a larger size tend to lose definition and become blocky, because these graphics file formats use *bitmaps* to define the images they contain. Bitmaps specify, line by line, the number, placement, and color of each pixel in an image. When you expand a bitmap image, you actually add more pixels to it, and the program that does the expansion has to *interpolate,* or guess, the color of those new pixels by reading the information from the pixels around it. Generally, the result is simply to create a bunch of pixels of the same color, creating a blocky appearance. Shrinking a bitmapped image, on the other hand, has just the opposite effect. Removing some of the pixels tends to tighten up the image, and an image that is less than perfect can be tremendously improved by minimizing it. If you must enlarge a bitmapped image, try to make the enlargement as slight as possible, to minimize the amount of the distortion.

This is one place where a quirk of the Clip Art Gallery is very handy. You may recall from Chapter 6 that the Clip Art Gallery comes with images in the Windows Metafile (WMF) format. Windows Metafiles are not bitmapped images, but *vector* images. Instead of mapping each individual pixel, vector file formats use a mathematical formula to describe the structure of the image. Because of this, they can be resized either larger or smaller with no loss to the image quality. If you plan to resize an image and are using the Clip Art Gallery as your image source, then by all means do the resizing before you convert the image to one of the usual Web graphics file formats.

TAKE NOTE

RESAMPLING VERSUS RESIZING

You can diminish the "blockiness" of an enlarged bitmap image somewhat by resampling it, which does a more sophisticated job of interpolating the fill-in pixels. Resampling is done via the Picture toolbar.

CROSS-REFERENCE

See the section on resampling later in this chapter.

FIND IT ONLINE

Try the GraphX Kingdom for free clip art at http://www.net-matrix.com/graphx/.

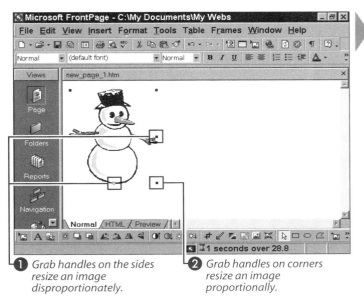

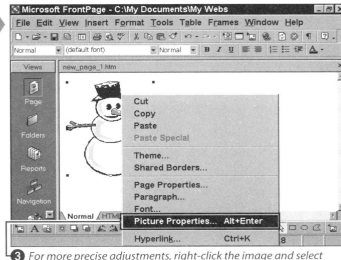

❶ Grab handles on the sides resize an image disproportionately.

❷ Grab handles on corners resize an image proportionally.

❸ For more precise adjustments, right-click the image and select Picture Properties from the popup menu.

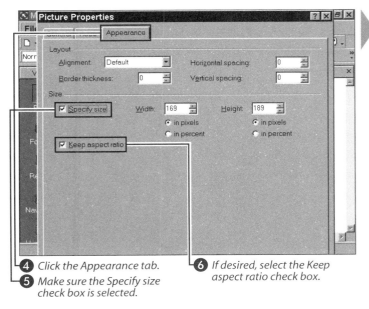

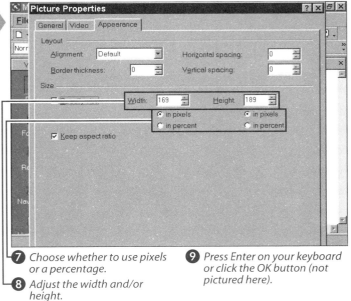

❹ Click the Appearance tab.

❺ Make sure the Specify size check box is selected.

❻ If desired, select the Keep aspect ratio check box.

❼ Choose whether to use pixels or a percentage.

❽ Adjust the width and/or height.

❾ Press Enter on your keyboard or click the OK button (not pictured here).

Adding Text to Images

In FrontPage, you can only add text to a GIF image. If you try to add it to some other type of image, the program will pop up a dialog box asking whether you want to convert the image to a GIF file. After you convert the graphics file format to GIF, you can add the text. If you later want to convert the file to another format, such as JPEG or PNG, you'll find that those options are grayed out in the Image Properties dialog box. The presence of the overlying text locks you into the GIF format. The only way to regain the file conversion options is to delete the text box from the image (the whole text box, not just the text itself). This is a peculiarity of FrontPage itself, not the file formats. If you want to add text to an image, and for some reason don't want the image to be in the GIF format, you can use practically any image editor to modify the original image by adding text to it.

After you work on the text, if you want to select the image instead of the overlaid text, you need to click the part of the image that's outside the text box. If you've expanded the text box to its fullest extent, however, it will be the same size as the image, and you won't be able to click the image after working on the text, because the entire image will be covered by the text box, with no part of the picture outside it. How do you switch from having the text box selected to having the image selected under these circumstances? Click the Web page outside the image, and then click the image again. The image will now be selected.

TAKE NOTE

THAT FIRST BUTTON

The first button on the Picture toolbar is the Insert Picture button. It looks just like the one in the standard toolbar, and it works the same way. Beware, however, of using this button. Since it doesn't show up unless you already have an image selected, using it to insert an image means you're getting rid of the selected one, not just adding a new one to the page. If you do use this option to replace an image, none of the old image's settings (like rotation, washout, and so on) will carry over into the new one. The whole thing gets overwritten.

ANOTHER WAY TO OVERLAY TEXT

You can always use a combination of regular text on the page and absolute positioning to make text overlie an image. You need to set the image's z-order so that it is behind the text and then maneuver the image so that it is in the same position as the text.

CHANGING FONTS AFTER MODIFICATIONS

If you intend to change the font face of your on-image text from the default, that should be your first move, because if you apply modifications to your text — such as changing the font size or making it bold — and then change the font face, you lose all of your modifications and have to redo them. This isn't a problem with normal text anywhere on the Web page, just the on-image text created with the Text button on the Picture toolbar. This reversion to the original settings only happens with font size and style settings, not with text alignment or font color.

CROSS-REFERENCE
See Chapter 6 for information on converting file types.

FIND IT ONLINE
Read more about Web graphics file formats at http://www.webresource.net/graphics/articles/format/.

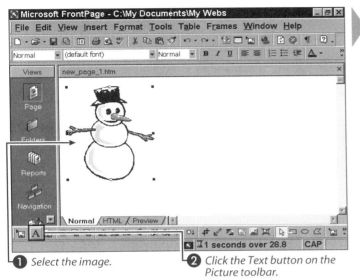

1 Select the image.

2 Click the Text button on the Picture toolbar.

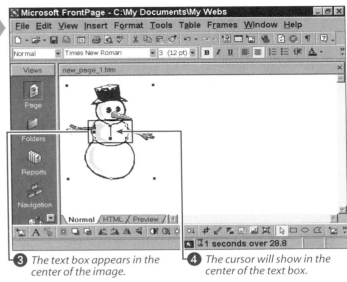

3 The text box appears in the center of the image.

4 The cursor will show in the center of the text box.

5 Enter the text.

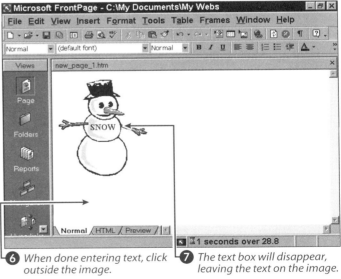

6 When done entering text, click outside the image.

7 The text box will disappear, leaving the text on the image.

Using Auto Thumbnail

As previously mentioned, one of the things that slows down Web page displays the most is waiting for image files to download, because the smallest image file tends to be many times larger than the largest HTML file. One of the ways that many Web designers have found to get around this problem is to use *thumbnails*—small versions of the images—instead of the full-size versions. Thumbnails aren't normal-sized images that are resized in the view presented by a visitor's Web browser—they are actually smaller files, thus speeding download time.

So far, that's not such an impressive concept. After all, smaller images usually have a smaller file size, but less detail, than the full-size image. Thumbnails, though, have a special function—they present the Web page visitor with an option. By creating a hyperlink from the thumbnail version of the image to the full-size version of the image, thumbnails enable visitors to download the page rapidly, but still view the larger, more detailed version of the image if they want to see it. They simply have to click the thumbnail image link to see the full version. Of course, at that point, they have to wait for the larger image to download, but the use of thumbnails gives them the *choice* of whether to wait for it to download. FrontPage's Auto Thumbnail button creates the thumbnail for you automatically, and it's the single easiest way we've ever found to create them.

CROSS-REFERENCE
See Chapter 8 for more information on image maps.

FIND IT ONLINE
There's more Web art at ArtToday: Online Image & Font Archive **http://www.arttoday.com/**.

❶ Select the image.

❷ Click the Auto Thumbnail button on the Picture toolbar.

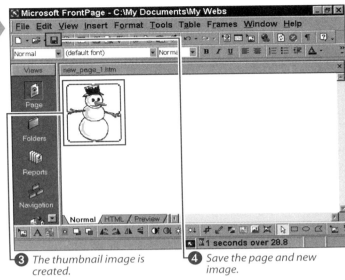

❸ The thumbnail image is created.

❹ Save the page and new image.

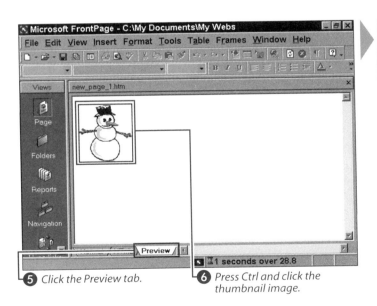

❺ Click the Preview tab.

❻ Press Ctrl and click the thumbnail image.

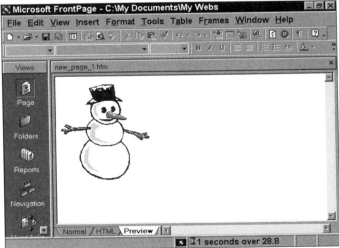

■ The full-size image is displayed.

Designing with Absolute Positioning

One of the major concepts behind the Hypertext Markup Language is that it merely describes the general layout and look of the materials on a Web page, but does not allow you to specify the absolute position of elements. The exact details of how to render the page are actually left to the specific user agent (such as a Web browser, for instance) that is used to interpret it. Thus, a particular agent is free to render text marked with, for example, the <STRONG< or <EM> (emphasized) tags in any way its designers feel is proper. Generally, these particular tags are taken to have the same meaning as the <B> (bold) or <I> (italic) tags, but the point is that nothing in HTML itself requires this interpretation. Any programmer is perfectly free to write a Web browser that displays those tags as upside-down, bright-red lettering if they feel like doing so; their browser, however odd, would still be in full compliance with the HTML standard. Likewise, nothing in the HTML code specifies the position of any element on the Web page. HTML coding can only specify the alignment of elements (such as to the left, center, or right of a page) and which element is to be the first viewable element displayed, which is to be the next viewable element, and so on. When the World Wide Web became popular with the general public, it passed beyond the province of being a mere plaything to technogeeks. At that point, graphics designers who were used to working in the more established area of magazine design wanted some way to use their customary approaches to page layout.

With traditional approaches to graphics design, you have to be able to specify the precise size of each page. Also, you need to be able to determine in advance the size and placement of each element on the page. The Web was obviously well on its way to replacing paper as the main graphical medium of our time. However, with the HTML standard's relatively lax approach to layout, these basic design factors were impossible to achieve.

Continued

TAKE NOTE

NEGATIVE NUMBERS AND ABSOLUTE POSITIONING

You can use negative numbers when positioning an object. A negative number in the vertical position value means that the image starts before the top of the Web page. A negative number in the horizontal position value means that it starts before the left side of the Web page. If you're going to write your own JavaScript programs for Web animation by using absolute positioning, you can use negative numbers to have images appear from or disappear into the margins.

CROSS-REFERENCE

See the following section on z-order.

FIND IT ONLINE

An article on absolute positioning is located at
**http://www.webresource.net/html/procenter/
articles/css_positioning/.**

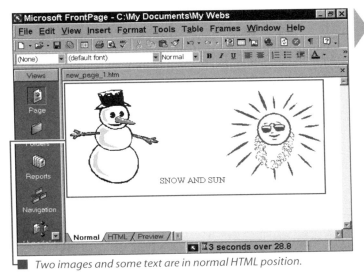

Two images and some text are in normal HTML position.

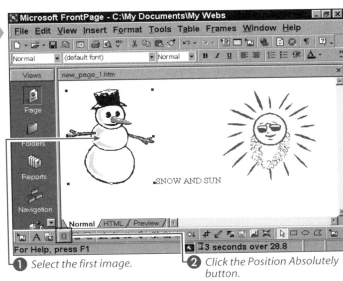

1 Select the first image.

2 Click the Position Absolutely button.

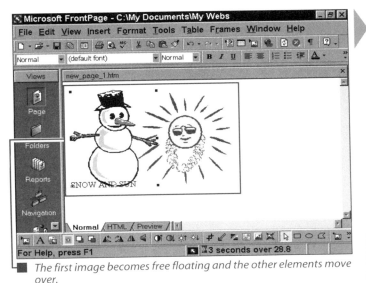

The first image becomes free floating and the other elements move over.

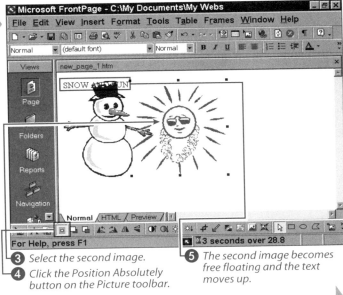

3 Select the second image.

4 Click the Position Absolutely button on the Picture toolbar.

5 The second image becomes free floating and the text moves up.

Designing with Absolute Positioning *Continued*

With the arrival of Cascading Style Sheets (CSS) and inline styles, though, the dream was realized. Not only could you stipulate the exact size of the fonts to be used in text, but the *position* style finally allowed Web designers to specify, right down to the pixel level, the exact location of every element on a page. For the first time, it became possible to design a Web page that would look exactly the same on every Web browser.

Technically, the "absolute" position of the image is relative to the container object, which means that an image all by itself on a page is positioned relative to the <BODY> element of the HTML page, whereas an image that's placed in the middle of some text and then absolutely positioned is really positioned relative to the paragraph that contains it. In FrontPage, this doesn't matter too much, because you don't ever have to work with the actual HTML or CSS code in positioning, but simply move the image at will by dragging it anywhere you want onscreen. From the time that you first apply absolute positioning to an image until the time, if ever, that you remove it, you'll notice that when you select it, you get a "move" crosshair cursor instead of the normal arrow cursor. To reposition the image, you simply hold down your left-mouse button and move the mouse; the image follows along.

The default behavior in FrontPage is to encapsulate any positioned element within its own <DIV> element, which is used to mark the extent of a segment of HTML code.

TAKE NOTE

WELL, ALMOST THE SAME COLOR

The problem of color representation still remains. No two computer systems are exactly identical in the way they show colors. But, even if your green fonts are different shades on different systems, they'll still be in the same spot.

A BIT UNDER THE HOOD

The default behavior in FrontPage is to encapsulate any positioned element within its own <DIV> or <SPAN> element. <SPAN> is identical to <DIV> except that it is an inline element, whereas <DIV> is a block-level element. You can override this setting if you want to. You get to the option by selecting Tools ⇨ Page Options from the main menu.

IT'S ALL RELATIVE

In addition to absolute positioning, *relative positioning* can be used, which is kind of a hybrid between the old-style HTML method of displaying things in the order they're listed in the source code, and the new idea of absolute control over position. You still have control over the exact placement of an image, but it's placed in reference to the preceding element rather than the page. FrontPage doesn't support relative positioning, however, only absolute positioning.

CROSS-REFERENCE

See Chapter 16 for more information on CSS.

FIND IT ONLINE

The official specification describing positioning is at http://www.w3.org/TR/REC-CSS2/visuren.html.

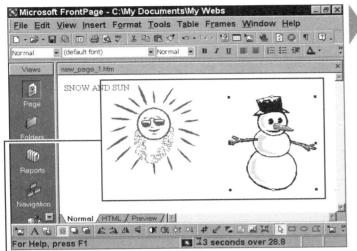

6 *The two images can be dragged anywhere on the page.*

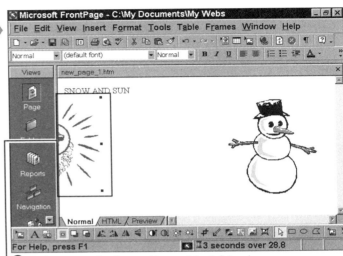

7 *An image can be dragged beyond the left border.*

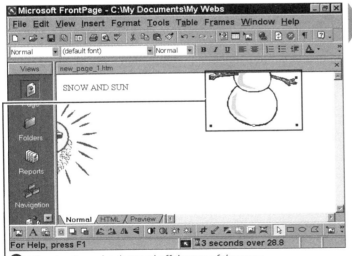

8 *Likewise, it can be dragged off the top of the page.*

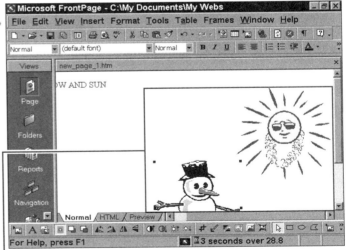

9 *Images dragged off the right or bottom, however, simply expand the Web page.*

Using Z-Order

In addition to setting the horizontal and vertical location of an element with absolute positioning, you can add a third dimension (depth) to the mix on your Web pages. Prior to the advent of absolute positioning, each element showed up on a Web page in the same sequence as it appeared in the HTML code on which the page was based. With the introduction of absolute positioning, any element could be put any place on the page. This created a situation that had never existed before—two totally different elements could be in the same place on the Web page. This added a new wrinkle to Web design. Without this possibility, designers had to consider only the X and Y axes, representing the horizontal and vertical positioning, respectively, of an element. These axes are not referred to in this way in Web page design, and are mentioned here only because the third axis is called the *Z axis*, and that terminology has worked its way into the world of Web design. The Z axis is perpendicular to both the X and Y axes, and can be visualized as running from the front of your monitor to the back. The positioning of elements on the Z axis is called their *z-order*.

Fortunately, this situation was foreseen and taken into account. The default behavior of elements that overlap is descended from the old-style HTML approach. The overlap is determined by the sequence in which the elements appear in the underlying HTML document—the first element in the HTML code is the one that's on the bottom of the pile, and the last one in the HTML code is the one that's on top of everything else. If only one positioned element exists, it's placed the same as if it were the last normal one.

However, to change the z-order of elements, you don't have to go into the HTML source code and cut and paste. You can, instead, specify a particular z-order value for any or all elements. The Bring Forward and Send Backward buttons on the Picture toolbar take care of this easily for images. Every time that you click the Bring Forward button, the z-order value of the image increases by one; every time that you click the Send Backward button, you subtract one from the image's z-order value. The larger the z-order value, the more forward the image is in the stack; the smaller, the more backward.

Continued

TAKE NOTE

IT'S NOTHING, REALLY

The z-order value of an image before you click the Bring Forward or Send Backward buttons is zero, even though nothing shows in the HTML code at this point. All elements, unless you assign a specific value to them, have a default z-order value of zero.

CROSS-REFERENCE

See the preceding section on absolute positioning.

FIND IT ONLINE

An interesting use of z-order appears at **http://wdvl. internet.com/Authoring/DHTML/CB/Cards/ index.html**.

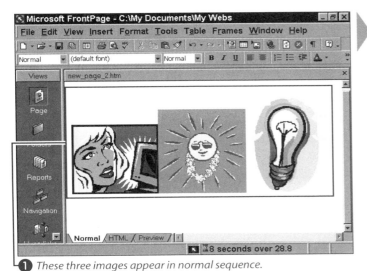

❶ These three images appear in normal sequence.

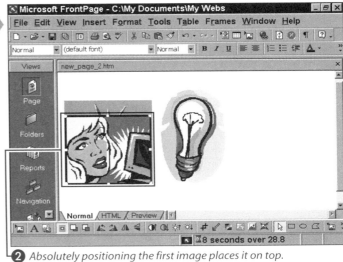

❷ Absolutely positioning the first image places it on top.

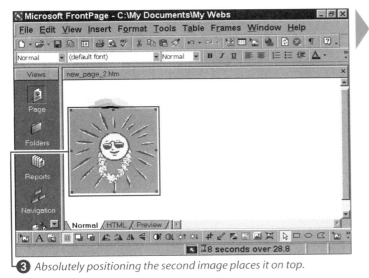

❸ Absolutely positioning the second image places it on top.

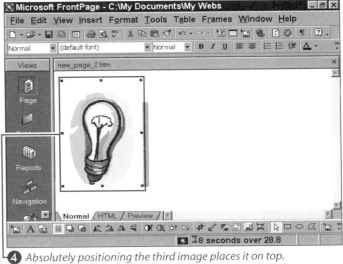

❹ Absolutely positioning the third image places it on top.

Using Z-Order

Continued

You can use negative values with z-order, just as you can with the other axes of absolute positioning. Unlike with the X and Y axes, though, assigning a negative z-order value doesn't cause the image to disappear behind a page margin. A negative number is simply lower than a positive number, and makes the image to which it's applied slide farther back than a positive number or a smaller negative number.

The Web page design possibilities inherent in overlapping images with images (and other elements) are limited only by your imagination. To start with, you might consider using images like you would a deck of cards, whereby the top image covers all the others underneath it. As each image is removed from the top — by changing either its horizontal and vertical position or its z-order value so that it drops underneath — the previously hidden images individually come into view. By combining absolute positioning with JavaScript, guessing games of the Concentration variety can be constructed in this way. You could create an onscreen book in which the pages are actually turned like they are in a physical book, allowing large amounts of information to be placed in a small area.

In animation, you can make images slide behind and before one another and move across the page, giving you yet another full dimension to play with. Although FrontPage doesn't yet offer anything remotely like collision detection in image movement, an enterprising programmer could use JavaScript to keep track of the sizes and positions of the various elements onscreen. The program could then calculate when an overlap takes place and react accordingly. This capability could make simple action games possible within the context of a Web page.

TAKE NOTE

▶ MOVEMENT VERSUS ANIMATION

To the purist, real animation requires more than simple change of position. For true animation, the image itself must be altered in some manner, and nothing in absolute positioning gives you this capability. Although writing a script that combines GIF animation with onscreen movement is technically possible via absolute positioning, the result would — with current scripting technology — be so slow and jerky that it would not be entertaining, to say the least.

▶ YOU DON'T NEED SCRIPTING

You can get a lot of use out of z-order without using any JavaScript. The placement of images behind other elements doesn't depend on movement, but can stand on its own. For instance, you can have an image underlying text locally, without committing to an overall background image for the page.

CROSS-REFERENCE

See Chapter 16 for more information on CSS.

FIND IT ONLINE

Read more about z-order at **http://www.w3.org/TR/ REC-CSS2/visuren.html#z-index**.

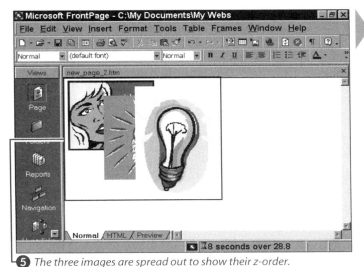

⑤ *The three images are spread out to show their z-order.*

⑥ *Select the second image.*

⑦ *Click the Bring Forward button.*

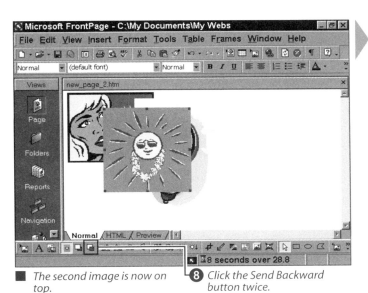

■ *The second image is now on top.*

⑧ *Click the Send Backward button twice.*

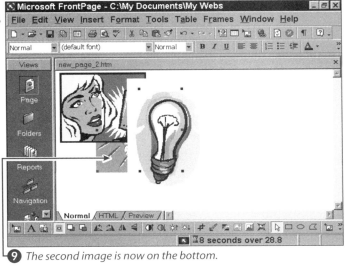

⑨ *The second image is now on the bottom.*

Rotating and Flipping Images

Sometimes, you may want an image to be viewed from a different angle than normal. Perhaps you have an image on disk or from a Web site that you think isn't shown in the right way, or perhaps you want to make some point by turning a shot upside down. You may want to make a copy of an image, paste it into your Web page alongside the original one, and reverse it so that you have a mirror image of one facing the other.

FrontPage has two different methods for controlling the orientation of images: rotation and flipping. You can rotate images to either the left or the right, and you can flip images either vertically or horizontally. Although the effects of the two techniques fit into the same broad category of altering an image's orientation on the screen, they do work a bit differently from one another.

If you click one of the rotation buttons endlessly, the image keeps rotating in the same direction. The rotation buttons cancel out each other. If you use the Rotate Left button, for instance, and then follow it by clicking the Rotate Right button, the image returns to its original state.

The flip buttons, on the other hand, are *toggle buttons*, which means that they can cause only two different states, between which they switch back and forth with each click (the term comes from electronics, in which toggle switches are used to shift between two states — the most common toggle switch is an on/off switch). If you click the Flip Vertical button,

you'll see this toggling effect in action. With the first click, the image turns upside down. With the second click, it turns right side up again. These are the only two things that can possibly happen with this button. Likewise, the Flip Horizontal button can only make a mirror image or return the image to its original state.

The four buttons can, however, be used in tandem with one another to create quite a few different states. By repeatedly flipping and rotating an image, it can be placed in a variety of different orientations.

TAKE NOTE

NO FINE-TUNING HERE

You can rotate images in FrontPage only 90 degrees at a time, so an image has only four possible rotational positions available to you. If you want a finer degree of control over rotation, you have to make the changes to the original image file in a separate graphics program that has more-sophisticated rotational capabilities.

CROSS-REFERENCE

See Chapter 6 for more information on images.

FIND IT ONLINE

Check out Cool Graphics at
http://little.fishnet.net/~gini/cool/.

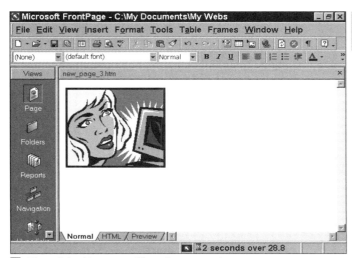

■ *The original image, unflipped, unrotated.*

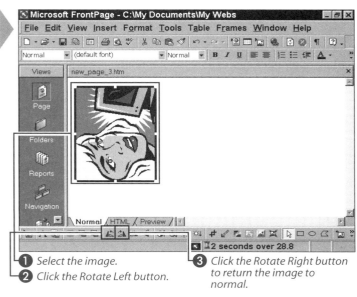

❶ *Select the image.*

❷ *Click the Rotate Left button.*

❸ *Click the Rotate Right button to return the image to normal.*

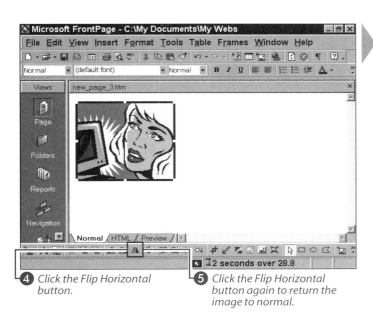

❹ *Click the Flip Horizontal button.*

❺ *Click the Flip Horizontal button again to return the image to normal.*

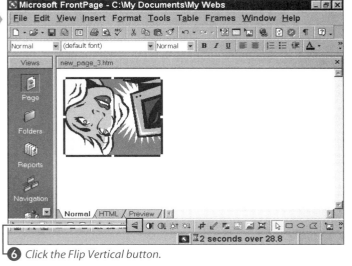

❻ *Click the Flip Vertical button.*

Changing Contrast and Brightness

The *contrast* of an image is the amount of difference between the various colors that make it up. With very high contrast, you lose absolutely all subtlety and have an image composed of strikingly different chunks of color. With very low contrast, you get the opposite effect, and the different parts of the image blend together to the point where all detail is lost.

Although high-contrast images generally are lighter than the original, and low-contrast images usually are darker than the original, this is not the same thing as controlling the brightness. Brightness affects the *saturation* of the colors in the image. Essentially, saturation is the amount of white that's mixed with the color.

Deeply saturated colors are more pure and have very little white diluting them (the rich blues of Victorian Christmas cards, for instance, are some of the most striking uses of saturation in art). By adding more brightness, you lower the saturation of the colors in the image. Pushed to its extreme, you can change any image to total white by raising the brightness to the maximum, or you can make it totally black, removing all white from it, by lowering the brightness all the way.

TAKE NOTE

▶ IT COULD BE EASIER

In FrontPage, you have to click the Contrast and Brightness buttons repeatedly to make major changes in the appearance of an image. If you have an image that's in serious need of such adjustments, your mouse finger will feel like it's about to fall off before you're done. In such a case, you are advised to work on the picture in an image editor. Most graphics programs enable you to adjust the brightness and contrast of an image by using slider bars or spinners, which are much easier to use than buttons for this type of work.

▶ WATCH OUT FOR OVERWRITE

When you make changes to an image, other than resizing it, you alter the actual file, not just its appearance on the Web page. When you save the changes, you permanently alter the image. If the same image is used on more than one of your pages, it is altered on all of them. If you want to use the same image on multiple pages, but just change its appearance on one or some of them, make sure that you save it under a new name when you save the page on which you made the changes. If you allow the default action of overwriting the old image file, you may regret the effects. Keeping a copy of the original file in another folder is a good idea, so that you can always get it back if you don't like the changes.

CROSS-REFERENCE

See the section "Black and White and Washout" later in this chapter.

FIND IT ONLINE

Try AndyArt at **http://www.andyart.com/**.

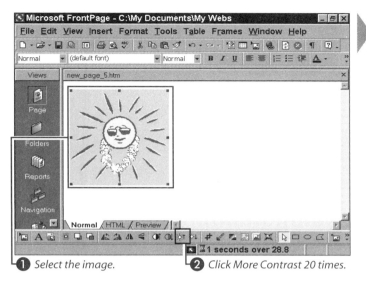

1 Select the image. **2** Click More Contrast 20 times.

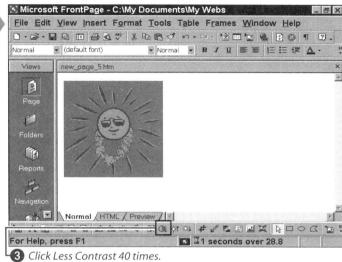

3 Click Less Contrast 40 times.

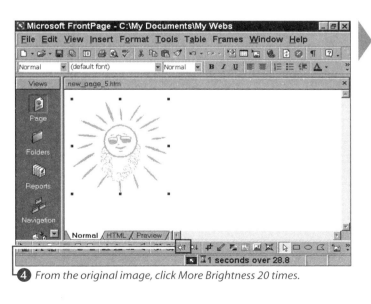

4 From the original image, click More Brightness 20 times.

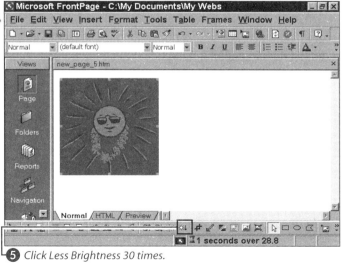

5 Click Less Brightness 30 times.

Cropping Images

Many times, you may disagree with the original artist or photographer about the total focus of a scene. Not that it's blurry, necessarily, but that it includes extraneous information that distracts from the main point of the image. Or, perhaps you want to extract one particular element from a montage. *Cropping* is the act of cutting out one particular part of an image and eliminating the remainder.

The cropping action in FrontPage is sensible, though not intuitive. It's the only button on the Picture toolbar that you have to click twice, once to initiate the cropping and again to complete it.

FrontPage offers no way to select and copy just part of an image. However, a workaround exists by using the cropping tool. Although this workaround is a bit awkward and requires a second program, it does the job. First, use the cropping tool to crop the image so that it shows only the part that you want to copy. Select the image and click the Copy button in the toolbar. Next, open any other program that accepts graphical input and paste the cropped image into it. Back in FrontPage, use the Undo or Restore buttons to return the original image to its uncropped state. You need to use a second program because FrontPage regards all copies of the image as the original image. If you paste into FrontPage, the pasted image will be restored along with the original one. However, if you first paste the cropped version into another program, you can then copy it from that program and paste it into FrontPage as a new image. FrontPage is fooled by this trick and does not restore the image to its original form.

TAKE NOTE

▶ DON'T CROP OUT HYPERLINKS

If you intend to crop an image map, you must take particular care not to eliminate any part of the image that has a hotspot on it. After you crop out a hotspot, it's gone. Fortunately, you can use the Undo button to reverse cropping, but remember that the Undo button has a limit of 30 actions to it. If you do 30 things after cropping, you won't be able to undo it. Even using the Restore button on the image won't recover a lost hotspot.

▶ YOU'RE CROPPING ALL THE COPIES, TOO

In common with nearly all image changes in FrontPage, if the same image is used on multiple pages, then you make the same changes on all the pages, even if you do it before the image is saved. This is true of all the Picture toolbar buttons except for the absolute positioning ones.

CROSS-REFERENCE
See Chapter 8 for information on image maps.

FIND IT ONLINE
Take a look at the Graphics Zone, located at
http://www.website-designs.com/graphic.html.

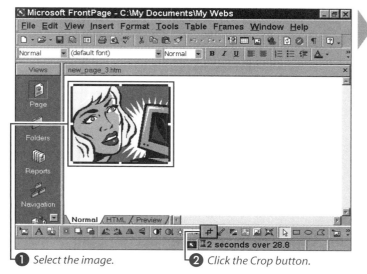

1 Select the image.

2 Click the Crop button.

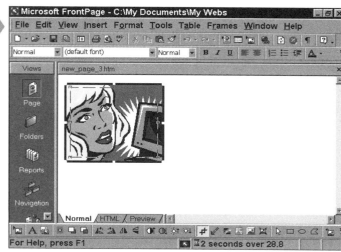

■ The crop box appears.

3 Resize the crop box to include the part of the image you want to keep.

4 Click the Crop button again.

■ The cropped image appears on the Web page.

Setting Transparency

One of the best features of GIF images is their ability to allow the background to show through part of the image. The transparency effect is limited to a single color, unfortunately, so not all images can take advantage of this feature to good effect. The best images to use transparency on are those in which the central part of the picture holds the focus, which is surrounded by a single solid color. Making that surrounding solid color the transparent color frees the image from the rectangular look that is forced on all computer graphics files by the exigencies of the graphics file formats.

You have to use a GIF image to set transparency, because transparency isn't supported by the JPEG file format. PNG images do support transparency, even on a pixel-by-pixel basis, but FrontPage doesn't utilize the PNG format, apparently deferring to the old tried-and-true standard instead (PNG files also tend to be very large).

A tradeoff is involved when switching to GIF format, unfortunately. GIF images support a maximum of 256 colors, whereas JPEGs and PNGs support 16.7 million colors. Although 256 colors is fine for most images, highly sophisticated, photorealistic images, when converted from truecolor to 256 colors, suddenly become much less attractive. However, many people on the Web have computer systems with video displays that show only 256 colors, anyway, so only more advanced users will even be able to notice the difference.

TAKE NOTE

▶ GET USED TO CLICKING THE BUTTON

One of the drawbacks — or benefits, depending on your point of view — to FrontPage is that the Set Transparent Color button deactivates itself every time that you use it. This means, in practical terms, that you get one shot at setting transparency. If the image you're working on presents a clear and simple situation, that's fine and useful, but it leaves you no room for experimentation. If you want to try one color first, and then another color, and so on, you can't just click them all in sequence and observe the effects of the different choices; you have to click the Set Transparent Color button, click the first color, click the Transparent button, click the second color, over and over until you achieve the effect that you want.

▶ ALPHA CHANNEL

Transparency is controlled by the alpha channel in graphics files, which technically sets the degree of opacity, not transparency. Less opacity means more transparency, and no opacity means totally transparent.

CROSS-REFERENCE
See Chapter 6 for more information on the effect of borders around images that use transparency.

FIND IT ONLINE
Check out the PNG specification at
http://www.boutell.com/boutell/png/png.html.

1 Select the image.

2 Click the Set Transparent Color button.

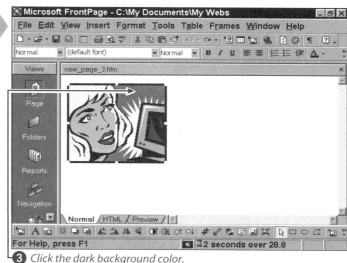

3 Click the dark background color.

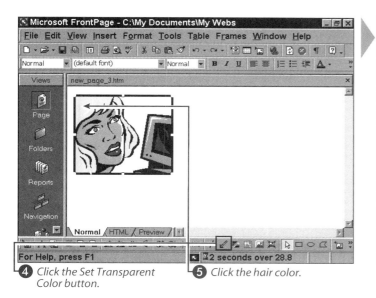

4 Click the Set Transparent Color button.

5 Click the hair color.

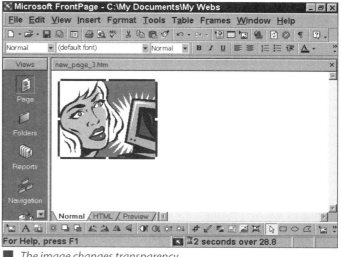

■ The image changes transparency.

Black and White and Wash Out

The Black and White button is used to convert an image from color to grayscale. As the term *grayscale* implies, the image isn't really converted to black and white, despite the name of the button. Instead, all colors in the image are converted to varying shades of gray, with white being the lightest form of gray, and black being the darkest form. In most images, though, not much (if any) actual black or white exists, just darker or lighter grays.

The Wash Out button is used to lessen both brightness and contrast in an image with one click, thus saving you a lot of trial and error and several clicks of both the Brightness and Contrast buttons.

Both the Black and White button and the Washout button are one-shot deals. You can't make a picture more grayscale than it is, of course, but the surprising thing is that a washed out image, even after it's saved and the file is reloaded, can't be washed out any more.

Both of these buttons have an unpleasant side effect on transparency in GIF images — they undo it. If you set a transparent color in a GIF image and then click one of these buttons for that image, you have to redo transparency after you convert the image to grayscale or apply wash out.

TAKE NOTE

BACKGROUND IMAGES

The washout effect is particularly useful for images that you're going to use as a background. Too often, a particular image that you want to use as a background is so dark that it would interfere with the other, overlying elements on a page. Text placed over such a background image is unreadable, and other images are interfered with as well. Creating a washed out version of the image usually solves this problem.

OH, YEAH, THE BEVEL BUTTON

The Bevel button, located next to the Wash Out button, doesn't deserve an entire section of its own, but should still get some mention. The Bevel button applies a thick, three-dimensional, gray-colored border to an image, shaded so that it appears to be beveled, with the lighting coming from the upper-left side. This is not the same thing as a regular border, and you actually can have both a bevel and a regular border on the same image simultaneously. The beveled border, unlike the normal one, doesn't have adjustable thickness. Also, its color is gray, regardless of the text color. The Bevel button shares with the Wash Out and Black and White buttons the problem of eliminating transparency in GIF images, so you need to reapply transparency after adding a beveled border.

CROSS-REFERENCE

See the section "Changing Contrast and Brightness," earlier in this chapter.

FIND IT ONLINE

For more information on grayscale, see **http://www.aa6g.org/Astronomy/Articles/grayscale.html**.

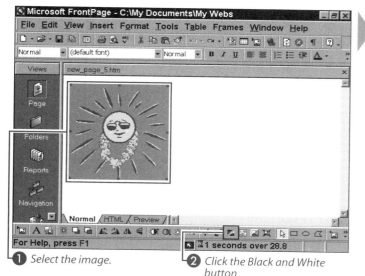

1 Select the image.

2 Click the Black and White button.

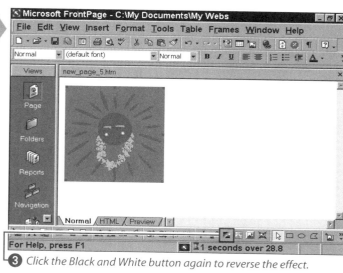

3 Click the Black and White button again to reverse the effect.

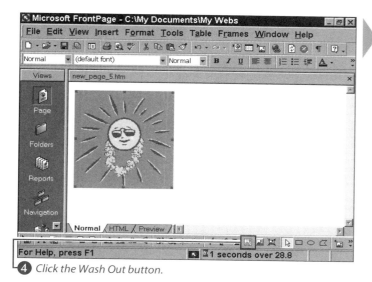

4 Click the Wash Out button.

■ The washed out image shows on the Web page.

Personal Workbook

Q&A

1 What file format is used when you add text to an image?

_____

_____

_____

2 Why can Clip Art Gallery images be resized without resampling?

_____

_____

_____

3 What is a *thumbnail image*?

_____

_____

_____

4 Why is the term *z-order* so appropriate?

_____

_____

_____

5 How many times do you need to rotate an image before it returns to its original position?

_____

_____

_____

_____

6 What is *saturation?*

_____

_____

_____

_____

7 What is the default z-order value?

_____

_____

_____

8 What does the Wash Out button do?

_____

_____

_____

ANSWERS: PAGE 326

EXTRA PRACTICE

1. Resize some bitmapped images.

2. Apply absolute positioning to an image, look at the HTML source code, and then move the image. Look at the code again.

3. Combine rotation and flipping. See how many different combinations there are.

4. Create a thumbnail image. Use Windows Explorer to see how much difference in file size exists between the thumbnail and the original image.

5. Try setting different transparency colors in an image to see the effects.

REAL-WORLD APPLICATIONS

✔ You like the bevel border, but wish it showed up better along the left and top sides. Try putting it against a dark background for a better appearance.

✔ You have a colorful Web page on which you want to use a background image. You might consider using the Black and White button on the image first so that it won't conflict with the page's color scheme.

✔ You're going to be making a lot of changes to an important image. It's a really, really good idea to make a backup copy of it first, just in case things go wrong.

✔ You have an image that you like, but it contains extraneous material. You may be able to solve the problem by cropping the image.

Visual Quiz

How do you create this thumbnail image?

_____

_____

_____

_____

_____

_____

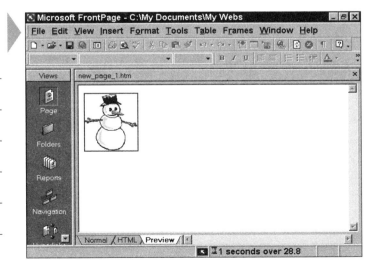

CHAPTER 8

MASTER THESE SKILLS

▶ Adding and Deleting Hotspots

▶ Modifying Hotspot Shapes

▶ Modifying Hotspot Links

▶ Using Text Hotspots

Using Image Maps

Image maps are a special kind of image-based hyperlink. Whereas a normal image link consists of a single figure that's linked to a single URL, an image map is a single figure that can link to many different URLs. With a regular image link, no matter where you click it, you'll go to the same place. With an image map, clicking on different areas — called *hotspots* — links you to different Web pages. And, just as a normal image link is not always a real improvement over a plain text link, an image map is useful on certain occasions and a waste of time and bandwidth on others.

A single image map can very effectively replace an entire menu of regular hyperlinks with one intuitive, easy-to-understand graphic. That is, it can if the graphic is well designed and the hyperlink menu it's replacing is within a particular range of URLs — not too many and not too few. What exactly is the right range for the number of links? It's not a hard and fast rule, but a good rule of thumb is that if you have less than four URLs to connect to, just use text hyperlinks. If you have more than ten URLs, then you should still stick with plain old text links because each link takes up a certain amount of space on the image, and the graphic you'd need to hold dozens of links would probably be a bit too large to be practical.

What types of images work the best as the basis for an image map? Ideally, they should be images that already convey a certain amount of information themselves. You might, for instance, use an actual geographical map, enabling visitors to your Web site to click on different countries to activate links to country-related Web pages. Many weather sites utilize this approach to enable visitors to get regional weather reports. A home page for a zoo might show a montage of animals, each one representing a separate hyperlink. Whatever the motif, the common feature is that image maps must provide a clearly discernible set of separate segments so that the user can understand at a glance that clicking here means one thing and clicking there means another.

Adding and Deleting Hotspots

Although image map hotspots — the areas on the image that correspond to different URLs — were originally rectangular, three different shapes exist today. Along with basic rectangles, you can make a circular hyperlink or one called a *polygon* that's shaped like just about anything you can imagine. Polygons are composed of a series of connected straight lines. By making the lines very short, you can simulate arcs and create a polygon that will closely follow a curved outline.

The three different shapes are created in slightly different manners. The rectangular shape is drawn from corner to corner; when you make the initial click, you hold the mouse button down and drag until you have the size rectangle you want. The process for creating a circle is pretty much the same, except that it expands outward from the initial point, which forms the center of the circle instead of the edge. Creating polygons, however, is a bit less intuitive.

To create a polygon shape, you click and release the button at the initial point, and then move the pointer to the next point and click again. You continue to do this until you've created the desired shape. At the final point, you double-click to complete the shape. Don't worry about getting the initial point and the last point exactly aligned; FrontPage takes care of that for you. You can double-click at the

next to the last point, since the final connection between points is automatic and closes the shape off.

Deleting hotspots is easy — just select the hotspot and press the Delete key.

TAKE NOTE

THE DEFAULT HYPERLINK

In addition to rectangles, circles, and polygons, you can create a fourth type of hotspot in an image map — *the default hyperlink*. This hyperlink is activated if a visitor clicks any area of the image outside the hotspots. While most image map creation programs specifically provide for establishing the default value, no such option exists in FrontPage. You must select the image and then make a regular image link. You should do this after the other hotspots are in place, or it won't be a part of the actual image map.

DELETING THE DEFAULT HOTSPOT

Since the default hotspot doesn't show up in FrontPage, you can't just highlight it and delete it the way you can with any of the normal ones. If you try this, you'll just end up deleting the entire image. To delete a default hotspot, right-click the image after the other hotspots have been deleted, and then select Hyperlink Properties from the popup menu. In the Hyperlink Properties dialog box, delete the URL, click the OK button, and the default hotspot setting is removed.

CROSS-REFERENCE

See Chapter 4 for information on how to make regular image links.

FIND IT ONLINE

You can find a FrontPage help Web site at
http://precisionweb.net/FrontPageHelp.htm.

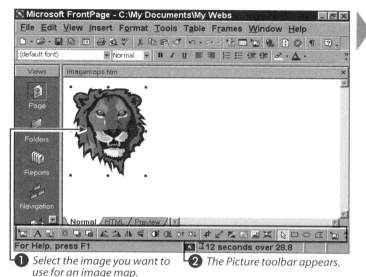

① *Select the image you want to use for an image map.*

② *The Picture toolbar appears.*

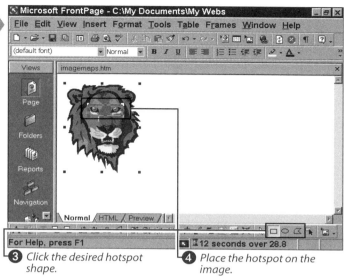

③ *Click the desired hotspot shape.*

④ *Place the hotspot on the image.*

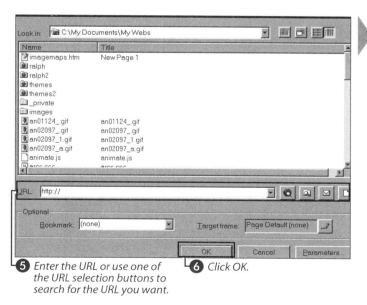

⑤ *Enter the URL or use one of the URL selection buttons to search for the URL you want.*

⑥ *Click OK.*

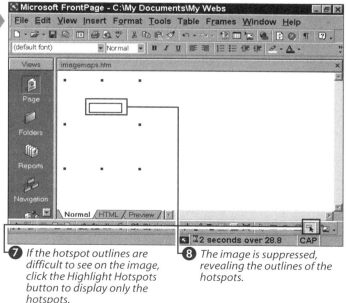

⑦ *If the hotspot outlines are difficult to see on the image, click the Highlight Hotspots button to display only the hotspots.*

⑧ *The image is suppressed, revealing the outlines of the hotspots.*

Modifying Hotspot Shapes

You'll sometimes want to adjust the exact coverage of the hotspots in an image map because the hotspots were placed inexactly to begin with or because some changes were made to the image itself. You can adjust the coverage by altering either the shape or size of the hotspots.

In fact, because you can adjust the location and extent of area coverage in a hotspot, you don't have to use exacting precision when you put them in. To a purist, this is blasphemy, but in the real world there are times when "quick and dirty" has to do, and it's nice to know that you can improve the situation later on. You can't, unfortunately, change the type of shape such as altering a circle to a more precise polygon shape.

The various hotspot shapes all have their quirks when it comes to making alterations. With circles, the only change you can make is to the size; the shape, of course, remains the same. With polygons, the only change you can make is to the shape since no provisions exist for altering the size while retaining the shape; nor can you add more lines to the polygon. Only with rectangles can you alter both size and shape at will, but of course the only possible alteration in the shape of a rectangle is to the length of its sides.

You can also make coverage adjustments by changing the location of a hotspot, even if you don't alter its shape or size. Just place the mouse pointer inside the hotspot, press the left mouse button and hold it while you drag the hotspot to its new location; then release the button. You're unlikely to need to do this with a polygon, since it will have been drawn to follow the edges of a particular image element in the first place, but circular and rectangular hotspots can often benefit by being nudged just a bit.

TAKE NOTE

▶ NO IMAGE LINK BORDER

One of the drawbacks to image maps is that nothing intrinsically identifies them as a source of hyperlinks. With a text link, you have underlining and color; with a regular image link, you have a colored border. An image map, however, is indistinguishable at a glance from a regular image. This is an odd failing in the HTML standards, but it is one you'll have to deal with. Some Web designers make an image map that has text included as a part of the image itself, making it clear that these are links. Others may specify in the text elsewhere on the page something like, "Click the image map below to go to different pages." Still others simply ignore the situation entirely.

CROSS-REFERENCE
See the following section on modifying hotspot links.

FIND IT ONLINE
You can find a FrontPage mailing list at
http://www.akorn.net/fpreffaq.htm.

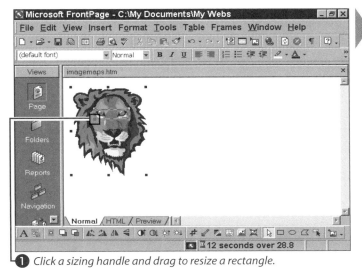

❶ *Click a sizing handle and drag to resize a rectangle.*

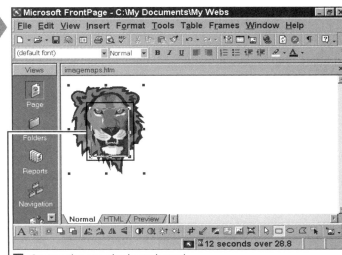

■ *Rectangles can also be reshaped.*

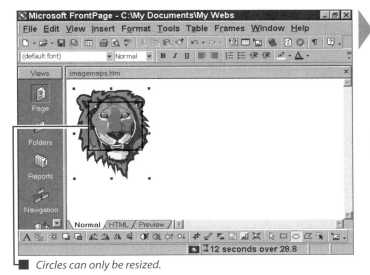

■ *Circles can only be resized.*

■ *Moving a sizing handle on a polygon changes the point where two lines intersect.*

Modifying Hotspot Links

As the saying goes, the only thing that is constant is change. This could easily be said of the World Wide Web. Web pages come and go. Some of them change addresses. Others drop off the World Wide Web entirely. Sometimes (not as often, but still enough to be a concern) a page changes its topic so drastically that a link is no longer valid although the connection still works. The problem is particularly prevalent in online communities like Geocities or Tripod, where the same Web address might be used over a period of time by several different people with extremely varied interests. Today, many Web sites offer free Web pages to the public, and when someone gives up one of those URLs, it's reassigned to the next person who comes along.

For a corporate Web site, you may be called the Webmaster, but if your bosses want a change, you have to make the change, no matter how it affects your image maps. Realistically, even if all your image map links are internal to your own personal Web site, and nobody else has any influence at all over its structure or content, something's bound to change at some point.

Regardless of the reason, sooner or later some of your links are bound to become obsolete. With a normal text link menu, it's a fairly simple matter to solve the problem — simply delete it and the rest of the links will automatically close up to fill in the gap. With an image map, you've got to deal with a whole other level of complexity, since at least part of the total image is keyed to the link. In a drastic situation, you may even have to can the image and replace it, but many times, the link information can simply be changed.

TAKE NOTE

▶ BLANKING THE URL

If you need to temporarily disable a hotspot URL, you have a couple of options. You could, of course, always point it to a page apologizing for the delay. You can also, however, simply remove the URL entirely, while leaving the hotspot itself in place. To do this, just completely remove all the text in the URL edit box (pictured in step 4 in the lower-left figure, facing page). The result will be that the hotspot will remain intact, but nothing will happen if someone clicks it.

▶ NOT JUST WEB PAGES

We've made many references in this chapter to using image maps to link to different Web pages. For the sake of readability, we have chosen to stick to this simple statement, and that's generally what people use them for. But you can, of course, use the hotspots in an image map to link to any resource on the Internet. A URL is all that's required. Use an image map to play different songs or videos. Use it to download different files. Use it to create a set of mailto links. Most of all, use your imagination — you don't have to do what everyone else does.

CROSS-REFERENCE

See the section earlier in this chapter, "Adding and Deleting Hotspots."

FIND IT ONLINE

You can subscribe to the FrontPage Friends mailing list at **http://www.purpleatpixie.co.za/frontpag.htm**.

1 Select the image containing the hotspots.

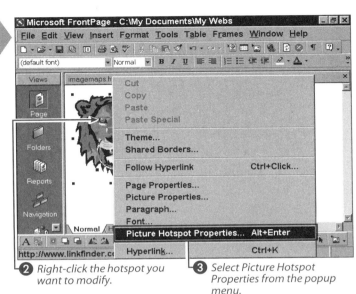

2 Right-click the hotspot you want to modify.

3 Select Picture Hotspot Properties from the popup menu.

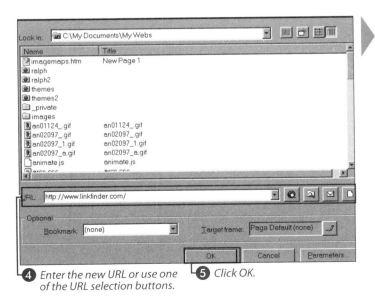

4 Enter the new URL or use one of the URL selection buttons.

5 Click OK.

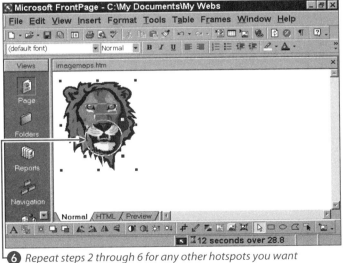

6 Repeat steps 2 through 6 for any other hotspots you want to change.

Using Text Hotspots

You can use text as a hotspot in an image in a couple of ways. One obvious way, of course, is to just have text on an image before you even import it (it would have to be added in a separate graphics program beforehand) and then to make a hotspot around it. However, FrontPage has its own way to include text hotspots.

Why would anyone want to use text in an image map? Isn't an image map designed to replace a plain text style hyperlink? One purpose might be for the sheer artistry of it. Using a textual overlay on an abstract image, for example, could create a hypertext link that is much more attractive than plain text. At other times, text is used to supplement images with ambiguous meanings. In the latter case, it would probably be better to use an image editor to apply the text before the image is used in FrontPage. If the image is a GIF file, you can use FrontPage to add the text to it after it is inserted on the Web page. After the text is in place on the image, you can use a hotspot to surround the text and the part of the image it is meant to clarify.

You might also use text in an image map because both regular text hyperlinks and the style of text hotspots created by FrontPage are limited to plain old horizontal placement. There are times when, for design purposes, you'll want to have text hyperlinks that are at odd angles. Since FrontPage doesn't offer any method of rotating text (it's true that you can

rotate entire images, but they can be rotated only in 90-degree increments), you'll need to use a more sophisticated external graphics program to do this. Once it's inserted into your Web page, you can turn the image containing text into a set of hyperlinks by using hotspots. Since the rectangular style of hotspots usually employed in the case of textual hotspots won't do the trick unless the text is either horizontal or vertical, you'll probably want to use the polygon shape to surround the text when creating the hotspot.

TAKE NOTE

NO CIRCLES OR POLYGONS

The FrontPage method of creating text hotspots that's detailed in the steps on the facing page always creates rectangular hotspots.

GET CREATIVE

Don't forget that you can manipulate the characters in a FrontPage-created text hotspot the same way you can any other characters on the Web page. Feel free to change font sizes, colors, and faces to suit your own tastes.

CROSS-REFERENCE
See Chapter 3 for more information on modifying text.

FIND IT ONLINE
You'll find FrontPage tips and a mailing list at
http://www.benway.net/frontpage.htm.

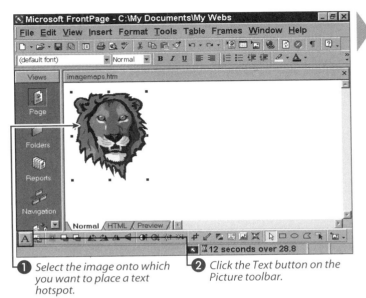

1 Select the image onto which you want to place a text hotspot.

2 Click the Text button on the Picture toolbar.

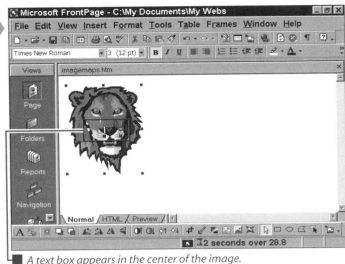

■ A text box appears in the center of the image.

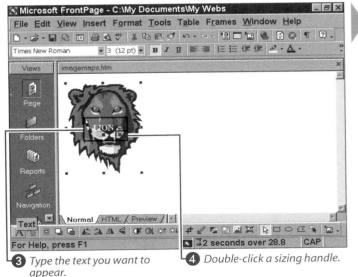

3 Type the text you want to appear.

4 Double-click a sizing handle.

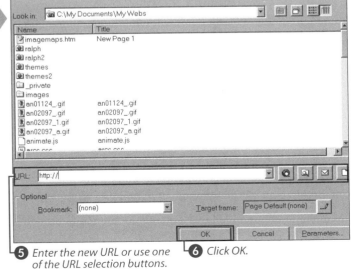

5 Enter the new URL or use one of the URL selection buttons.

6 Click OK.

Personal Workbook

Q&A

1 What is an *image map*?

_____

_____

_____

2 What is a *hotspot*?

_____

_____

_____

3 How many hotspot shapes are there?

_____

_____

_____

_____

4 What can a hotspot link to?

_____

_____

_____

5 How many hotspots can be used in one image map?

_____

_____

_____

6 What happens when you move a sizing handle on a polygon?

_____

_____

_____

7 What is the main difference between client-side and server-side image maps?

_____

_____

_____

_____

8 What is the default hyperlink?

_____

_____

_____

ANSWERS: PAGE 326

EXTRA PRACTICE

1. Place a rectangle hotspot, and then resize and reshape it.

2. Use a polygon hotspot to trace an irregular shape.

3. Overlap two hotspots and see which one is activated when you click the overlap area.

4. Consult a book on drawing to see how images are created from basic shapes like circles. Ponder which hotspot shapes would best delineate portions of various images.

5. Create a text hotspot. Afterward, attempt to modify the URL. See what happens if you double-click inside or outside the border of the text box.

6. Modify the text inside a hotspot. Use different font sizes and colors.

REAL-WORLD APPLICATIONS

✔ You have several links you'd like to put into a menu. You might consider using an image map instead.

✔ You want to make an image map, but don't have one image that will carry the meaning you want. In an external graphics program, you can combine several different images into a montage to create the image to be used for the image map. Then import it into FrontPage.

✔ You've created an image map, but its colors make it difficult to see the hotspots. Try using the Highlight Hotspots button.

✔ When you're finished with the image map, your client decides the image should be smaller. You can resize the hotspots after the image is resized.

Visual Quiz

What are these three shapes? How do you get this display?

_____

_____

_____

_____

_____

_____

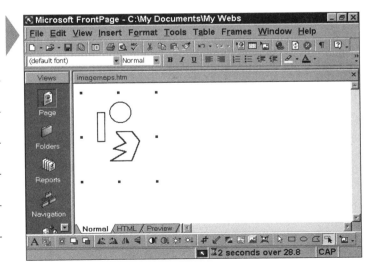

PART

III

Intermediate Web Design

The chapters in this section cover the use of those elements of Web page design that are normally the province of the advanced Web page designer. Chapter 9, "Getting Information from Forms," provides instruction on inserting forms in a FrontPage web, saving form fields, setting field names, and using hidden fields and confirmation pages.

In the tenth chapter, "Customizing Forms," you'll learn how to use the tab order, make clickable labels, and set the validation rules for various form elements.

Chapters 11 and 12 provide information and instruction on using various FrontPage components, ranging from hit counters and search functions to meta variables and hover buttons.

The thirteenth chapter covers how to use tables to structure Web pages, and the fourteenth chapter covers the more advanced functions of tables, which add to the functionality of your Web site.

CHAPTER **9**

MASTER
THESE
SKILLS

▶ **Inserting Forms**

▶ **Saving Form Fields**

▶ **Setting Field Names**

▶ **Using Hidden Fields**

▶ **Using Confirmation Pages**

▶ **Assigning a Custom Confirmation Page**

Getting Information from Forms

Forms are the most common method for interacting with visitors to your Web site. In fact, prior to the development of JavaScript and Dynamic HTML, forms were the *only* means of interacting with your users. They're still the preferred approach for interactivity in Web page design, simply because they have, so to speak, a degree of seniority over the newer methods.

However, the older method is not going to be supplanted by newer techniques as so often happens. Forms have their specific uses on the World Wide Web just as their paper equivalents do in the world of business and commerce, and they will always be needed. No one yet has come up with a better technique for getting such information as names and addresses for placing orders. Even if digital IDs eventually enable any commercial Web site to reliably identify a shopper, information will still be needed to make decisions about matters such as form of payment, shipping address for purchased merchandise, and user e-mail address to send requested information to. Form input will be necessary to process such information properly.

You have only two choices when it comes to collecting online survey data — you can use simple forms or you can perform an elaborate job of custom programming. Since the latter would be expensive and time consuming and would only succeed in duplicating the functionality of the existing HTML form approach, the winner is clear.

The most common form elements should already be familiar to you even if you've never done any HTML programming before. The forms that you'll use on your Web pages are virtually identical to the forms you fill out for everything from job applications to income tax. They utilize variations on text boxes and check boxes, and yes or no responses are covered by radio buttons. Beyond that, you don't need any specialized knowledge because FrontPage will automatically supply your forms with Reset and Submit buttons the instant that you put any form element on your Web page.

Inserting Forms

In FrontPage, every form has at least three elements — the FORM element itself, a submit button, and a reset button. Visitors to a Web site use the submit button to send information they've entered; they can use the reset button to clear that information and set all the options back to their default values. That raw, minimal form is, of course, utterly useless. It needs to offer some method for visitors to your site to either enter information or indicate choices between available options. Without those additional elements, there's no data to either submit or reset.

The elements that you can use in a form are:

▶ **One-Line Text Box**. Used to hold textual data such as name and address. Although you can enlarge a text box, there is no real need to, since the data will scroll if it won't fit the visible part.

▶ **Scrolling Text Box**. Used for longer textual input, such as comments and shipping directions. Also known as the <TEXTAREA> element in HTML parlance.

▶ **Check Box**. Used to indicate a non-exclusive choice among multiple options or a single yes/no choice. You can choose as many check boxes in a group as you want.

▶ **Radio Button**. Used to indicate a choice among multiple mutually exclusive options. You can only choose one radio button in a group; choosing one automatically deselects the others.

▶ **Drop-Down Menu**. Used to present a series of options in a compact space.

▶ **Push Button**. Used to launch a custom JavaScript program.

▶ **Picture**. Used to place an image in the form. You can't do anything with an image unless you want to write a custom script, but they are often used to include logos and other such images.

▶ **Label**. Used to make text associated with another form element clickable.

TAKE NOTE

IN HTML, YOU ONLY NEED ONE

The three-element basic form is an invention of FrontPage. Technically speaking, HTML's only requirement for a <FORM> element on a Web page to be valid is the element itself; no contained elements are actually necessary. Of course, just like FrontPage's basic form, it would be useless. The functionality of a form comes not from the container, but the contents.

THE FAST WAY

If you want to create a form and save a step, you can go right ahead and insert the first element. If you insert, say, a radio button onto a page in FrontPage, the form will automatically be created around it. If you don't want it to work this way, select Tools ⇨ Page Options, click the General tab, and clear the check box labeled "Automatically enclose form fields with a form."

CROSS-REFERENCE
See Chapter 10 for how to modify form elements.

FIND IT ONLINE
You will find FrontPage tips, including forms info, at
http://www.purpleatpixie.co.za/frontpag.htm.

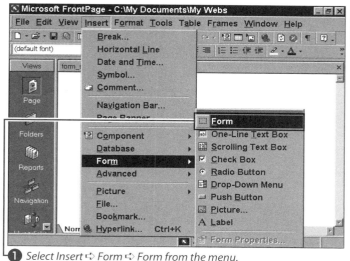

1 Select Insert ⇨ Form ⇨ Form from the menu.

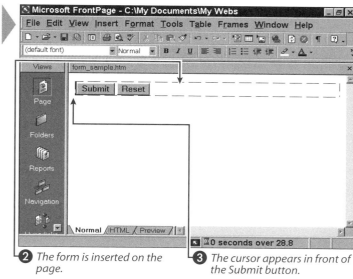

2 The form is inserted on the page.

3 The cursor appears in front of the Submit button.

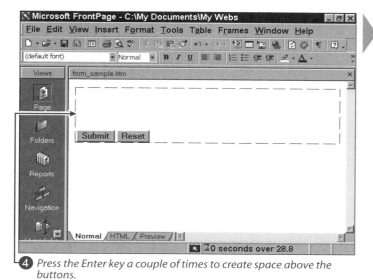

4 Press the Enter key a couple of times to create space above the buttons.

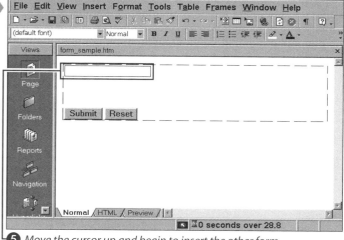

5 Move the cursor up and begin to insert the other form elements.

Saving Form Fields

By default, the data from every form field is saved. The only exception is the Reset button, which by the very nature of its function does not have any data to present to the form handler. FrontPage enables you to control the information that is saved from the various fields in your forms.

Why would anyone want to limit the amount of information saved from a form? After all, a properly designed form should contain every field that's needed to gather the desired data, no more and no less. Generally speaking, that's true, of course, but specialized situations exist in which a subset of the total data is more useful than all of it would be. It is fairly common in surveys or psychological testing, for instance, to only care about the answers to a few questions. In order to keep the subject from attaching any particular importance to the key questions and thereby skewing the results, a number of other questions are mixed in for the purpose of distraction. Thus, the subject has no idea which are the important questions, and the researcher doesn't care about the responses to the diversions. In such a case, you would want to set up the form so that it only recorded the responses to the key questions.

It's what FrontPage allows you to add to the saved fields, however, that's of more interest to the average Web page designer than what it allows you to leave out. If it is important to you to know what day and time the form data was processed (as, for instance,

with an order on a commercial Web site), then you need to set a date and time format. The "Additional information to save" elements will be familiar to anyone who has used environment variables while working with UNIX or doing CGI programming. The "Remote computer name" is provided by the REMOTE_HOST variable, "Username" is the REMOTE_USER variable, and "Browser type" is HTTP_USER_AGENT. Although many other environment variables exist, most of them are strictly technical material. These three variables will provide you with the most useful information in a commercial situation or in any other situation in which you want to know a bit more about the people who are using your site.

TAKE NOTE

WHAT'S A FORM HANDLER?

It's the program that actually processes the data from the form's input. FrontPage takes care of that little detail for you, but if you are familiar with the Common Gateway Interface (CGI) and want to write your own form handler programs, FrontPage won't stand in your way.

CROSS-REFERENCE
See Chapter 10 for more information on form fields.

FIND IT ONLINE
A free FrontPage hosting is available at
http://www.superdomain.com/free-1.htm.

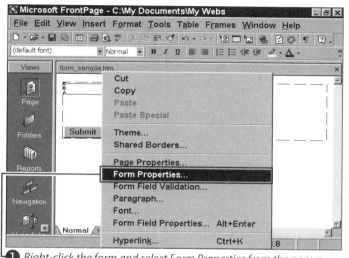

1 Right-click the form and select Form Properties from the popup menu.

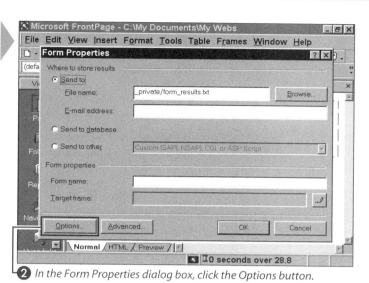

2 In the Form Properties dialog box, click the Options button.

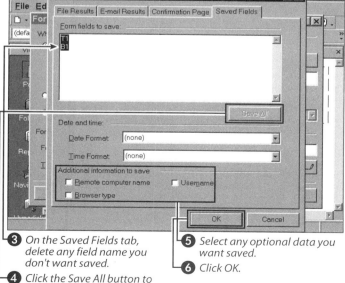

3 On the Saved Fields tab, delete any field name you don't want saved.

4 Click the Save All button to restore all field names to the list.

5 Select any optional data you want saved.

6 Click OK.

7 In the Form Properties dialog box, click OK.

Setting Field Names

Every element within a form has a *field name* that is used to identify it as a unique part of the form. This name is matched up with the data represented by that field in what's known as a *name/value pair*. You don't have to worry about assigning field names manually if you don't want to, because FrontPage automatically assigns arbitrary ones for you. FrontPage isn't very imaginative or descriptive when it comes to field names, however. It simply uses a letter and a number to identify the form elements. If you give more meaningful names to your fields, you'll make your life a lot easier.

In the following table summarizing the FrontPage naming system, the letter x represents the number in the letter/number combination:

Field	Standard Name
One-Line Text Box	Tx
Scrolling Text Box	Sx
Check Box	Cx
Radio Button	Rx
Drop-Down Menu	Dx
Push Button	Bx (including the Submit and Reset buttons)
Picture (Image)	Ix
Label	No field name is associated with a label.

Faced with a set of names like T1, C3, and B1, it can be very difficult to comprehend the output of a form submission. Manually assigning new names like FirstName, Yes, and Submit instead of settling for the standard ones can vastly increase the ease of understanding. Even if you have no trouble remembering which form element is S2 and which one is T7, you should still take the time to fix the field names. The field names are included in the confirmation form that your users will see after they submit the form, and they can't confirm what they can't understand.

TAKE NOTE

NOT ALWAYS THE SAME

The Form Field Properties dialog box varies somewhat from one type of form element to another, but all of the dialog boxes include the name/value pair. If you want to, you can set the initial value as well as the name in this dialog box. This simple approach can vastly increase the user's understanding of the form's purpose and meaning, as well as improve the odds that you will get back the kind of input that you intended when you designed the form. People everywhere are notoriously sloppy when it comes to following directions, and any assistance you can give them toward supplying the kind of response you need or want will repay your effort. Of course, there's always the possibility of the reverse happening, and people have been known to look at an incorrect default value and leave it intact instead of changing it (this results in such addresses as Boston, MA, and UK). In the end, it's another value judgment.

CROSS-REFERENCE

See Chapter 6 for information on pictures.

FIND IT ONLINE

The FrontPage2000.org Web site is located at **http://www.frontpage2000.org/default.asp.**

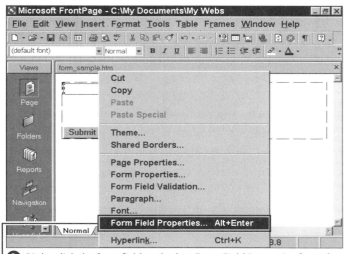

1 *Right-click the form field and select Form Field Properties from the popup menu.*

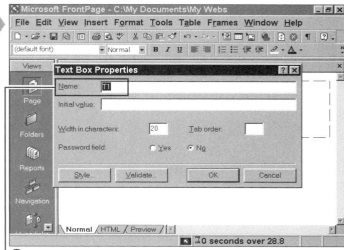

2 *The name currently assigned by FrontPage will show.*

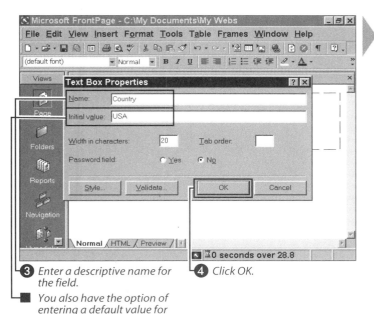

3 *Enter a descriptive name for the field.*

4 *Click OK.*

■ *You also have the option of entering a default value for the field.*

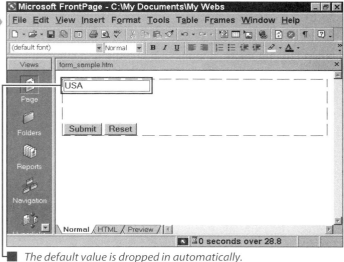

■ *The default value is dropped in automatically.*

Using Hidden Fields

The normal fields in your form are, of course, fully visible to your users. Fields composed of form elements such as check boxes and radio buttons would be totally useless unless they could be seen so that data could be entered or they could be clicked. But what if you want to have information included in a form's output that isn't visible or accessible to users and can't, therefore, be changed by them? For this reason, FrontPage offers hidden fields.

What are some of the situations for which you might want to use hidden fields in your forms? You may wish to include a form number, for example, as well as the date and time of the latest revision. Large corporations and government agencies are particularly likely to need such hidden fields in order to keep the form in strict compliance with the organization's standard operating procedures.

You might also want to use hidden fields if you have an arrangement with Webmasters of different sites for them to take orders for your product. You would most likely have the same form in use on several different Web sites and would need to track from which one an order was placed in order to determine which Webmaster should get the credit for the referral. In this case, you should probably assign a unique code identifier to each of your affiliates for the purpose of tracking the origins of the orders. You can place the code identifier in a hidden field in order to quickly and easily distinguish the originating form

page and the representative's identity. And remember that hidden fields cannot be manipulated by the person filling out the form, so that gives both you and your affiliates an extra level of security.

For product ordering, you might also include the price, product number, shipping and handling charges, and the like as hidden fields. In such instances, your goal in using hidden fields is not necessarily to hide the fields, but to make them unchangeable. Information in these hidden fields should certainly be shown on the confirmation page.

TAKE NOTE

THEY DON'T STAY HIDDEN

FrontPage's default confirmation page automatically lists all fields, even the hidden ones. If you use it, then the hidden fields and their values will be displayed to your users, although they still can't change the values or contents of them. To avoid this, you'll have to create your own custom confirmation page, which doesn't list them.

PUT THEM IN ORDER

The hidden fields will not show up on a confirmation page or form submittal in the same order in which you enter them. They are automatically sorted into alphabetical order, both in the Advanced Form Properties dialog box and in the HTML source code.

CROSS-REFERENCE

See the following section on custom confirmation pages.

FIND IT ONLINE

Datasync has a FrontPage forum at
http://www2.datasync.com/forum/.

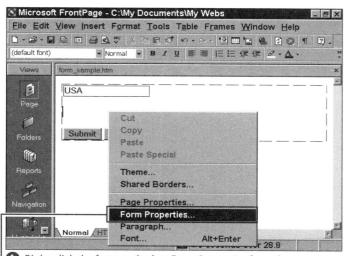

1 Right-click the form and select Form Properties from the popup menu.

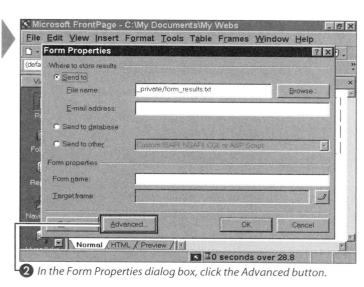

2 In the Form Properties dialog box, click the Advanced button.

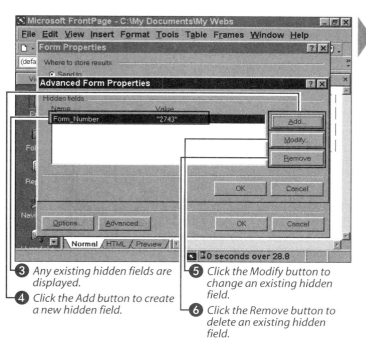

3 Any existing hidden fields are displayed.

4 Click the Add button to create a new hidden field.

5 Click the Modify button to change an existing hidden field.

6 Click the Remove button to delete an existing hidden field.

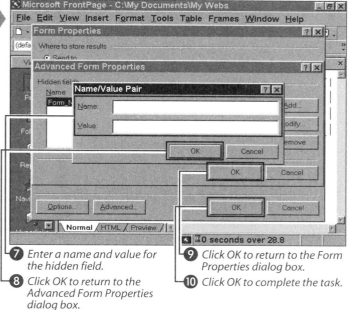

7 Enter a name and value for the hidden field.

8 Click OK to return to the Advanced Form Properties dialog box.

9 Click OK to return to the Form Properties dialog box.

10 Click OK to complete the task.

Using Confirmation Pages

When a visitor to your site fills out and then submits a form, FrontPage automatically displays a second confirmation Web page that shows all the fields from the form and the values (or responses) associated with them. The nice thing is that you don't have to do any work at all on it — FrontPage takes care of it for you.

That's the good news. The bad news is that the FrontPage default confirmation page is really a bare bones, no frills approach. Also problematic is that it lists *all* the fields — even hidden ones. But if you don't have any hidden fields and if you've carefully worked on the names for all the fields in your form, then you might find that the default FrontPage form confirmation page will do just fine for your purposes.

A confirmation page enables visitors to your Web site who have filled out a form to confirm that the data is correct before it is actually submitted. If visitors see that the information is incorrect, they can just hit the Back button in their Web browser and correct the form.

Fortunately, you can create a custom confirmation page. Of course, keep in mind your reason for having a confirmation page in the first place. You should instruct visitors to use the Back button to correct any errors. Also make certain that you have provided meaningful and coherent names for every single field in the form or your visitors won't have any idea what it is they're supposed to be confirming.

Finally, make sure that the layout of the confirmation page is easy for the people who are going to be filling out your forms to understand. Put each different field on a different line, at the very least.

TAKE NOTE

MAKE A LIST

FrontPage will not provide you with a list of field names to choose from, so if you have more than you can comfortably remember, you'd better write up a list of them ahead of time. Even if you don't have too many to comfortably keep track of, a written list will enable you to check them off as you take care of each one, thus providing you with a double check on the efficacy of your confirmation page.

CUSTOM FORM HANDLERS

If you create a custom form handler, then you'll lose the advantage of having FrontPage automatically create a default confirmation page. In that case, you'll have to make your own.

CROSS-REFERENCE
See the preceding section on hidden fields.

FIND IT ONLINE
Webs Unlimited has a FrontPage Web site at
http://websunlimited.com/.

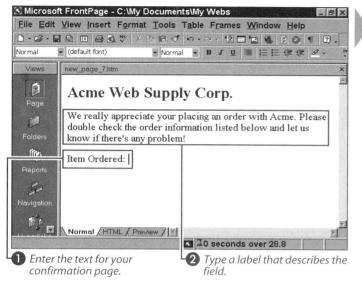

❶ Enter the text for your confirmation page.

❷ Type a label that describes the field.

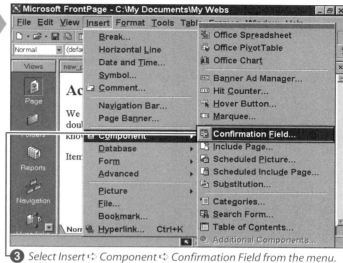

❸ Select Insert ➪ Component ➪ Confirmation Field from the menu.

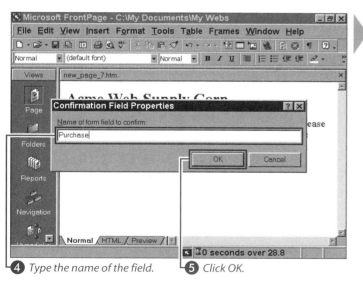

❹ Type the name of the field.

❺ Click OK.

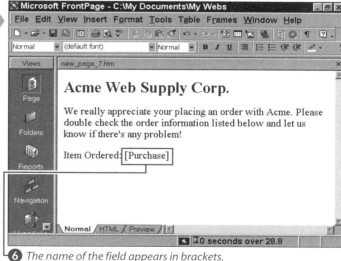

❻ The name of the field appears in brackets.

Assigning a Custom Confirmation Page

Now that you've got your own custom confirmation page for your form, you need to put it to use so that it shows up in their Web browsers when visitors to your site submit form data. To accomplish this, you must first assign it to a form as its confirmation page. If you skip this step, then the form will use the FrontPage default confirmation page and all your efforts in creating a customized confirmation page will be totally and utterly wasted. If you're using a custom script for handling your form data, you should also be aware that you must create and assign a custom confirmation page for that form or it won't have any confirmation page at all.

Make a note of the exact filename of the confirmation page you create *before* you assign it. If you fail to do this, you can use the Browse button in the Form Properties dialog box to locate it, but it will be a lot easier to simply make a note of it. It's a really good idea to follow basic FrontPage procedures, those simple steps that confirm that the processes you're involved in run more smoothly. Just as a piano maestro spends a great deal of his or her time in practicing scales, you must pay attention to the basic procedures in order to be a true Webmaster.

TAKE NOTE

GETTING BY WITHOUT A CONFIRMATION PAGE

If you deliberately decide that you don't want any confirmation page to be presented to the people who fill out your forms, then you have to use a custom script of your own as a form handler. In the absence of one, FrontPage will display either the default confirmation page or, if one exists and has been assigned, a custom confirmation page.

ANOTHER WAY TO GO WITHOUT

If you don't want to be bothered with a custom script to get around the confirmation page display, but still don't want a real confirmation page, there's a simple way out. Create a meaningless confirmation page. It is, after all, just a Web page that's automatically displayed after a form submittal — and that particular page is displayed because you assigned it. There's nothing in the rule book that says you can't make it a page that says nothing but "Click here," supplying a link to wherever you want to send the person who filled out the form.

MAKE IT A DIFFERENT COLOR

Some users are confused by confirmation pages. In addition to making it as functional and useful as possible, it's usually a good idea to provide the confirmation page with a different background color or background image than the Web page that contains the form itself. You might want to use a different font as well, to make the confirmation page as different as possible from the form page. With all these visual cues, the user will instantaneously recognize it as a different page.

CROSS-REFERENCE

See Chapter 10 for more information about customizing forms.

FIND IT ONLINE

Prometheus provides FrontPage training at http://www.prometheus.co.uk/.

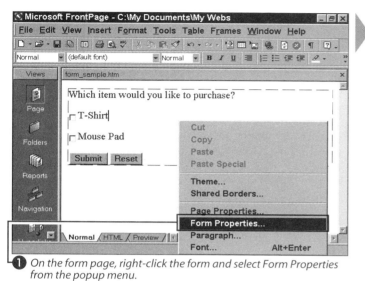

1 On the form page, right-click the form and select Form Properties from the popup menu.

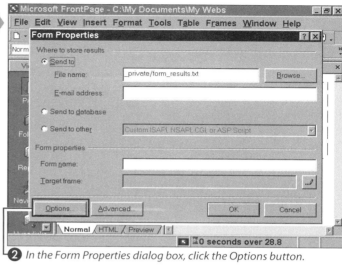

2 In the Form Properties dialog box, click the Options button.

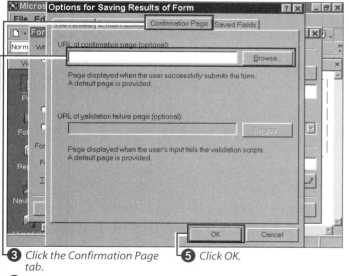

3 Click the Confirmation Page tab.

5 Click OK.

4 Type the URL of the confirmation page, or click the Browse button to locate the URL.

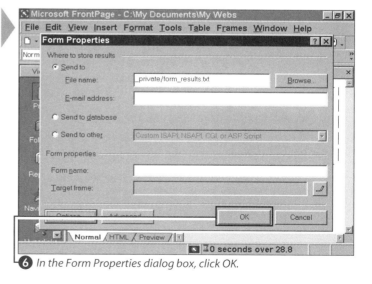

6 In the Form Properties dialog box, click OK.

201

Personal Workbook

Q&A

1 What is a *confirmation page*?

_____

_____

_____

2 What are the three environment variables which can be saved along with form data?

_____

_____

_____

3 What is the HTML name for the scrolling text box?

_____

_____

_____

4 Describe the difference between the way check boxes and radio buttons work.

_____

_____

_____

5 Which fields are displayed to a user in FrontPage's default confirmation page?

_____

_____

_____

6 Text in a form that responds to a mouse click is called what?

_____

_____

_____

7 What are *hidden fields*?

_____

_____

_____

8 What is the standard name for the Picture field?

_____

_____

_____

ANSWERS: PAGE 327

EXTRA PRACTICE

1. Design a form to collect name and address data.

2. Change the names of the form elements so they have more easily recognizable meanings.

3. Make a custom confirmation page and assign it to a form.

4. Create a form that uses a drop-down menu.

5. Make a form that uses every possible form element.

6. Experiment with check boxes and radio buttons to see how they are both similar and different.

REAL-WORLD APPLICATIONS

✔ You need to get a large amount of text in a form. Instead of using a plain text box, consider using a scrolling text box.

✔ You want to know which Web browser the people who fill out your form are using the most. You can keep track of this by setting the Browser type as an included field.

✔ You have a form that contains confidential information in hidden fields. You'll probably want to create a custom confirmation page so they won't be revealed.

✔ You have several options to choose from, but don't want to use up much space on your form. You might want to try the drop-down menu approach.

Visual Quiz

How do you get to this dialog box?

_____

_____

_____

_____

_____

_____

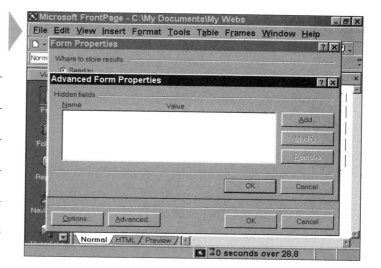

CHAPTER **10**

MASTER
THESE
SKILLS

▶ **Setting Tab Order**

▶ **Making Clickable Labels**

▶ **Setting Validation Rules for Drop-Down Menus**

▶ **Setting Validation Rules for Radio Buttons**

▶ **Setting Validation Rules for Text Boxes**

Customizing Forms

Once you have your basic form in place on your Web page, you can use FrontPage to modify it to suit your exact needs. You can control the order in which keyboard tabbing moves the cursor among the various form fields, even adjusting the effects if you've used absolute positioning to structure your form. You can add dynamic labels to your Web page forms, bringing them up to date with the same kind of functionality you're accustomed to in the programs you use.

The most powerful of the modifications you can make, however, is the addition of data entry validation rules to your form fields. Three form field elements support validation rules, and they are by far the most important ones: drop-down menus, radio buttons, and text boxes. All three support the most basic validation rule, that they must have some sort of selection or entry made before the form can be submitted. In fact, this is the only validation option available for radio buttons. Drop-down menus add more functionality in keeping with their more complex nature. It is ironic, however, that the most complex of all the data entry validation

rules are utilized for what is probably the single simplest data entry method — the one line text box (no data validation is available for the scrolling text box, or text area element).

The one line text box, despite its simple nature, is capable of holding the most varied types of data, ranging from simple text to integers and decimals. Even within the realm of text alone, permutations include white space, letters, numbers, and the odd characters that don't fit into any of those categories.

Certain form entries require some of these variations; others may not permit them at all. With phone numbers alone, you face a myriad of choices. Will you choose to allow the use of parentheses around the area code in a phone number? Do you limit the area code to three digits and the phone number to seven? Or is your business an international one and do you take into account the infinite variety of international calling codes and local phone number variations? The potentially endless combinations of data which can be input from the keyboard into a text box are what makes such a variety of data entry validation rules necessary.

Setting Tab Order

Tab order, as you might expect from the phrasing, has to do with using the Tab button on the keyboard. Although most people when filling out a form on the World Wide Web will use their mouse to move from field to field by sheer force of habit, basic form functionality does include the ability to move the cursor from one form field to the next by pressing the Tab key. That way, you don't have to take your fingers off the keyboard to move the cursor. Of course, this is more important for the parts of the form where you're filling out textual data.

By default, the tab order is the same as the order in which the fields show up in the HTML source code and, under normal circumstances, the fields will go in the same order as you want them to show up in the finished form. Even if you move a field during the design phase or after the form is completed, FrontPage will automatically adjust the source code to reflect its new position.

If you should decide to use absolute positioning for your form elements, however, the onscreen order and the order in the source code may not be the same at all. In that case, you'll need to use the tab order settings for the affected form fields to make things work the way you intended.

What if two form fields have the same tab order value? In that case, it's the same as the default behavior — the one that's first in the HTML source code is the one that comes first in the tab order.

TAKE NOTE

LABELS ARE FIELDS, TOO
Clickable labels are form fields, of course, and as such they are included in the tab order just like all the other form fields.

IF YOU DON'T WANT A FIELD INCLUDED
What if you don't want a particular form field to be a part of the tab order at all? Is there any way to set it so that a Tab won't select that field? Yes. Just set its tab order value to a negative number.

WHAT'S THE HIGHEST TAB ORDER?
Well, pure HTML has no real limit, but FrontPage will only accept numbers as high as 999. Granted that you'll probably never design (or even see) a form with 999 elements in it, but you may not want to use sequential numbers for the tab order values. That way, you can leave yourself a little bit of room for maneuvering. There's no requirement that two tab order values have to be sequential, anyway, just that one be higher or lower than another.

CROSS-REFERENCE
See Chapter 2 for information on how to view HTML source code.

FIND IT ONLINE
To see the configuration data FrontPage hosts use, go to http://www.starboardtack.com/_vti_inf.html and select View ⇨ Source from your menu.

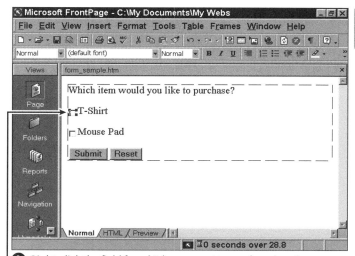

❶ Right-click the field for which you want to set the tab order.

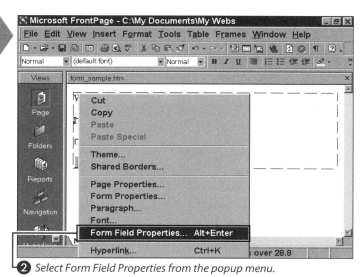

❷ Select Form Field Properties from the popup menu.

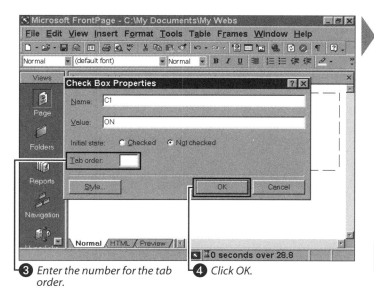

❸ Enter the number for the tab order. ❹ Click OK.

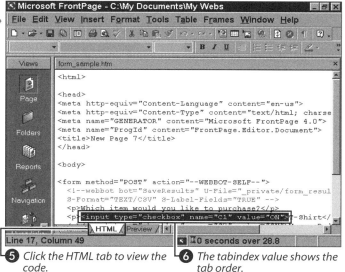

❺ Click the HTML tab to view the code. ❻ The tabindex value shows the tab order.

207

Making Clickable Labels

You can add text to a form simply by typing in it just as though the interior of the form were the same as a blank part of the Web page. All forms require some text, of course, since otherwise most elements would communicate no meaning to the user. Check boxes, radio buttons, and the like have no real value without some kind of labeling (buttons, obviously, don't require any labels since they have words on them already).

Simple labels are really all that's needed, but you'll find a variation on them that's still fairly new to HTML — clickable labels. A *clickable label* (also called a *dynamic label*) is one that's attached programmatically to another form element so that clicking on the label causes the exact same action as if you had clicked the element it's linked to; thus, clicking on a label that's attached to a radio button will select that radio button. In FrontPage, the "Label" element on the form submenu refers to a clickable label. Although these have been around in most professional programs for quite a while, they're still fairly new to the World Wide Web.

With clickable labels, you can also create a keyboard shortcut to the associated field. You're accustomed to using keyboard shortcuts (or at least they're available to you) in every Windows program you have. The underlined letters on your menu options provide the information you need for the keyboard shortcuts (for example, the *F* in File is underlined so you would use Alt+F to access your File menu). Once you've created a label, you can create your own shortcut by selecting the letter you want to use and clicking the Underline button on FrontPage's toolbar (this won't work on regular text in the form — it has to be an attached label). You should bear in mind, however, that the letter you choose shouldn't be the same as one that's already in use for another shortcut.

TAKE NOTE

THE DOTTED LINE

Although the form — the actual containing element — is invisible on a Web page and only its contents appear, you can see it in FrontPage as an outline of dashes that surround all the included elements. Clickable labels, like the overall form element itself, are also delineated by a dotted line.

REMOVING A CLICKABLE LABEL

To remove a clickable label, you simply place the cursor anywhere within it and follow the same procedure as for putting it there in the first place. Another removal option exists as well, but it's nonstandard. Simply move the form field that the label is attached to without moving the label, too. That will break the connection between the two, even if you later return the field to its former location.

CROSS-REFERENCE

See Chapter 9 for more information on forms.

FIND IT ONLINE

SMSU provides a FrontPage course at **http://fidelity. smsu.edu/ShortCourses/IntroFrontPage/index.html.**

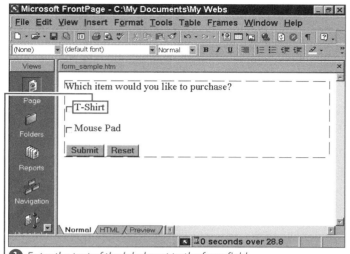

1 Enter the text of the label next to the form field.

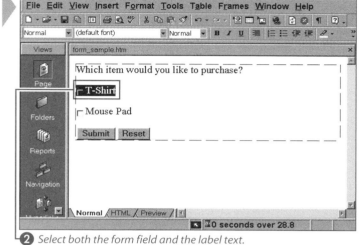

2 Select both the form field and the label text.

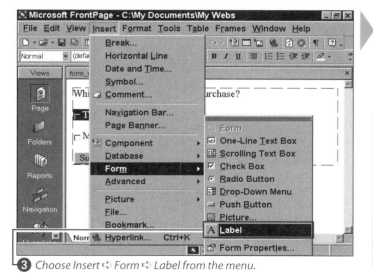

3 Choose Insert ➪ Form ➪ Label from the menu.

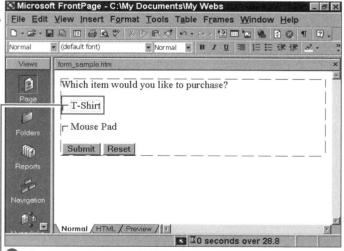

4 The text is now surrounded by a dotted line to signify that it's clickable.

Setting Validation Rules for Drop-Down Menus

A basic form simply has elements in it, and users can fill in those elements in any old way they want, including in ways you don't want them to be filled in. You can take more control over the form and how it's filled out, however, by utilizing the power of data validation rules. When users who are filling out your form violate the data validation rules, they won't be able to submit the form. Instead, they'll get an error message telling them to fill it out the way you designed it.

Only two data validation rules exist for a drop-down menu. As with radio buttons, there is a "data required" option, which means that the person filling out the form must make some choice from this form field and is not allowed to just ignore it.

In addition to this, however, and very important to the functionality of a drop-down menu, is to disallow the first option offered in a drop-down menu. In the example in the figures to the right, the first option is to "Pick a size" of T-shirt, and the choices include Small, Medium, and Large. Since we obviously want them to pick one of the three sizes, the function of the first "choice" is actually the same as would be that of a label with another form field. The first choice provides a brief instruction as to the use of the field. Not all drop-down menus, of course, have such an option in place, nor is it any kind of a requirement.

Using the first choice as a label, however, does add a nice touch to the menu, and using the data validation rule to override it as a valid choice preserves its true purpose.

TAKE NOTE

▶ MINIMUM AND MAXIMUM ITEMS

You'll find one change in the available options in the validation dialog box for drop-down menus if that menu allows more than one selection to be made. In that case, you'll have the option to specify the largest and smallest number of items the user can select.

▶ THERE'S NO VISIBLE CHANGE

You won't be able to tell by looking at the form which fields have had validation rules attached to them. You won't see a color change, dotted line, or other visible indicator, so you'll have to either keep careful track of the fields as you enter the rules or go through the fields one by one after the fact to verify that the rules are in place.

▶ FRONTPAGE ONLY

If you take a look at the source code for data entry validation rules, you'll see that it's not pure HTML or even an HTML extension, but a webbot, which means that it will only work on servers that support the FrontPage extensions.

CROSS-REFERENCE
See Chapter 2 for how to view HTML source code.

FIND IT ONLINE
You can also find FrontPage training at
http://aainet.com/Training.htm.

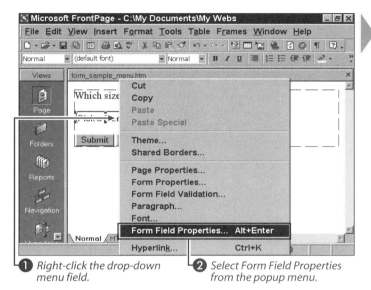

① *Right-click the drop-down menu field.*

② *Select Form Field Properties from the popup menu.*

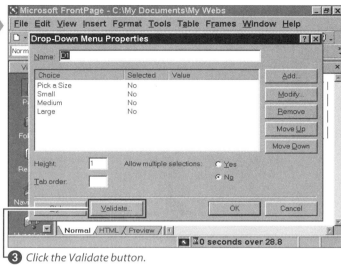

③ *Click the Validate button.*

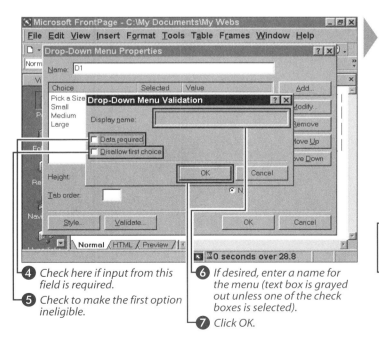

④ *Check here if input from this field is required.*

⑤ *Check to make the first option ineligible.*

⑥ *If desired, enter a name for the menu (text box is grayed out unless one of the check boxes is selected).*

⑦ *Click OK.*

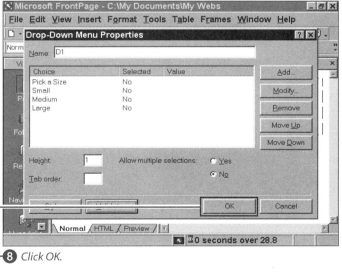

⑧ *Click OK.*

Setting Validation Rules for Radio Buttons

Radio buttons are a bit different from all of the other form elements. Radio buttons work together as a group while all the other elements are stand-alone versions. You can put two or three check boxes or text boxes together without creating any synergistic effect, but multiple radio buttons placed together always act as a group, with the choice of one radio button negating the choice of any other of the radio buttons in that group.

For this reason, radio buttons are the fields of choice whenever you have a mutually exclusive set of choices to be made in a form. You might, for instance, have users select the color of a carpet they are buying. Obviously, there can be only one color, so the use of check boxes would be futile, since users can check as many check boxes as they want. If you received form input that said the carpet should be red, blue, and green, you'd have to put the order on hold until you could contact the person for clarification. Radio buttons, by their very exclusion of one another, solve this problem quite neatly.

Radio button data validation, like the radio buttons options, applies to the entire group of radio buttons, so you can select any of them to set the rule for the group.

CROSS-REFERENCE
See Chapter 9 for how to set field names.

FIND IT ONLINE
There's a good FrontPage site at **http://www.smcvt. edu/authors/frontpage/index.htm**.

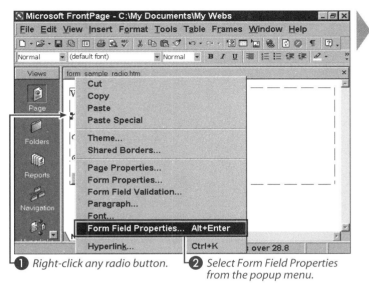

❶ Right-click any radio button. ❷ Select Form Field Properties from the popup menu.

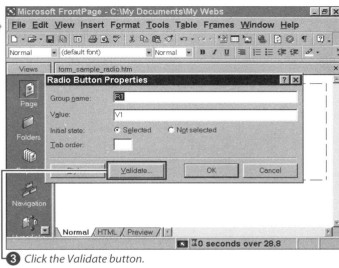

❸ Click the Validate button.

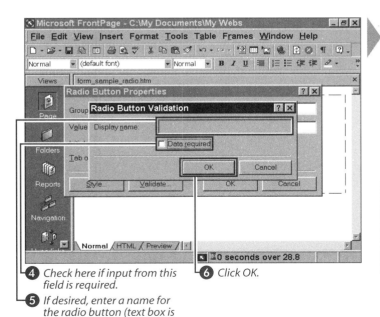

❹ Check here if input from this field is required.

❺ If desired, enter a name for the radio button (text box is grayed out unless the check box is selected).

❻ Click OK.

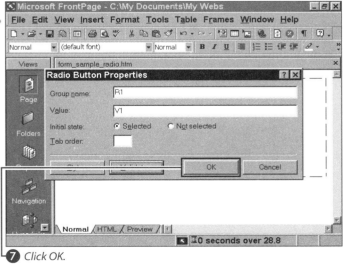

❼ Click OK.

Setting Validation Rules for Text Boxes

Text boxes are arguably the simplest type of form field — nothing but a blank rectangle into which the user types. It's ironic that the data validation rules for text boxes offer the most complex possibilities among all the form fields.

The following list describes the uses of the various data validation rules for text boxes:

- ▶ **Display name**. Gives a name to the text box (not necessarily the same as the field name) which will be used if an error message results from the form submission.
- ▶ **Data type**. Sets constraints on the kind of data permitted in the text box. You can set text, integer, number, or no constraints as the data type.
- ▶ **Text format**. Used to specify exactly what type of text the user is permitted to type in. You can set it for letters, white space, digits, or other. ("Other" means anything that can be typed, but doesn't fit in the other three categories, such as exclamation points, colons, and so on.) Since these are check boxes, you can select any combination, or all of them.
- ▶ **Numeric format**. Sets the way in which thousands ("grouping") and decimals are displayed. Thousands can be grouped by commas, periods, or nothing. Decimals can be displayed with the usual decimal point (period) or a comma.
- ▶ **Data length**. Used to set a minimum and/or maximum length for the entry.

- ▶ **Data value**. Enables you to set a range or limit upon the entered value. The options are less than, greater than, less than or equal to, greater than or equal to, equal to, and not equal to. This is of more use with numerical entries than with text, although it can be used in either case. In the case of numbers (whether integer or decimal), the comparisons are strictly mathematical. With text (which includes, in this case, the "No constraints" option), the comparisons are done in ASCII order.

TAKE NOTE

▶ USE MORE THAN ONE

You can use multiple text boxes placed in a row, each with its own data entry validation rules, to achieve a single purpose. For instance, you could use two different text boxes to get one telephone number, requiring three numbers in the first one for the area code and seven numbers in the second one for the actual telephone number.

▶ WHERE'S THE "DATA REQUIRED" CHECK BOX

In the Text Box Validation dialog box, the "Data required" check box is hard to spot. It's simply labeled "Required" and it appears as if it's merely a part of the Data Length requirements. While the data length settings aren't activated until this check box is, they don't have to be filled out.

CROSS-REFERENCE

See the section on radio buttons earlier in this chapter for a discussion of field names.

FIND IT ONLINE

CartIt plug-ins for FrontPage are found at http://www.cartit.com/index.html.

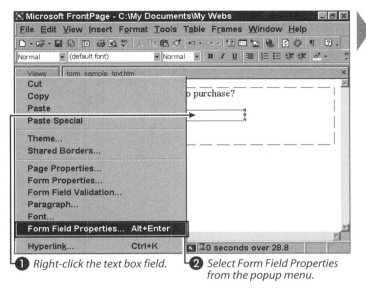

1 *Right-click the text box field.*

2 *Select Form Field Properties from the popup menu.*

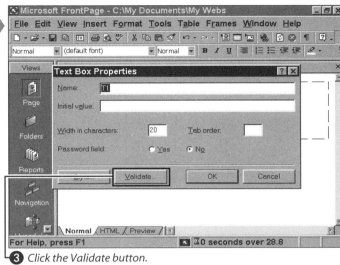

3 *Click the Validate button.*

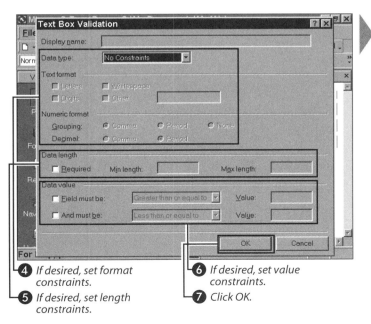

4 *If desired, set format constraints.*

5 *If desired, set length constraints.*

6 *If desired, set value constraints.*

7 *Click OK.*

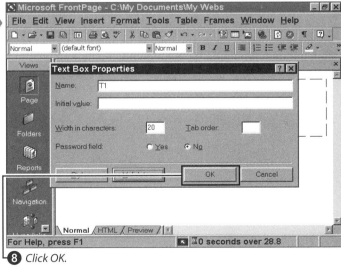

8 *Click OK.*

Personal Workbook

Q&A

1 How do you make text in a form respond to a mouse click?

_____

_____

_____

2 How can you tell if a form field has validation options in place?

_____

_____

_____

3 What does a negative tab order value do?

_____

_____

_____

4 Which form field has the most complex validation rule options?

_____

_____

_____

5 What visual cue tells you a label is assigned to another form field?

_____

_____

_____

6 How does a display name differ from a field name?

_____

_____

_____

7 How are radio buttons different from the rest of the form fields?

_____

_____

_____

_____

8 How many form fields have validation options available?

_____

_____

_____

ANSWERS: PAGE 328

EXTRA PRACTICE

1 Create a form and then assign clickable labels for each of its elements.

2 Remove a clickable label from a form.

3 Alter the tab order of the elements on your form.

4 Add a keyboard shortcut to a label.

5 Assign validation options to a text box.

6 Set the tab order so that labels are skipped.

7 Move one radio button out of a group to someplace on the other side of another element and see what effect this has on the radio button.

REAL-WORLD APPLICATIONS

✔ You're using a form with absolute positioning to give the fields the best possible appearance. Try double-checking how this affects the tab order.

✔ You have a form that won't give useful information unless all the form fields are properly filled out. Consider using validation rules to force the type of responses you want.

✔ You have a form with several fields. Although you might want to use clickable labels for it, you may find that you should set their tab order values so as to remove them from the tab function.

✔ You're using data validation rules for your form. You might want to make a point of using some nice, descriptive display names to make things easier on your users.

Visual Quiz

How do you get to this dialog box? What does the number 9 in the Tab order box mean?

_____

_____

_____

_____

_____

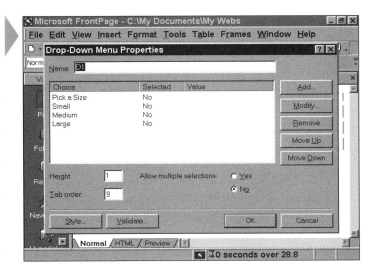

CHAPTER 11

Adding FrontPage Components

Although most basic Web pages are composed of only simple text and, in the vast majority of cases, some images, you can do a lot more to enhance the appearance and functionality of your Web sites. FrontPage offers several easy ways to add components to your site that will prove useful and beneficial to both you and your users.

In this chapter, we deal with the simplest components and enhancements; in the next chapter, we'll deal with some others that are also useful but somewhat more complex.

First, we take a look at using *hit counters*, those little extras that keep track of how many times a particular Web page is loaded into someone's browser. Next, we dig into something that's useful to your users — a search form that will enable them to quickly locate whatever terms they're looking for and then jump to the pages containing those terms.

We also cover *rotating banner ads*, which are used to provide multiple linked images in a common format for advertising. You'll see how easy FrontPage makes the installation of banner ads, and you'll see FrontPage's shortcomings as well.

If you want to emphasize something, using marquees is one of the best ways. *Marquees* are scrolling lines of text that you can add to your pages, controlling the speed, direction, background color and size of the page, among other factors. We show you the proper uses of marquees and provide a few cautions about their misuse.

Finally, we introduce you to background sound and time stamps, which, unlike hit counters, rotating banner ads, and marquees, are not true FrontPage components. But they are still nice little add-ons that can vastly improve your site with very little effort on your part. *Background sound* is the audio equivalent of background color, adding a new element to your entire page instead of existing as a single component contained within it. *Time stamps* offer a simple method of letting your users (and clients) know exactly when the page was last updated.

Adding a Hit Counter

Hit counters are a popular but inexact way to show how many people have visited your Web site. Since they only show how many times a particular Web page has been accessed, the numbers are potentially misleading. For example, if one person loads your page 800 times, it looks the same as when 800 people each look at it once. If you want to put together some statistics that will be of use and interest in a commercial setting, such as impressing would-be advertisers or sponsors with your traffic, you should use a more sophisticated tracking program (such as Statbot) that will filter all the hits you get and count only those Web page accesses from a unique source during a particular time period. Check with your ISP or Net Administrator for specifics on how to utilize such a program with your particular server configuration.

Still, if you don't need professional results from your hit tracking software, hit counters are a fun and easy method to get a general idea of how many visitors you're seeing.

FrontPage provides a decent selection of number types for your hit counter, but you can also create your own custom number styles if you want. You simply create a single GIF file with the numbers 0 through 9 from left to right, and make sure that the numbers are evenly spaced. You'll need to make a note of the exact location and filename, however, since the Hit Counter Properties dialog box does not, for some inexplicable reason, have a Browse button to help you locate it. You'll have to type it in by hand.

TAKE NOTE

ONLY ON FRONTPAGE SERVERS

The hit counter component only works on Web servers that run the FrontPage extensions. It won't work for an individual page, either, except for ones that are part of a FrontPage web. If either of these possibilities describes the project you're working on, then you'll probably want to use one of the many easy-to-install CGI hit counters that are available (see Find It Online below).

FIXED DIGITS

The "Fixed number of digits" option enables you to set your hit counter so that it will display a minimum number of digits, not a maximum number of them. In effect, this simply puts a number of leading zeroes ahead of your hit count in the early stages. Thus, if you set the number of digits to 2, your first visitor will be number 01 instead of number 1.

RESETTING THE NUMBER

There are a number of cases in which you might want to use the "Reset Counter To" option. Some people use it to just plain old cheat and show a large number of visitors when they're just getting started. Others find it handy when they change service providers and don't want to start from scratch — they just make a note of how many people visited their old site and start the counter from there. And, of course, it's a nice feature to have on hand if a system crash screws up your old data — although you'll have to have some idea of what the number was.

CROSS-REFERENCE
See Chapter 6 for more information on GIF images.

FIND IT ONLINE
Selena Sol's scripts can be found at http://www.wownet.co.uk/mirror/selena/Scripts/.

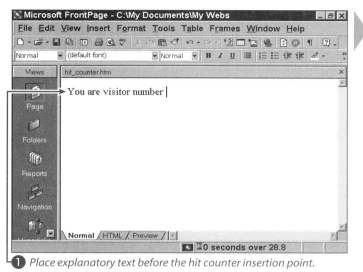

1 *Place explanatory text before the hit counter insertion point.*

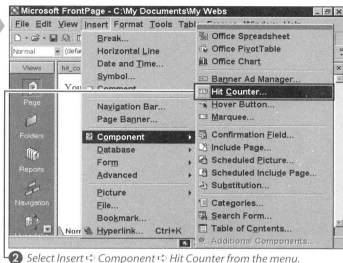

2 *Select Insert ⇨ Component ⇨ Hit Counter from the menu.*

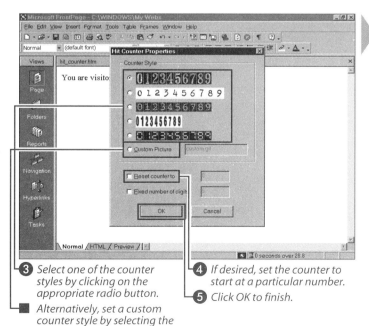

3 *Select one of the counter styles by clicking on the appropriate radio button.*

Alternatively, set a custom counter style by selecting the Custom Picture radio button.

4 *If desired, set the counter to start at a particular number.*

5 *Click OK to finish.*

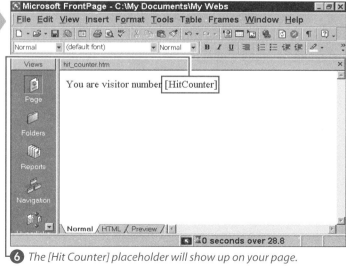

6 *The [Hit Counter] placeholder will show up on your page.*

Adding a Search Function

If your site is composed of only a single Web page, then visitors to it can search the entire page by using the Find function in their Web browsers. Even if only a couple of pages are involved, they can still search the entire site without much difficulty. If it's a complex Web site, however, you'll need to give them a hand when it comes to finding what's where.

Searches are performed by comparing search terms (called *keywords*) that are entered into the search form against a list of all the words in your entire FrontPage web. You don't have to worry about creating that list, since FrontPage does it for you automatically. The list isn't actually a concordance, however, since common words that are of no value in searches (such as *a*, *an*, *the*, and so forth) are automatically excluded from the word list.

When you're first putting the search form in place, don't be overly concerned with the exact look of it, since you can always change it to suit your preferences later on. You can access the same Search Form Properties dialog box that you used to create the form by double-clicking on the search form. Even though this is called a form and it comes complete with labels, text boxes, and Submit and Reset buttons (called "Start Search" and "Clear" buttons), you can't select and modify the individual form field elements, just the search form as a whole. If you check out the HTML code, you'll see why — it's not coded as a form, but as a *webbot* component (a predesigned, self-contained, drop-in program).

TAKE NOTE

ANOTHER FRONTPAGE-ONLY OPTION

The search function, like the hit counter, only works on servers that are running the FrontPage extensions. If you're using FrontPage to develop a Web site for a different server, then you'll need to use a different search program, like Simple Search (see the listing under Find It Online below).

HOW WIDE SHOULD THE KEYWORD TEXT BOX BE?

It's a matter of the designer's personal taste, since the text boxes will scroll any entries that are too long to fit in the visible area. The search is conducted on the entire entry, not just what shows in the visible area.

CONTENTS OF THE WORD LIST

The word list is updated every time you save a page. FrontPage adds any new words from the saved page to the list. However, it will never remove any words by this process, so if you delete a page from your web, then you'll end up with an incorrect list. To solve this problem, you'll have to manually select Tools ⇨ Recalculate Hyperlinks from the menu.

CROSS-REFERENCE

See Chapter 9 for more information on forms.

FIND IT ONLINE

Matt's Script Archive can be found at
http://worldwidemart.com/scripts/.

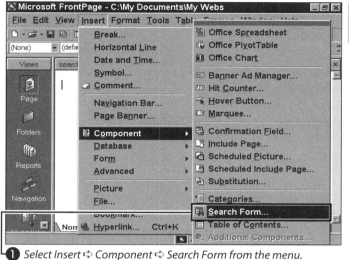

1 Select Insert ➪ Component ➪ Search Form from the menu.

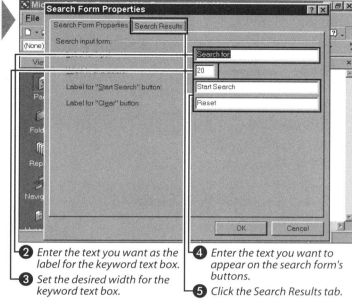

2 Enter the text you want as the label for the keyword text box.

3 Set the desired width for the keyword text box.

4 Enter the text you want to appear on the search form's buttons.

5 Click the Search Results tab.

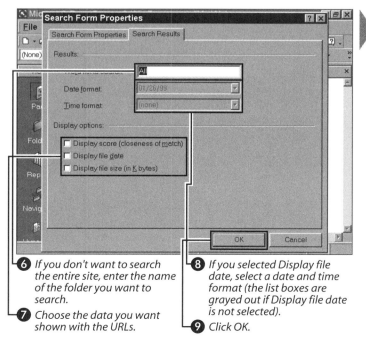

6 If you don't want to search the entire site, enter the name of the folder you want to search.

7 Choose the data you want shown with the URLs.

8 If you selected Display file date, select a date and time format (the list boxes are grayed out if Display file date is not selected).

9 Click OK.

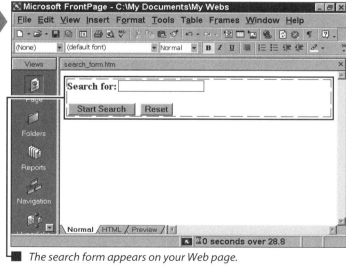

■ The search form appears on your Web page.

Using Banner Ads

Many Web sites utilize banner advertising to generate extra revenue for their operations. With this technique, an image that is small enough not to detract from the basic design of the Web page, yet large enough to be noticed, is inserted. Usually it's placed at the top of the page, but you'll find them all over some Web pages. If it's a very successful site with lots of traffic coming through, then you usually find a fair amount of advertising, and the banners at the top of the page are charged at a higher rate than the ones lower on the page. When users see a banner ad for a product or service they're interested in, they click it and follow the link to the sponsoring company's Web page.

Some Web sites show different banner ads in a rotating sequence, thus enabling advertisers to pay for the top spaces at a lower rate, since they don't occupy the space to the exclusion of all other advertisers. See the first Take Note for the problem with using FrontPage for this. Advertisers can also use the rotation sequence to provide a series of images that tells a story about the product or service.

For banner rotation, FrontPage utilizes a Java applet to manage things, which provides a half dozen different transition effects. Of those transition effects, *None* simply means that the image changes with no intervening state; the *horizontal* and *vertical-blind* effects gradually cover over one image with strips of the succeeding one until it is complete; the *dissolve* effect does more or less the same thing, but instead of

strips, random series of pixels gradually replace one image with another; the *box in* and *box out* effects draw the new image in chunks of about one third each, one starting from the center, and the other from the outside edges.

TAKE NOTE

▶ YOU CAN'T LINK EACH IMAGE

When you select a Web page (or other file) to link your banner ads to, you don't have the capability to link each separate image in the banner ad rotation to a different Web page. It's kind of unbelievable, since the whole idea of using rotating ad banners is to show multiple advertisements from different clients, but it's true. No matter how many different banners you put into the rotation, they all have to link to the exact same place.

▶ USE ANIMATED GIFS

If you want to get the most out of your banner ads, using animated GIF files can create a very professional appearance while taking up much less file space than any other form of animation.

▶ ENTER IMAGE SIZE

The default size of a banner ad image is 320×100 pixels. However, your images may well be a different size, and you'll need to enter that size when you create the ad banner. Or you can alter it afterward by right-clicking it and selecting Banner Ad Manager Properties from the pop-up menu.

CROSS-REFERENCE

See Chapter 6 for more information on images.

FIND IT ONLINE

There's a FrontPage tutorial at
http://moon.jic.com/hptutorials/index.html.

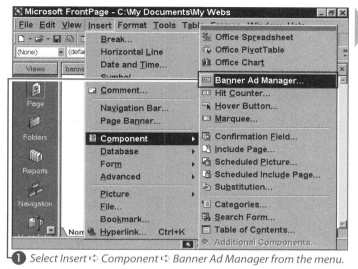

1 Select Insert ⇨ Component ⇨ Banner Ad Manager from the menu.

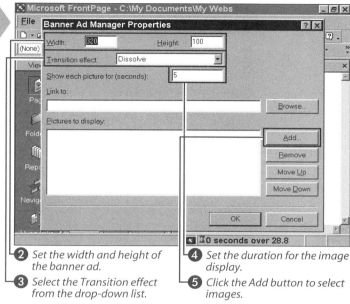

2 Set the width and height of the banner ad.

3 Select the Transition effect from the drop-down list.

4 Set the duration for the image display.

5 Click the Add button to select images.

6 Select an image from the current web.

7 Click OK.

■ Alternatively, browse the World Wide Web for an image or select an image from another folder.

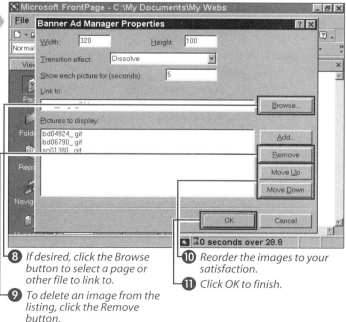

8 If desired, click the Browse button to select a page or other file to link to.

9 To delete an image from the listing, click the Remove button.

10 Reorder the images to your satisfaction.

11 Click OK to finish.

Adding Marquees

Marquees are areas of scrolling text on Web pages much like the scrolling news headlines you see in Times Square or scrolling stock ticker data on Wall Street. As with any repetitively moving Web page element, it's a pretty good idea to use marquees sparingly, since many people find that sort of onscreen action on a Web page to be an annoying distraction. One of the best uses of marquees is to draw attention to something that has legitimate urgency, such as an impending change of the site's URL or a rapidly approaching deadline as with auction bids. In such cases, the marquee is a much better choice for drawing attention than the BLINK element, since it's a lot easier to read scrolling text than it is to read blinking text.

You can, by the way, have more than one marquee on a page. All the marquees will scroll simultaneously, and you can create some interesting effects by having multiple lines of text all moving at the same time. You can use different background colors for each of the marquees to interesting effect. With a fast computer, visitors to your Web site won't suffer any significant degradation of the motion with multiple marquees, but those with slower computers will find that the movement becomes much jerkier than normal.

TAKE NOTE

▶ SLIDING VERSUS SCROLLING

When a marquee *scrolls*, it comes out from one side of the Web page, moves across the screen, and then disappears into the other side of the page, repeating the process as often as you have set it to. When it *slides*, on the other hand, it comes out from the side of the page, moves across the screen, and stops at the page's edge without continuing on out of sight, and the repeat setting has no effect at all; it will slide only once. The "Alternate" option actually doesn't do anything that you'd expect. It sounds like the marquee would first scroll, then slide, then scroll, and so forth. In fact, the marquee under these circumstances simply bounces back and forth between one side of the page and the other, constantly reversing its direction.

▶ SPEED SETTINGS

The Delay setting sets how many milliseconds pass between moves of the marquee. The Amount setting determines how many pixels it moves at a time. The default settings of 90 milliseconds and 6 pixels create a smoothly moving marquee. If you alter either of these settings, you may want to experiment with different combinations of the other to produce the best effect.

▶ MAKING IT MORE DISTINCTIVE

The fact that a marquee scrolls across the Web page makes it stand out, of course. You can also use standard font modification methods to make it stand out even more. Simply right-click it and select Font from the popup menu to access the same font options as you have with regular text.

CROSS-REFERENCE

See Chapter 3 for information on blinking text.

FIND IT ONLINE

You'll find the FrontPage Problem Solving page at **http://precisionweb.net/additionalfrontpagehelp. htm**.

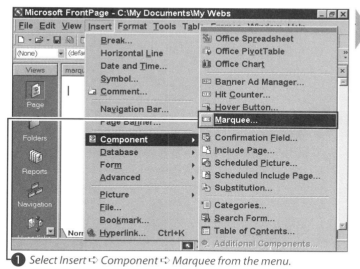

➊ Select Insert ➪ Component ➪ Marquee from the menu.

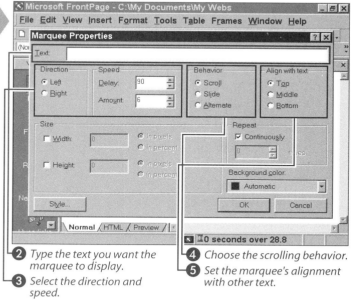

➋ Type the text you want the marquee to display.

➌ Select the direction and speed.

➍ Choose the scrolling behavior.

➎ Set the marquee's alignment with other text.

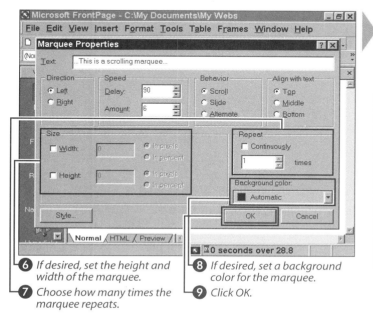

➏ If desired, set the height and width of the marquee.

➐ Choose how many times the marquee repeats.

➑ If desired, set a background color for the marquee.

➒ Click OK.

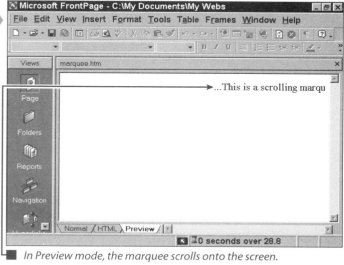

■ In Preview mode, the marquee scrolls onto the screen.

Adding Background Sound

Web pages were originally a purely visual phenomenon, consisting of only text and images, but that's all changed. There are many different ways to add sound to Web pages, but the easiest is to use background sound. Strictly speaking, it's not actually a FrontPage component, and you won't see any visible change to the Web page when you add it. Like background color, background sound is a property of the page itself, and it's put in place via an HTML tag. However, you should bear in mind that it's not standard HTML, but an HTML extension that's supported by Microsoft's Internet Explorer (version 4.0 or later). You don't have to be concerned with the actual HTML code implementation (although you can view it by clicking on the HTML tag if you want), since FrontPage enables you to use a simple menu approach to insert it.

Depending upon whom you talk to about it, background sound for Web pages is either a fabulous and beneficial example of technical progress or one of the greatest curses ever inflicted on the world. In order to avoid convincing people to move from the first opinion to the second one, it's a really, really good idea to avoid setting the music's Loop setting to "forever." If you do that, then your visitors who don't want to hear the music endlessly will be forced to either turn off their speakers or leave your Web page behind and go somewhere else. If you have any skill with

JavaScript programming, you can even set up your page so that your visitors can click an option button to shut the sound off or turn it back on.

TAKE NOTE

▶ WATCH OUT FOR THE COPYRIGHT PROBLEM

Most of the music created in the last several decades is still under copyright. It's highly unlikely that you'd have any problems using something written by Beethoven or Bach, since they're both long dead and their music has been in the public domain longer than any of us have been alive. If you want to add something from the Spice Girls, on the other hand, you're looking for trouble. While you'll have no difficulty in finding thousands of sites that use copyrighted musical works without permission (it's about as common as you can get), if you do the same and one of the law firms representing the artist or one of the music industry groups that are concerned with collecting royalties decides to make an example of you, you'd better have a good lawyer and a healthy bank account.

▶ SOUND FILE FORMATS

Although there are several other methods for adding sound to Web pages, including RealAudio, you're limited to certain types of sound files with the Page Properties approach in FrontPage. The background sound that you can use with this setting needs to be in one of three formats — midi, wav, or au.

CROSS-REFERENCE
See Chapter 3 for information on background color.

FIND IT ONLINE
There's a FrontPage FAQ at **http://support.rapid system.net/index.html#frontpage.**

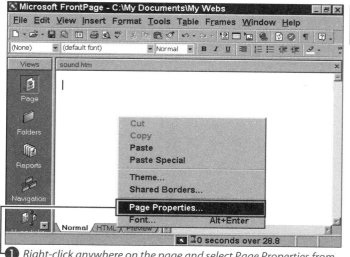

❶ Right-click anywhere on the page and select Page Properties from the popup menu.

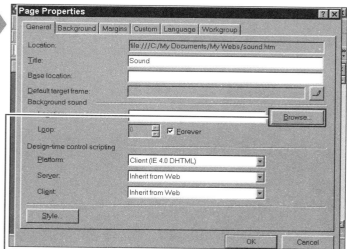

❷ In the Page Properties dialog box, click the Browse button.

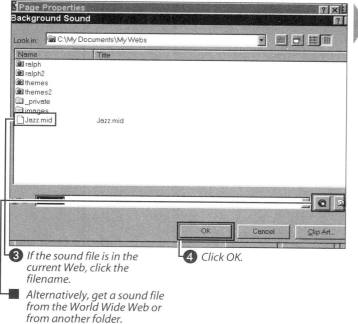

❸ If the sound file is in the current Web, click the filename.

■ Alternatively, get a sound file from the World Wide Web or from another folder.

❹ Click OK.

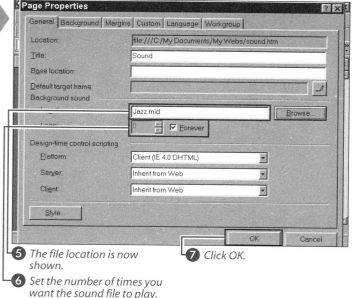

❺ The file location is now shown.

❻ Set the number of times you want the sound file to play.

❼ Click OK.

Adding a Time Stamp

If you've ever been to a Web page and had to look the whole thing over to see if anything had changed since the last time you'd been there, you'll really appreciate the simple and useful functionality of the time stamp, which lets your visitors know right off the bat exactly when the page was last updated. If a visitor sees that the time stamp has a date older than the date of the last time they visited, they can just ignore the page and move on. Time stamps are generally found at the bottom of a Web page, separated from the rest of the material by a horizontal line.

Of course, if you update your pages infrequently, you may not wish to advertise that fact to the world. This is not to say, of course, that those who don't update their sites frequently are lazy. There are many cases where a page seldom or never needs updating. Many reference sites, for example, change their data very infrequently, and there's a big difference between the usefulness of year-old data for stock prices versus year-old data for a dictionary. In the first example, the age of the data makes it useless for anything but historical purposes; in the second, there probably hasn't been that much change in the language over the period of a single year. Even so, the dictionary's Webmaster may not want to put in a time stamp since the overall impression given by an old date is that the site is not as useful as it could be if it were more recent.

The time stamp isn't just for the use of Web site visitors. A quick surf of your own sites to check the time stamps can give you a good idea where you need to put in some work. If you have clients for whom you perform Webmaster duties, then looking over the sites you have responsibility for can even generate some new business for you, since you'll be able to use the time stamps to point out to your clients where they need to update their Web presence.

TAKE NOTE

THE "NONE" OPTION

By default, FrontPage shows "none" for the time format, which means that only the date format will be included in a time stamp. To include the time as well, simply select any time format. Likewise, if for some strange reason you need to put in the time but not the date, select "none" for the date format. If you select "none" for both of them, however, then you'll have a blank time stamp, which won't do anyone any good.

TIME ZONES

Some of the time format options include the letters *TZ* after them. This abbreviation stands for time zone, and shows the time difference between your time zone and Greenwich Mean Time. In the figure in the lower-right corner of the facing page you see a time difference of five hours ("-0500"). The screenshot was taken on the East Coast, which is 5 hours off from GMT.

CROSS-REFERENCE
See Chapter 2 for information on horizontal lines.

FIND IT ONLINE
The Web Academy provides FrontPage training. You can find them at **http://www.webacademy.com/**.

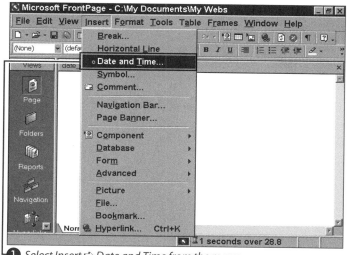

❶ Select Insert ➪ Date and Time from the menu.

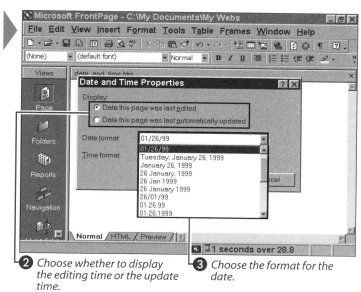

❷ Choose whether to display the editing time or the update time.

❸ Choose the format for the date.

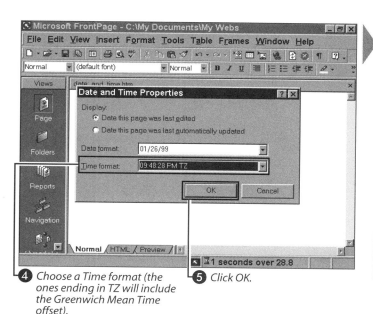

❹ Choose a Time format (the ones ending in TZ will include the Greenwich Mean Time offset).

❺ Click OK.

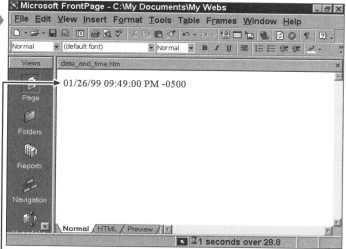

■ The date and time are inserted on the page.

Personal Workbook

Q&A

1 What is a *hit counter*?

_____

_____

_____

2 What kind of component is background sound?

_____

_____

_____

3 What is a *marquee*?

_____

_____

_____

4 Can you alter the fields in a search form?

_____

_____

_____

5 What list do you need to create in order for the search form to work?

_____

_____

_____

6 On what kind of servers does a FrontPage hit counter work?

_____

_____

_____

7 What FrontPage limitation keeps the ad banners from being as useful as they could be?

_____

_____

_____

8 What is a *time stamp*?

_____

_____

_____

ANSWERS: PAGE 329

EXTRA PRACTICE

1 Create a series of marquees with different background colors.

2 Experiment with different transition effects in banner ads.

3 Recalculate the hyperlinks to update a search form word list after deleting several pages.

4 Set a hit counter to show 0001 for the first hit.

5 Add a hit counter that will work on non-FrontPage servers.

6 Experiment with different background sounds for your Web pages.

REAL-WORLD APPLICATIONS

✔ Your boss wants background sound on the company Web page, but the other employees complain that it drives them nuts. You might want to consider limiting the number of times it plays.

✔ You want to use FrontPage's hit counter, but don't like any of the supplied digital graphics. Take a shot at creating your own.

✔ You want to use the search function, but not to search your entire Web site. You may want to limit it to a particular folder.

✔ You want to add a search function, but the server you're using doesn't support the FrontPage extensions. You might want to use one of the common CGI search programs.

Visual Quiz

What requirements are there to use the Custom Picture option in this dialog box?

_____

_____

_____

_____

_____

_____

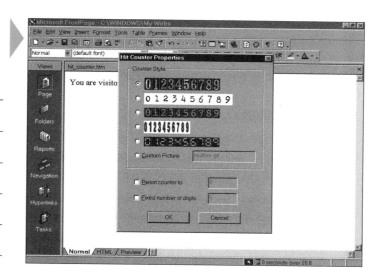

CHAPTER 12

Advanced Components

Chapter 11 covered the simpler and less technical components that FrontPage can add to your Web pages. In this chapter, we look at some of the more complex features that you can use to increase the functionality — and sometimes the beauty — of your Web pages.

For starters, we cover the relatively simple, yet extremely powerful, Include Page feature. An *include page* enables you to put an entire second Web page into an existing Web page. Although the idea may sound just a little bit on the nutty side at first, you'll soon begin to see many instances in which you can use this new capability to great advantage in your Web page design decisions.

A more sophisticated variation on this theme enables you to schedule the times and dates during which the pages are included, and a very similar approach enables you to include scheduled images as well. The latter approach is especially useful in commercial situations where you are selling blocks of time to various sponsors and need to automatically change the advertisements at specified times.

Substitution, another of FrontPage's innovations for the Web, brings the power of variables out of the often confusing realm of computer programming and enables you to use them right in your Web pages. You'll be able to instantly alter any value you have set on every Web page in your site all at once.

Meta variables are a bit more complex than plain substitution. They use the Hypertext Transfer Protocol — the basic method by which Web browsers ("clients") and Web servers communicate with one another — to advantage by enabling you to either alter existing HTTP header information or to include your own user defined header data.

Finally, we look at *hover buttons*. Hover buttons are a bit tricky to use at first, but can add a good bit of fun and glitz to your Web pages. Although they serve no greater purpose than plain hyperlinks, connecting your users to other Web pages (or any other file with a URL), they can add quite a bit to the appearance of your pages. They bring special effects like glows and color gradients to your hyperlinks, and you can even use them to add images and sound effects to your hyperlinks.

Including Another Page

If you've ever done any programming, especially in the C language or anything remotely like it, then you're already familiar with the idea of including one file as a functional part of another one. While the Include Page function in FrontPage isn't for the purpose of adding value assignments or code routines, the concept and the method of using it are very similar.

In FrontPage, the Include Page function inserts a stretch of text in the middle of another Web page. It doesn't have to be text, however, or just text. The page that's included is another complete Web page, and it can be absolutely anything that is on the original Web page, including hyperlinks, sound files, images, and so forth. If the Web page you want to include consists of nothing but an image, however, you're probably better off using the scheduled Include Image approach, which is detailed later in this chapter.

You can best use an include page for large stretches of elements that will change from time to time. Say, for example, that you're running a news site. The top story for the day always goes in the same place on the main page. While you could manually delete the old story and then insert the new one, you risk messing up your main page every time you edit it. One solution to the problem would be to use frames for the different parts. However, an include page is much faster and easier to maintain, and it doesn't require splitting up your main page's screen

for people to view your stories. Using an include page means that the main page and the included top story present a seamless interface to your audience. And your main page is never offline this way, not even for a second.

TAKE NOTE

YOU CAN USE LOTS OF THEM

You're not limited to just one include page on a Web page. You can use an unlimited number of them. In fact, there's no reason why your main page has to be anything but a series of headings, each with its own include page underneath. That way, you can change any part of it at any time without affecting the remainder.

FEEL FREE TO MIX AND MATCH

Include pages don't demand all-or-nothing choices. You can mix regular page content with include pages, scheduled images, scheduled include pages, and anything else you can fit on a Web page. Scheduled include pages, by the way, work just like scheduled images, and the process is covered in the following section.

CROSS-REFERENCE

See the following section on scheduling image displays.

FIND IT ONLINE

There are more components available at
http://websunlimited.com/fpjbotsv2/fp-jbots.htm.

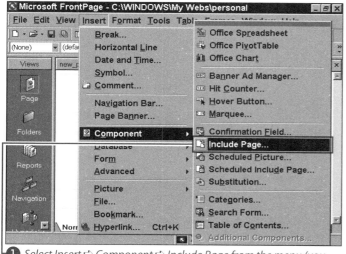

1 Select Insert ⇨ Component ⇨ Include Page from the menu (you must have a web open or this will be disabled).

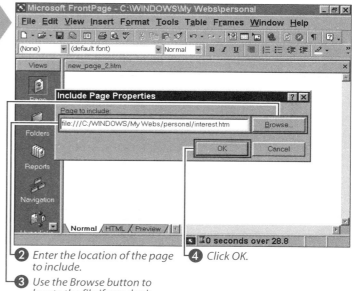

2 Enter the location of the page to include.

3 Use the Browse button to locate the file if you don't know the location.

4 Click OK.

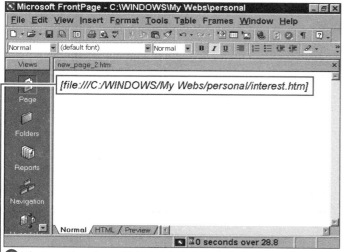

5 The insert location will show briefly, so briefly that you might not even see it.

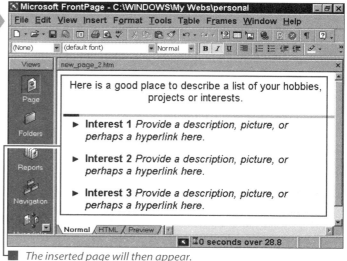

■ The inserted page will then appear.

Scheduling Image Displays

Although FrontPage's usefulness when it comes to rotating banner ads tends to fall a bit short of perfection for commercial purposes, its scheduled image display more than makes up for it. In fact, you really should use scheduled image display if you're seriously interested in using FrontPage for creating and managing a Web site that has paying sponsors.

A scheduled picture works just like a normal Web page image — to all outward appearances, at any rate — and visitors to your Web page won't be able to tell the difference. As far as your work is concerned, however, it's a different matter. A scheduled picture is a webbot, not a regular image, and you will not be able to manipulate it in any of the ways you're used to. Selecting the image will not bring up the image toolbar, and the image properties aren't available by right-clicking on it, either. Since this is the case, you should do any image handling or alteration before you use it as a scheduled picture. The best way to do this is to create another page in your FrontPage web, insert the image onto it, make any changes such as contrast enhancement that you want, and then save that page, including the altered image. That puts the image into your web, where you'll find easy access when you want to use it for the scheduled picture, and you can just delete the old page afterward.

There's tremendous flexibility in the scheduling itself. You can set things up years in advance if you want to, although most commercial applications would be scheduled for a matter of months, at most.

As far as the alternate image that appears before and after the scheduled one is concerned, you should set one up as a placeholder even if you don't have any specific purpose in mind for it. Even an image that says nothing but "This space for rent" is better than nothing.

TAKE NOTE

▶ INCLUDE PAGES, TOO

You can schedule include pages as well as images. The process is absolutely identical, except that you need to click Scheduled Include Page instead of clicking on Scheduled Picture. You might use a very short scheduled include page at the top of your regular page as a greeting to say, "Good Morning" during the early hours and "Good Day" or "Good Evening" later on.

▶ ADDING A LINK FROM A SCHEDULED IMAGE

To put in a hyperlink on a scheduled image, right-click it and select Hyperlink from the popup menu.

CROSS-REFERENCE
See Chapter 11 for information on rotating banner ads.

FIND IT ONLINE
El Scripto has some components at
http://www.elscripto.com/info/index.htm.

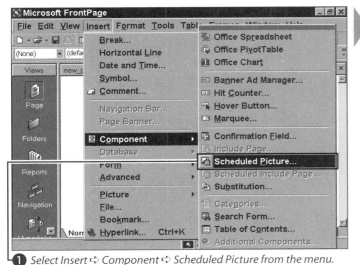

❶ Select Insert ➪ Component ➪ Scheduled Picture from the menu.

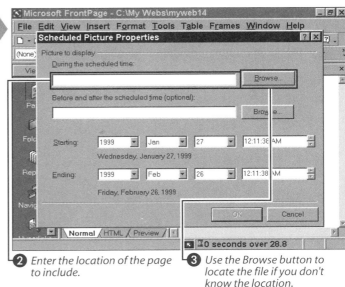

❷ Enter the location of the page to include.

❸ Use the Browse button to locate the file if you don't know the location.

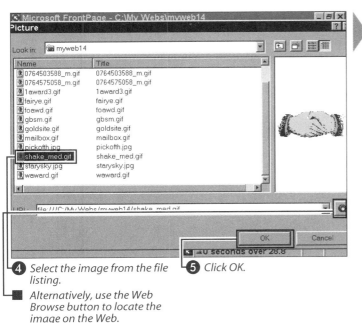

❹ Select the image from the file listing.

■ Alternatively, use the Web Browse button to locate the image on the Web.

❺ Click OK.

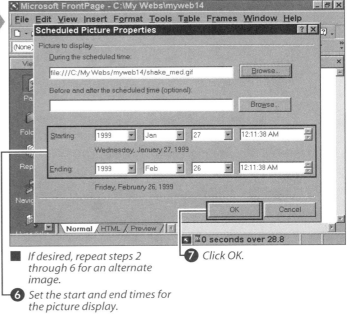

■ If desired, repeat steps 2 through 6 for an alternate image.

❻ Set the start and end times for the picture display.

❼ Click OK.

Using Substitution

substitution is one of the most powerful approaches to Web page design FrontPage offers. Once again, it's a standard computer programming technique that has been applied to Web page design. And thanks to Front-Page's ease of use, you don't have to have any computer programming experience or skills in order to use it.

Substitution is a two-step process. First, you define a variable. A *variable* represents the value of a changeable item. If you want to change all the instances in which that item appears, then all you have to do is change the value of the variable once, and all the places where it shows up will be changed without any further effort or action on your part.

In order to make it worth your time to set up and alter the variable, however, it should be an item that shows up in several different places instead of just a few.

For example, let's say you have a single item that you're selling. Its price may change from time to time, but if you only have the price in one place on a single Web page, it's a lot easier for you to just retype that part of the page occasionally than it is to set up a variable and alter its value later.

On the other hand, you may have a whole Web site with dozens of pages on which the price is mentioned over and over again. In that case, it can be a major pain in the mouse to track down each and every occurrence of the price and alter it by hand

every time it changes. Missing even a single instance of the price can lead to confusion on the part of your users, too, and may lead to financial loss if someone insists on paying the old price that you accidentally left in place in one part of your advertisement. But if you assigned a variable to the value of the price, you'd simply need to make one change in that variable. Every single instance of the price would be changed by one action, thus avoiding any possible chance of confusion or loss of income.

Continued

TAKE NOTE

CHANGING THE VALUE

How do you change the value of a variable once it has been defined and displayed? That's the easiest part. Just go through the same process as you did for defining it, but click the Modify button instead of the Add button and only alter the value in the dialog box.

CROSS-REFERENCE

See the section on meta variables later in this chapter.

FIND IT ONLINE

The FrontPage Support Home is located at **http://support.frontpage.u-net.com/**.

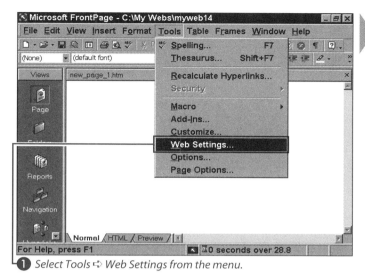

① Select Tools ➪ Web Settings from the menu.

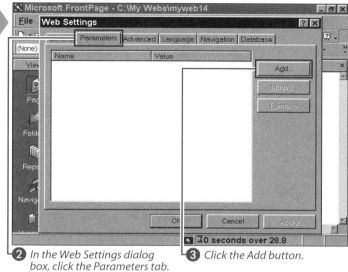

② In the Web Settings dialog box, click the Parameters tab.

③ Click the Add button.

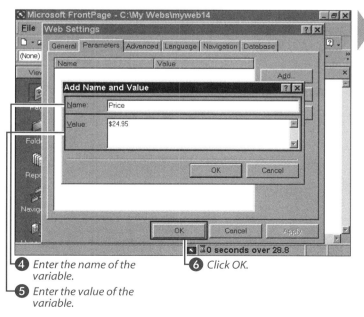

④ Enter the name of the variable.

⑤ Enter the value of the variable.

⑥ Click OK.

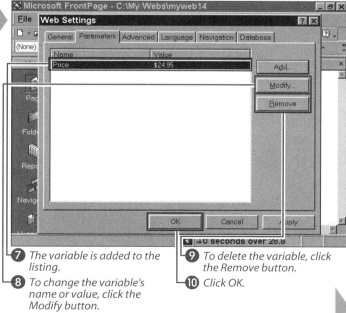

⑦ The variable is added to the listing.

⑧ To change the variable's name or value, click the Modify button.

⑨ To delete the variable, click the Remove button.

⑩ Click OK.

Using Substitution

Using the Variable

Once you've got the variable defined, you have to put it onto your Web page in order for it to be displayed and for any changes in its value to be reflected. Of course, changes in the value take effect the instant you make them whether the variable is displayed anywhere or not, but nobody but you will know it if it doesn't show up somewhere on a Web page.

You should keep in mind when you put in a variable that it is an insertion, and it will move any other elements or content that follow it (at least within the same block level containing element). You can even insert a variable in the middle of another word if you want. If you want to use a variable to replace another element, like some text for instance, then you'll need to select that text prior to performing the variable insertion. When you do insert the variable, it will then replace the selected text or other element instead of being inserted before it.

Don't neglect the possibility of using substitution for approaches other than normal text. There's no reason you can't use it for replacing the URLs that are displayed when you make a hyperlink, for instance. Let your imagination and experimentation take it as far as it can go. When using it for URLs, however, you'll need to play around a bit. If you just select the entire displayed URL for a hyperlink, and then attempt to replace it with the substitution, you'll actually delete the hyperlink. You need to select all but the first letter in the displayed part of the URL,

then perform the variable insertion, and then delete the first letter that wasn't selected. Using this two-step process, the hyperlink itself will remain intact, but the text of the display will be altered.

TAKE NOTE

▶ MAKE SURE YOU LEAVE ENOUGH SPACE

Many people tend to leave either too much or too little space between the variable and any surrounding elements. Don't make the mistake of treating a variable like some strange and mysterious thing from another planet — it's just another word on your Web page and should be treated exactly like the others.

▶ WATCH THAT CURSOR PLACEMENT

The variable insertion will occur wherever your cursor is at the time you click the menu selection to start the process. If it isn't where you want it to be, you're going to have to manually move the variable after it's inserted. To do so, simply drag it to where you meant to put it.

CROSS-REFERENCE
See Chapter 4 for information on hyperlinks.

FIND IT ONLINE
The FrontPage Support Web site is at
http://www.planetnet.com/frontpage.htm.

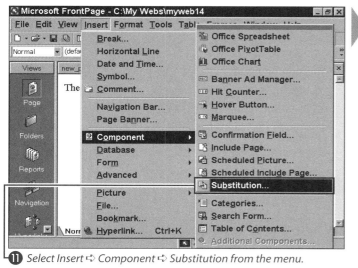

11 Select Insert ➪ Component ➪ Substitution from the menu.

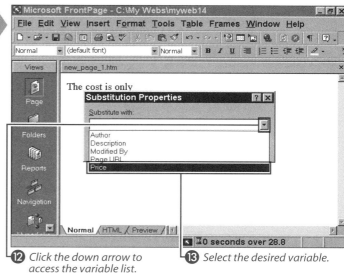

12 Click the down arrow to access the variable list.

13 Select the desired variable.

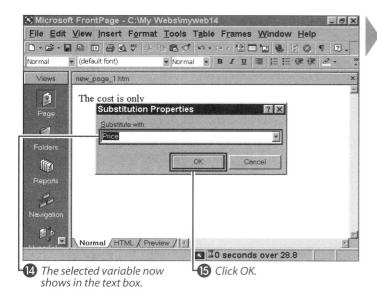

14 The selected variable now shows in the text box.

15 Click OK.

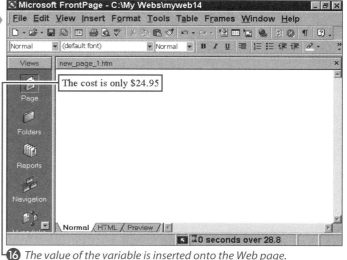

16 The value of the variable is inserted onto the Web page.

Using Meta Variables

Meta variables may at first appear to be the same as substitution, but there's a world of difference beyond the surface similarities, as well as a different method of utilizing them. Meta variables do not show up on the visible part of your Web pages, and while they are indeed variables and work just like any other variable in any other programming application, they have a very special function.

Meta variables are used to communicate directly through Web servers using the HTTP (Hypertext Transfer Protocol) header information. This is not an area for the faint of heart or the amateur Web page designer to mess with, however. If you're not thoroughly familiar with the exact variables that your particular Web server uses (and they are somewhat different, in many cases from one server to another), you can really confuse the software in question. You should not override the normal HTTP header information without fully understanding exactly what the consequences of your actions will be.

The Hypertext Transfer Protocol is the heart of communication between Web clients (such as browsers) and Web servers. When a Web browser connects to a Web server, the browser sends the server certain information via HTTP. This is known as the *client request*. The Web server processes this information and sends back what is appropriately enough known as a *server response*. The client request contains such data as the type and version of the Web browser, the kinds of file types it's capable of displaying, and the name and (alleged) location of the file it's requesting from the server. The server response gives the browser the same sort of information about the server and includes any additional header information, and then sends the requested file (assuming everything goes well and the file is where it's supposed to be, that is). The HTTP header information you'll be including on your Web page is to be included in the server response, and it allows you to communicate directly with the Web browsers that people are using when they visit your site.

TAKE NOTE

▶ **CREATE YOUR OWN**

In addition to overriding the values of established HTTP header variables, you can create your own meta variables. The process is exactly the same as for existing ones, except that you click the Add button next to User Variables instead of the one next to System Variables. Again, be sure you know which ones your Web server uses so you don't duplicate them unintentionally. Many people use this functionality to add new information such as the name and e-mail address of the Web page's author or such details as copyright information.

CROSS-REFERENCE

See the section on substitution earlier in this chapter.

FIND IT ONLINE

There's an interesting META tag program for FrontPage at **http://www.hisoftware.com/hiverscr.htm.**

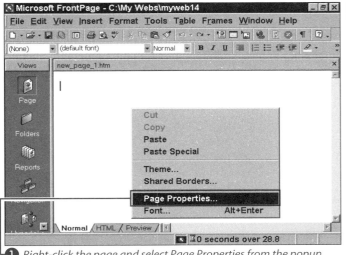

1 Right-click the page and select Page Properties from the popup menu.

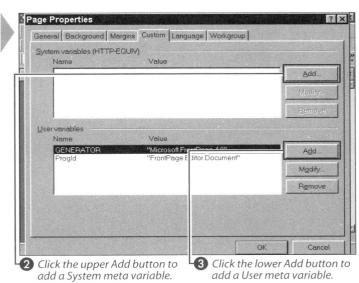

2 Click the upper Add button to add a System meta variable.

3 Click the lower Add button to add a User meta variable.

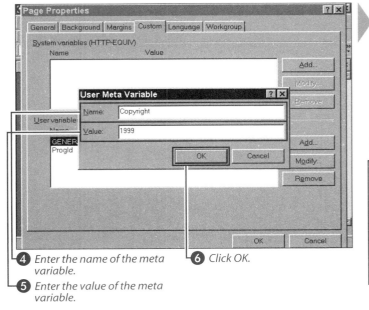

4 Enter the name of the meta variable.

5 Enter the value of the meta variable.

6 Click OK.

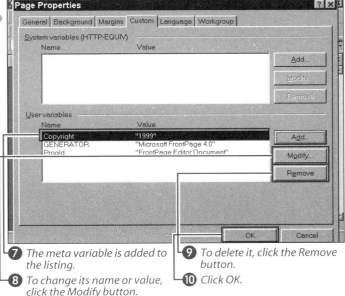

7 The meta variable is added to the listing.

8 To change its name or value, click the Modify button.

9 To delete it, click the Remove button.

10 Click OK.

Using Hover Buttons

According to some people, hover buttons are nothing more than a passing fancy. Others think they add beauty and fun as well as functionality to their Web page design. Whichever school of thought you finally settle on, the one thing that's certain is that you really should try hover buttons out before you make up your mind.

Hover buttons are a special kind of hyperlink that perform a variety of special effects when either a mouse pointer is placed over them ("hovering") or when they are clicked. In fact, you can set different effects for each of those actions if you want. The special effects can include visual or audio changes (the default special effect is a glowing appearance). Of course, the hover button still acts just like a regular hyperlink when it's activated; it switches a Web browser to the linked page from the one the hover button was on.

Even though hover buttons don't use JavaScript, if you're familiar with JavaScript programming, you'll find yourself comfortable thinking about the "On click" setting as the onclick event and the "On hover" setting as an onmouseover event. Of course, thanks to FrontPage's ease of use, you don't have to do any actual programming; the events are built in, and the effects are simply chosen from a drop-down list.

If you do use images for your hover buttons, you'll need to make sure that you adjust the height and width settings to accommodate the images or you won't get the desired effect, thus robbing your Web page of the creative effort you've put into it. In fact, you should thoroughly familiarize yourself with the variety of effects the hover button can give in order to integrate it into your design in the most pleasing ways.

TAKE NOTE

▶ NOT FOR EXPLORER ONLY

Hover buttons are not specific to Microsoft's Internet Explorer, so you can use them on your site regardless of what Web browser your visitors use. They're Java applets, however, so they have some restrictions on which files you can use with them. The sound effects files have to be .au files in 8-bit, 8000Hz, mono, u-law format.

▶ TEXT DOESN'T ALIGN

The text for a hover button is centered within the hover button itself. Even if you set the background color so that the text appears to be on a normal part of the Web page instead of against a colored local background, the text will not be on the same level as that of the sentence in which the hover button is placed.

CROSS-REFERENCE
See Chapter 11 for information on sound files.

FIND IT ONLINE
There's a FrontPage shopping cart at
http://www.salescart.com/.

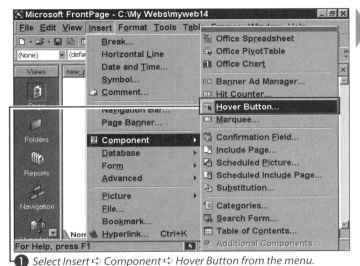

❶ Select Insert ➪ Component ➪ Hover Button from the menu.

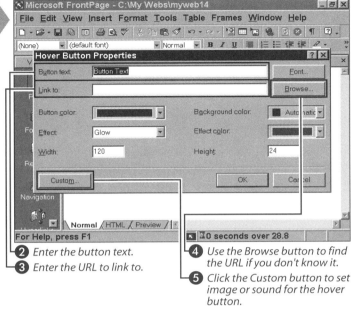

❷ Enter the button text.
❸ Enter the URL to link to.

❹ Use the Browse button to find the URL if you don't know it.
❺ Click the Custom button to set image or sound for the hover button.

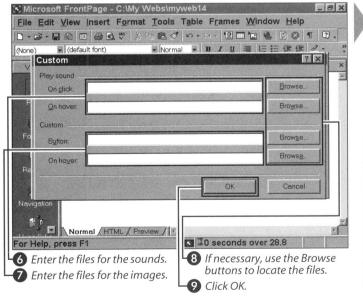

❻ Enter the files for the sounds.
❼ Enter the files for the images.
❽ If necessary, use the Browse buttons to locate the files.
❾ Click OK.

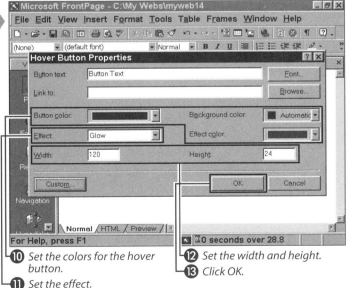

❿ Set the colors for the hover button.
⓫ Set the effect.
⓬ Set the width and height.
⓭ Click OK.

Personal Workbook

Q&A

1 What items can be scheduled for display?

_____

_____

_____

2 What Web page elements can be used in an include page?

_____

_____

_____

3 How many variables can you use on one Web page?

_____

_____

_____

4 What is the primary difference between substitution and meta variables?

_____

_____

_____

5 What is the purpose of the alternate image in a scheduled picture?

_____

_____

_____

6 What two events does a hover button respond to?

_____

_____

_____

7 What does HTTP stand for?

_____

_____

_____

8 What is the basic function of a hover button?

_____

_____

_____

_____

ANSWERS: PAGE 330

EXTRA PRACTICE

1 Set up a Web page that uses at least three include pages.

2 Insert a hover button and experiment with the different visual effects.

3 Use a scheduled picture on one of your pages. Set the time for a few minutes and watch it change.

4 Create a meta variable to include your name.

5 Use a variable to change four words on a Web page.

6 Compare the speed of a hover button with a regular hyperlink.

REAL-WORLD APPLICATIONS

✔ Your Web page has a large number of repetitive items that constantly need updating. You may want to consider the value of substitution and make variables for those items.

✔ You have three different sponsors, each of which is willing to pay for a different time slot. You'll probably want to use scheduled image displays and perhaps scheduled include pages to accommodate their needs.

✔ You have some data you want to put into your Web pages, but you don't want it displayed. You might want to use meta variables to add it.

✔ You're happy with your Web page design, but feel it could use a little bit of something extra. You may wish to try some hover buttons for added glitz.

Visual Quiz

How do you get to this dialog box?

_____

_____

_____

_____

_____

_____

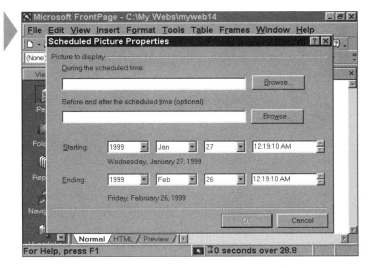

CHAPTER 13

**MASTER
THESE
SKILLS**

▶ **Inserting Tables**

▶ **Inserting and Deleting Rows, Columns, and Cells**

▶ **Using Text in Tables**

▶ **Using Images in Tables**

▶ **Adding Background Color and Images**

Structuring Pages with Tables

Without a doubt, tables are among the most versatile of all the Web page elements. Although they were originally designed and intended simply for the display of tabular data — a functional but rather dull application — tables can contain any element that can be contained within a Web page. This makes them a tremendously valuable resource for graphic designers working on the World Wide Web. Until the advent of absolute positioning, tables were the only method of adding real structure to a Web page. Many designers still utilize this technique instead of bothering with the more cumbersome and difficult approach inherent in absolutely positioning several different elements (although there's no reason why you can't mix both techniques).

Of course, you can still use a table to show the growth rate of a stock or the decline of Bohemian fruit farming if that's what you need to use it for. Rows and columns of raw data are still among the most comprehensible ways to present some types of information, and that's what tables consist of.

This chapter will introduce you to the basic techniques of creating and utilizing tables. The chapter that follows will delve more deeply into some of the more sophisticated techniques First, we cover how to insert tables into your Web pages and you'll learn a couple of tricks that will make your life a bit easier. Next, we take a look at the different ways you might want to modify the structure of a table once it's already in place. You'll learn how to add and delete individual cells as well as entire rows or columns. (Columns of cells, by the way, don't really exist in HTML, which is limited to dealing with rows and cells, but FrontPage enables you to work as though they do exist, anyway.)

From there, we'll move on to the items you'll be populating your cells with: images, text, and even features like hyperlinks and bulleted lists. Finally, we'll wrap up this chapter with a discussion of the uses of background color and background images in tables and cells.

Inserting Tables

Before you insert a table, it's a good idea to first carefully design — at least in your mind — exactly what the table's purpose will be. In many cases, its structure will be perfectly obvious. If you're making a standard, run-of-the-mill table to hold rows of data, you'll know precisely how many columns you'll need, what their contents will be, and how much space the table will take up on the Web page. But you can use tables for so much more than simple data display. In fact, many of the best Web page designers use tables for structural purposes, since the contents of table cells can be placed accurately and precisely. With symmetrically placed rectangles, everything in a column or row will be exactly aligned with everything else in that column or row (unless, of course, you deliberately make each cell in the column or row have a different alignment scheme). Using invisible borders (borders whose width is set to zero), you can gain the structural qualities without anyone ever realizing that a table provides the foundation for the Web page.

By default, a table will take up the entire screen width. You can alter this behavior by setting a particular width, either as a percentage of the screen or in pixels. Most Web page designers prefer to use the percentage route, since tables will remain constant from one monitor to the next, whereas a fixed-pixel width results in the use of a variable amount of screen space, dependent entirely upon the video capabilities of each user's computer system.

TAKE NOTE

INVISIBLE TABLES

If you've just inserted a table and can't see a thing, right-click the area where the table is supposed to be. If the table's there, but invisible, the popup menu should include a Table Properties selection. Clicking this will bring up the Table Properties dialog box. Check the border width setting. If it's at zero, then that explains why you can't see anything.

TABLES WITHIN TABLES

When we said that a table could hold anything a Web page could hold, we meant *anything* — and that means that tables can hold tables. Just put the cursor in the cell where you want to insert the table and proceed as if you were working on a normal Web page. This capability enables you to subdivide the structure of a table without inserting a whole series of cells, since you can insert a cluster of cells at one time as an individual table.

TABLE WIDTH AND ALIGNMENT

As with horizontal rules, the default table width of 100 percent of the Web page's width creates an interesting situation. If the table stretches across the entire screen, then no alignment is possible, since alignment depends on the possibility of the table moving in reference to the page's edges. Try it. No matter if you align left, right, center, or whatever, it will have no effect unless the table width is set for less than 100 percent. The same situation exists when a particular pixel width is specified and that pixel width equals or exceeds the screen width.

CROSS-REFERENCE

See Chapter 14 for information on drawing tables.

FIND IT ONLINE

There's a FrontPage FAQ at http://www.global-trades.com/frontfaq.htm/.

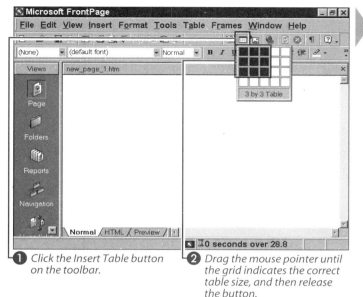

① Click the Insert Table button on the toolbar.

② Drag the mouse pointer until the grid indicates the correct table size, and then release the button.

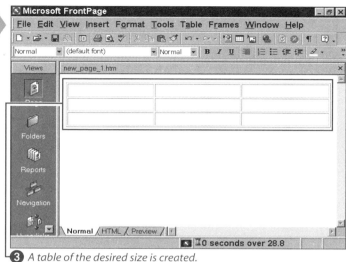

③ A table of the desired size is created.

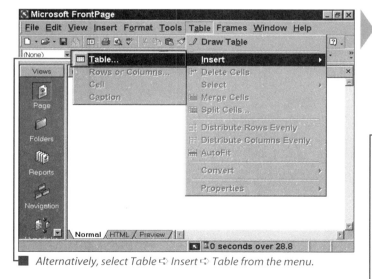

■ Alternatively, select Table ➪ Insert ➪ Table from the menu.

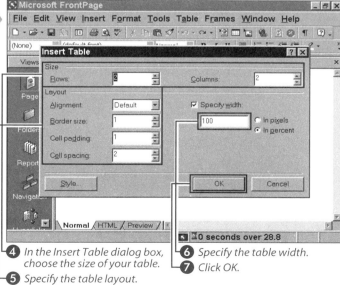

④ In the Insert Table dialog box, choose the size of your table.

⑤ Specify the table layout.

⑥ Specify the table width.

⑦ Click OK.

Inserting and Deleting Rows, Columns, and Cells

Even with the best of intentions and planning, you'll sometimes find that you need to modify your table due to alterations in the type and amount of data or new design considerations. Some table elements must either go or be added.

In fact, many Web designers will deliberately set up an entire page that is nothing but one large table. Obviously, if the page is to be anything but a series of equally spaced and sized rectangles, then some cells will have to be removed and others added. You can structure the entire page in this manner, with some rows having but a single large cell and others having three or four cells of varying sizes.

You can't, unfortunately, design such a table from scratch; you have to start with a normal table. A table, when it's first created, is completely symmetrical. When you insert or delete entire rows or columns, that symmetry is maintained. When it comes to cells, however, making numerous changes can result in a drastic loss of symmetry, with some rows having more cells than the others in the table do. If this is a deliberate design decision, then everything's just fine, but you do need to be aware that it will happen.

Bearing in mind the Take Note about cell deletion problems in FrontPage, you might want to simply

start with a table that has only a single column. Then you could add cells as needed to flesh out your intended design, altering the cell width and span (see Chapter 14) to suit your intent. You might also want to consider the simple approach of leaving some cells with no content at all. That way, you don't always have to be so concerned with the exact number and width of the cells in your Web page design, and can simply use the blank cells as spacing elements.

TAKE NOTE

► DELETING SINGLE CELLS

Believe it or not, FrontPage won't let you delete a single cell. In order to select cells for deletion, you have to drag the pointer across them while holding the left mouse button down. If you do this within a single cell, all you're selecting is its contents, not the cell itself. So what do you do if you have three cells in a row and want to have only two cells there? Brace yourself. You insert a new cell, and then select both it and the one you originally wanted to delete. Now, with both unwanted cells selected, you can delete them by using either the main menu or by right-clicking and using the popup menu, whichever you prefer.

CROSS-REFERENCE

See Chapter 14 for more information on manipulating cells.

FIND IT ONLINE

Check out **http://dostal.da.ru/mindshare/ office2000/fp2000/** for a sneak peek at FrontPage 2000.

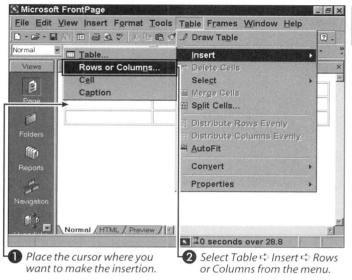

1 Place the cursor where you want to make the insertion.

2 Select Table ➪ Insert ➪ Rows or Columns from the menu.

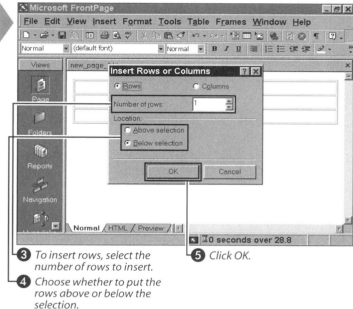

3 To insert rows, select the number of rows to insert.

4 Choose whether to put the rows above or below the selection.

5 Click OK.

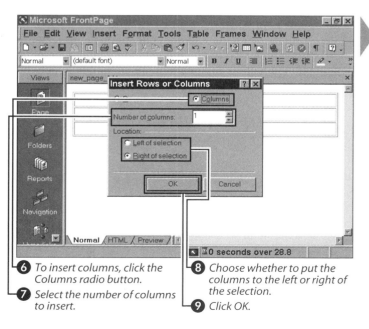

6 To insert columns, click the Columns radio button.

7 Select the number of columns to insert.

8 Choose whether to put the columns to the left or right of the selection.

9 Click OK.

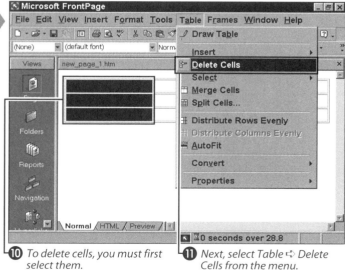

10 To delete cells, you must first select them.

11 Next, select Table ➪ Delete Cells from the menu.

Using Text in Tables

Even with all the marvelous things you can do with tables, they're still used primarily to hold text ("text" in this context is defined as either letters or numbers). As with any alphanumeric characters anywhere else on a Web page, you can format the text in tables. Feel free to color it, make it bold or italic, change the font face or size — whatever strikes your fancy. And, as with text elements anywhere else on a Web page, you can work your formatting changes right down to the individual character level. You can use this capability to create some nice effects by varying the size and color of various characters. You can also select the entire table and alter all of the text simultaneously.

Text in a table is found not just as contents in its cells, by the way, but in the caption as well. The caption, even though it stands above or below the table on the page, is still a part of the table element, as you can see if you click the HTML tab and take a look at the source code. Captions, by the way, are always placed by FrontPage at the top of a table, and you won't have the option to put a caption at the bottom of the page during the creation stage. If you want to move it, you'll have to right-click it, select Caption Properties from the popup menu, and choose Bottom of Table as the option.

TAKE NOTE

▶ ### USING FORM ELEMENTS IN TABLES

You can use tables to make form elements line up neatly with one another. For instance, by right-aligning textual labels in the left-hand column and left-aligning text boxes in the right-hand column, you can create forms that look much nicer than the standard. Many designers use this technique in regular HTML, but FrontPage has a problem in that the form element itself begins and ends in the first cell when you try this. You can still use the technique, but you'll have to understand HTML and use some cutting and pasting in the HTML source tab to make the form begin right after the table and end just before it does.

▶ ### WHAT'S A HEADER CELL?

A *header cell* is one that is used to title a column or row. The text in header cells is automatically formatted as bold and centered within the cell. While you can change the alignment if you want to, and add italic or underline formatting to the text in a header cell, you can't get rid of the bold formatting.

▶ ### A SNEAKY WAY TO CREATE NEW TABLES

If you already have a table on your Web page, you can create a new one from it. Just copy a row or column and paste it into a blank area of your Web page. A new table will appear, and the contents and settings (such as background color) of the original table will go along with it. Cut and paste works the same way except, of course, that it also deletes the selected area from the original table.

CROSS-REFERENCE
See Chapter 3 for information on modifying text.

FIND IT ONLINE
SKW Communications specializes in FrontPage sites. Find them at **http://www.skw.com.au/**.

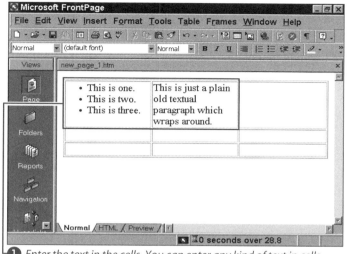

① *Enter the text in the cells. You can enter any kind of text in cells, including bulleted lists.*

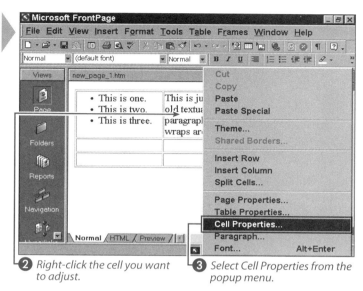

② *Right-click the cell you want to adjust.*

③ *Select Cell Properties from the popup menu.*

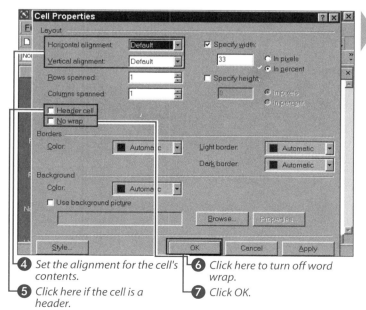

④ *Set the alignment for the cell's contents.*

⑤ *Click here if the cell is a header.*

⑥ *Click here to turn off word wrap.*

⑦ *Click OK.*

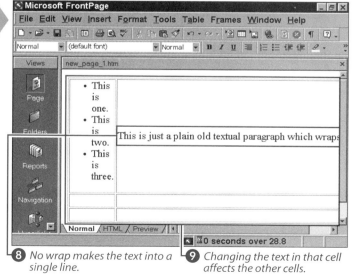

⑧ *No wrap makes the text into a single line.*

⑨ *Changing the text in that cell affects the other cells.*

Using Images in Tables

You can, of course, include images in the cells of your table, just as you can include any other type of Web page element. We're talking about foreground images here, although you can also have background images, both in individual cells and for the table as a whole (see the following section for details on background images).

The use of table cells as image containers is a Web page graphic designer's dream. By using the alignment properties of the individual cells, you can make images relate to one another in space in ways that they can't in normal HTML, no matter how much you monkey with their placement. With creative usage of alignment, borders, intervening blank cells, and perhaps a proper mix of textual elements, you're just beginning to explore the possibilities.

The "blank" spacing cells can, if you wish, contain their own background colors to emphasize their role as separators. Although the use of a background color in this case means that you must, because of the rectangular shape of cells, settle for a rather harsh, straight-line appearance between images. You can get around this by using your own softer, more curved images in the separator cells. If the images are GIF files, you can make use of transparency to soften the edges to a great degree. In this case, you may or may not want to have the background color as an added design element.

One of the nicest features of using table cells as image containers is the relative ease of changing the layout. When you want to move an image on a regular Web page, all the other elements alter their positions as a consequence (unless they're absolutely positioned), which can wreak havoc on your careful designs. With a table, however, everything is neatly constrained within the cells, and moving an image from one cell to another will affect, at most, the two cells involved.

> ## TAKE NOTE
>
> ### ▶ FAKING AN IMAGE MAP
>
> You can use images in tables to create an image-map-like display. Most people don't realize that tables can contain hyperlinks, but they can, and those hyperlinks — just like regular ones on the Web page — can be image-based as well as text-based. Use of a table whose cells contain a series of image-based hyperlinks can result in the appearance and functionality of an image map, especially if you use a border width setting of zero and the cell spacing and padding is set to allow the images to exactly abut one another.

CROSS-REFERENCE
See Chapter 8 for more information on image maps.

FIND IT ONLINE
You'll find information on FrontPage server extensions at **http://www.internet-central.net/front.htm.**

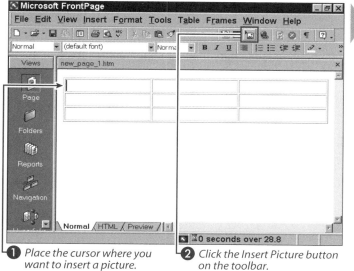

1 Place the cursor where you want to insert a picture.

2 Click the Insert Picture button on the toolbar.

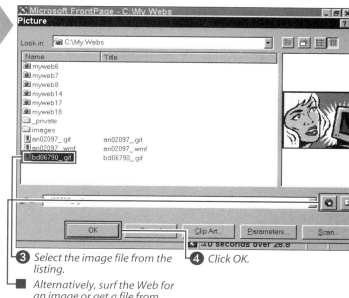

3 Select the image file from the listing.

■ Alternatively, surf the Web for an image or get a file from disk.

4 Click OK.

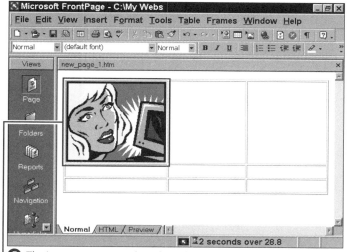

5 The image appears in the selected cell.

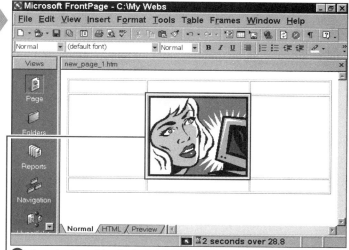

6 Once in the table, the image can be moved to another cell by dragging.

Adding Background Color and Images

In addition to normal content, tables can have their own background color or background images (as opposed to regular images, which you can think of as "foreground images," in this context). While normal table content is restricted to individual cells, the background color and background image settings are interestingly different. The table as a whole can have both background color and images underlying all the cells at once, and each individual cell can also have both on its own.

Background images, of course, are tiled in a table or cell just as they are on a Web page, repeating as many times as the width of the containing element will permit them to. Although you can plan the exact size of Web page background images with a fair degree of ease as we explained in Chapter 6, it's usually a bit more difficult with tables. Even though a normal table is the full width of the screen, due to the interference of cell spacing, padding, and borders, you can't just assume that the an image that tiles perfectly on a Web page will do so in a table. Of course, if you're dealing with a single cell that's set to a specific pixel width, it's a lot easier. Practically, though, you'll find that things don't always work out exactly as planned, and you may have to do a bit of cropping of your original image before you have it all worked out. Probably the simplest approach to this problem is to just use an image for your backgrounds that is indefinite in its details, so that any fitting problems won't show up well.

TAKE NOTE

▶ **CELL BACKGROUND SIZES**

Background image size in tables becomes extremely difficult to handle when you're dealing with a cell background image. The cell's smaller size magnifies the enormity of the fitting problem. Although the background image in the figures on the bottom of the facing page works reasonably well when applied to the table as a whole, it would be intolerably cropped if applied to an individual cell. The caveat that you should use more abstract background images is even more applicable to cell backgrounds.

▶ **YOU CAN'T REALLY USE BOTH**

Although it's technically possible to have both a background color and a background image, they are, in practical terms, mutually exclusive. A *background image* will cover over a *background color*, rendering it invisible in a table just as it does on a Web page. Also, bear in mind that a cell's background settings will override the table's background settings within that cell. Thus, if you have a background image for the table as a whole, and then set a background color for a particular cell within the table, the background color for the cell will be what you see in that cell. The table's background image, however, will still be visible in the other cells. Likewise, a cell's background image will also override any background settings for the table as a whole. And, of course, within a cell, the cell's own background image will override its own background color, as in a table or a Web page.

CROSS-REFERENCE

See Chapters 3 and 6 for information on background color and images.

FIND IT ONLINE

For a site on sound, FrontPage, and Netscape surf to http://dynamicnet.net/support/fp/back groundsound.htm.

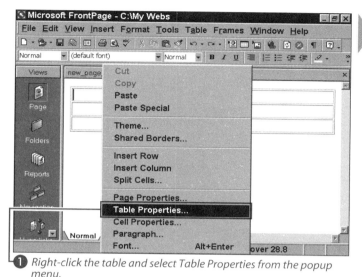

❶ Right-click the table and select Table Properties from the popup menu.

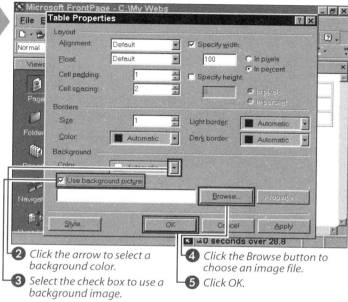

❷ Click the arrow to select a background color.

❸ Select the check box to use a background image.

❹ Click the Browse button to choose an image file.

❺ Click OK.

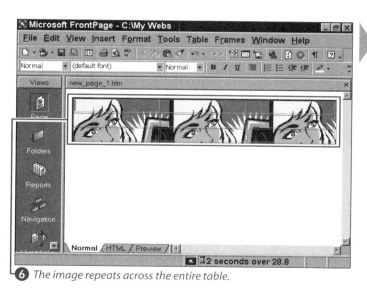

❻ The image repeats across the entire table.

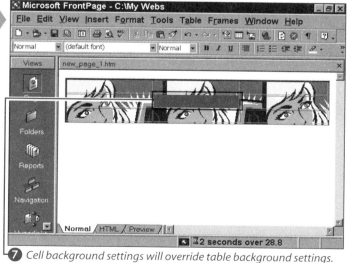

❼ Cell background settings will override table background settings.

Personal Workbook

Q&A

1 What kinds of elements can be contained within a table?

_____

_____

_____

_____

2 How many cells can be inserted into a single row?

_____

_____

_____

3 In FrontPage, where is a caption placed by default?

_____

_____

_____

4 What happens when you specify both a background color and a background image?

_____

_____

_____

5 How do you remove the bold formatting in a header cell?

_____

_____

_____

6 What is the minimum number of cells you can delete? The maximum?

_____

_____

_____

7 What table elements can be inserted into a table?

_____

_____

_____

8 What does the No Wrap option do?

_____

_____

_____

ANSWERS: PAGE 330

EXTRA PRACTICE

1. Place an image into a table cell, and then move it to another cell by dragging and dropping it.

2. Use the Table menu to insert a caption, and then move the caption to the bottom of the table.

3. Make a table that contains one of each kind of HTML element.

4. Create a table, insert a form into it, and use Cut and Paste on the HTML tab to make the form fit within the table.

5. Experiment with using background images in tables and cells. See if you can find ones that complement one another rather than clash.

6. Insert a table within a table.

REAL-WORLD APPLICATIONS

✔ You have a list of information you want to present. Consider using a table to organize it into rows and columns.

✔ You have a series of images you want to use as an image map. Rather than pasting them together in a paint program and then converting the resulting image into an image map, consider using a table to put them together as a group of image-based hyperlinks.

✔ You want to create a Web page that exactly duplicates a magazine layout. Instead of working with CSS and absolute positioning, you might want to try designing a table to block off parts of the page.

Visual Quiz

What can you do in this dialog box that we've covered in this chapter?

_____

_____

_____

_____

_____

_____

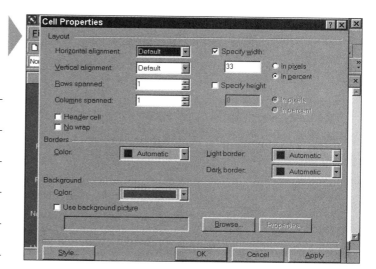

CHAPTER 14

MASTER
THESE
SKILLS

▶ Converting Between Text and Tables

▶ Setting Cell Width, Height, and Span

▶ Setting Cell Padding and Spacing

▶ Merging and Splitting Cells

▶ Drawing Tables

Advanced Tables

Chapter 13 introduced you to using FrontPage to put tables into your Web pages. In this chapter, we take a look at some of the more obscure and unusual ways to manipulate tables.

First, we cover the capability to convert back and forth between text and tables. This technique enables you to take an existing table from any program that can generate delimited ASCII files, paste that text version of the table into your Web page, and convert it to an HTML table right in FrontPage. Or, if you're an intrepid and careful typist, you can even create such a delimited data source yourself onscreen and do the conversion after that. The conversion routine is most useful, though, when you're working with existing data. The reverse operation—converting an HTML table to text that is split into paragraphs based on the original table cells—is extremely useful when you're working with a Web page designed by somebody else that requires such modifications. The one-step table-to-text conversion routine makes your life much easier than it would be if you had to cut out the cell contents one at a time and paste the material into place on the Web page to create the new design.

Next, you'll learn how to alter the way cells themselves fit into the table. Each individual cell in the table can have its own settings for width and height (although all the other cells in the same row are affected by a height setting). You can also vary height and width by setting how many rows or columns a particular cell will span. Cell padding affects the amount of space between cell walls and their contents, whereas cell spacing changes the amount of space between the cells themselves. Adjusting either of these settings affects every cell in the table.

Cells can also be merged together, making the contents of multiple cells fit into one larger cell. Cells may also be split apart, cutting the original cell in half and creating a new cell of the same size, both of which fit into the same space as the original cell.

Finally, you'll learn to create tables by drawing them by hand instead of using FrontPage's insertion approach.

Converting Between Text and Tables

If you have some text that you would like to put into a table, you could create a table of the desired size and characteristics, and then laboriously cut and paste the text into the various cells. You'd probably also have to resize some of the cells after the fact to make the table look better. Fortunately, FrontPage has a nice feature that can save you from having to face this arduous task. Not only can you convert text to tables, you can also do the reverse — convert your HTML tables to text that is separated into paragraphs instead of into table cells.

Generally speaking, text that is to go into a table on a Web page should already be in some sort of tabular format to begin with (at least to be compatible with FrontPage's table-conversion feature). For example, if you have a table from a database or spreadsheet program, you could save it in a delimited format such as CSV (see the first Take Note). The CSV text could then be placed directly on your Web page within FrontPage and converted to an HTML table on the spot. Of course, if your table is in Microsoft Excel, then you can simply insert it directly as a component without worrying about converting it at all. The drawback to inserting an Excel table directly as a component is that it can only be done by users of Microsoft Internet Explorer.

Continued

TAKE NOTE

WHAT IS CSV?

CSV is short for *comma separated values*, and it's also commonly referred to as *comma-delimited* data. In this type of file, the individual elements of the table (the cell contents) are distinguished from one another by having commas placed between them. Thus, a set of locations might be represented as "Wyoming,Florida,New York". Note that there are no spaces after the commas because the space would then become part of the data itself.

WHAT IF THE TEXT INCLUDES COMMAS?

Some cell data, such as names or certain addresses, includes commas as part of the normal grammar of the data. Most programs that use comma-delimited format allow you to use quotation marks around data that already includes commas. Those commas are differentiated from the delimited ones. FrontPage does not allow this. If your data itself must include commas, then substitute some other delimiter instead. The default "Other" replacement in FrontPage is a period, which creates its own conflicts with normal grammar (a name with middle initials, for instance). It's better to use a really obscure character such as the caret (^) for a separator if you cannot use commas.

CROSS-REFERENCE
See Chapter 3 for more information on text handling.

FIND IT ONLINE
Check out the Table Tutor at **http://junior.apk.net/~jbarta/tutor/tables/index.html**.

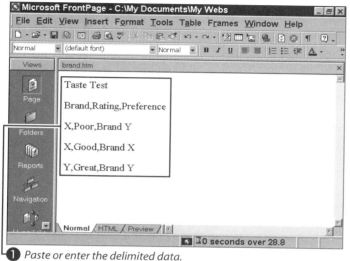

1 Paste or enter the delimited data.

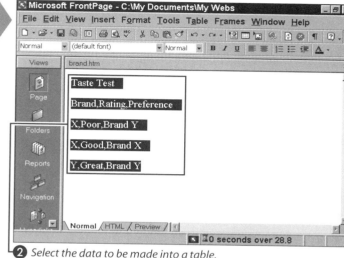

2 Select the data to be made into a table.

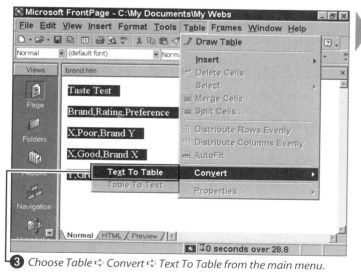

3 Choose Table ➪ Convert ➪ Text To Table from the main menu.

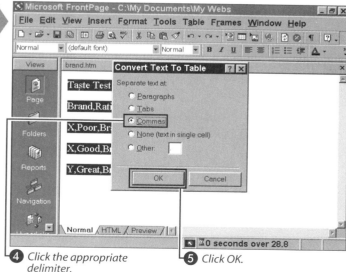

4 Click the appropriate delimiter.

5 Click OK.

267

Converting Between Text and Tables *Continued*

Because your data is all on different lines, you can structure the table by simply selecting "Paragraph" as the delimiter. This will maintain the line-by-line arrangement of your data, creating a single cell per line, with all the data from one line in one cell. Paragraphs are also recognized in other delimitation options, even though this option is not specified. Any time there is a paragraph break, a new row of cells begins. In other words, if you have several items on a line, each separated by commas, and there are several lines of this sort, then the table made from them will consist of several rows of cells, each cell containing one of the items.

When the table to text conversion is performed, paragraph delimitation is the only output option. You unfortunately cannot have FrontPage create a CSV set of text for you, or use any of the other options available when converting from text to a table. The upshot of this is that you cannot actually reverse a text to table conversion by using the table to text conversion. Regardless of the form of input when converting to a table, the output when converting back to text will always be a series of separate lines, with each line holding the contents of the former table cells.

As far as the option to keep all text in a single cell, there's not much apparent use for this. Although

Microsoft notes in its help file that you may want to use this option "if you are using a table for page layout," there is actually no layout you can do with a single cell. You would still have to add other cells within the table and populate them with contents.

TAKE NOTE

▶ TABS DON'T WORK SO WELL

You can use tabs for your delimiters. However, there is really no such thing in HTML as a tab. FrontPage handles this by entering three nonbreaking spaces and a regular space in the HTML source code when you press the Tab key. Although FrontPage will interpret this as a tab for the purposes of making a table, it also leaves some debris behind. Two of the nonbreaking spaces and the regular space remain after the table is created, thus adding invisible characters to the data in each cell except the last one in a row. This is a design/implementation flaw within FrontPage because tab-delimited files are a cross-platform standard for textual representation of tabular data, and can be the source of all sorts of headaches when you're trying to resize the table. The only resolution is to manually edit the HTML source code.

CROSS-REFERENCE

See "Inserting Tables" in Chapter 13 for more information on table size.

FIND IT ONLINE

You'll find another table tutorial at **http://wysiwyg.future.easyspace.com/table.html**.

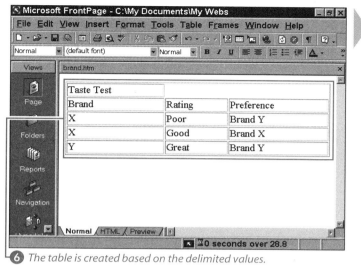

6 The table is created based on the delimited values.

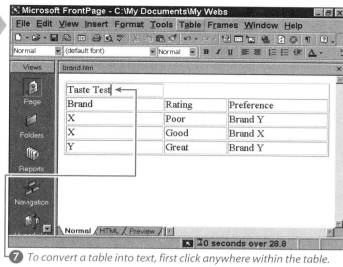

7 To convert a table into text, first click anywhere within the table.

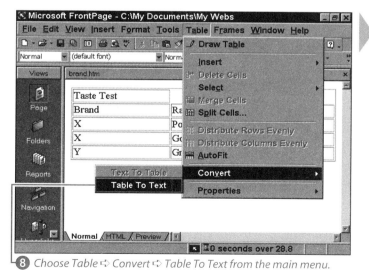

8 Choose Table ⇨ Convert ⇨ Table To Text from the main menu.

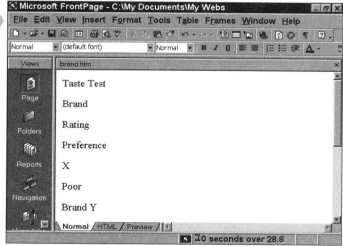

■ The table is broken into separate paragraphs.

Setting Cell Width, Height, and Span

Using the Cell Properties dialog box, you can adjust the width and height of each individual cell in a table either by a percentage of the table's overall width or height, or by an absolute value in pixels.

Also, you can set the number of rows or columns spanned by a particular cell in the table. For instance, the top row can be made to consist of a single cell that spans all the columns in a table. You'll notice, no doubt, from the images in the lower-left and lower-right figures on the facing page, that setting cell span to more than one column or row distorts the table's symmetry. The solution is as simple as it is drastic — you must delete any and all of the cells in the row or column that violate the overall symmetry of the table. The only alternative is to accept a table that has an unequal coverage in either rows or columns.

Of course, if you are using the table for other than data presentation purposes, you may wish to deliberately create an asymmetrical table. For example, if you are using a table for page layout purposes, and you wish to include each different page element within its own cell in the table, then an asymmetrical table is probably exactly what you desire. Fortunately, FrontPage is flexible enough to accommodate vastly different design tastes.

CROSS-REFERENCE

See "Using Horizontal Lines" in Chapter 2 for a discussion of pixels versus percentages.

FIND IT ONLINE

There's a good article on cell span at **http://builder.cnet.com/Authoring/Htmltips/ss02j.html**.

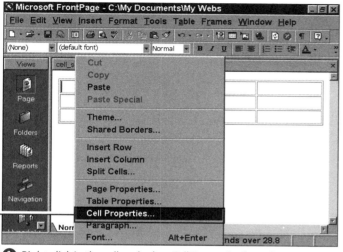

❶ Right-click in the cell and select Cell Properties from the popup menu.

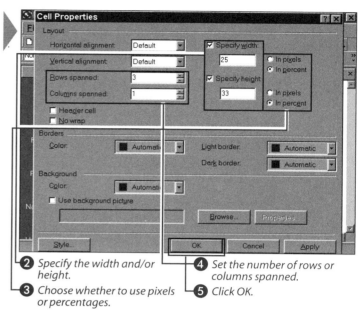

❷ Specify the width and/or height.

❸ Choose whether to use pixels or percentages.

❹ Set the number of rows or columns spanned.

❺ Click OK.

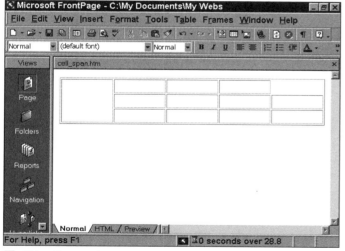

■ This cell spans three rows.

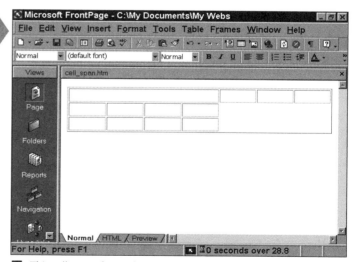

■ This cell spans four columns.

Setting Cell Padding and Spacing

Cell padding is the distance between the edges of the cell's borders and its content. *Cell spacing*, on the other hand, is the distance between individual cells in the table. The default value for cell padding is a single pixel, and the default value for cell spacing is 2 pixels. The contents of cells is pretty much right up against the cell walls, and the cells themselves are pretty much abutting one another.

This setting, fortunately, is very flexible and, depending upon your design needs, you can set the spacing and padding to much higher amounts. Although there is no theoretical limit in the HTML standard itself, FrontPage will only scroll to settings of 100 at the maximum for both attributes, and you cannot enter any number larger than that. However, it is certain that no normal Web page design would benefit from cell padding or spacing greater than 100 pixels, and much less will probably suffice. It is important to note, too, that the settings for cell padding and spacing are tablewide, and cannot be set for an individual cell. All cells must share the same settings for these attributes.

Cell spacing not only moves the cells apart from one another, but moves them apart from the outer border of the table as well — and by the same amount, of course, as the cells are from each other.

TAKE NOTE

USING PADDING WITH IMAGES

Most images look best in a table when there is no padding at all between them and the edges of the cells that contain them. Thus, you should generally make it a practice to set the cell padding to zero in cells that contain images. Cells that contain text, on the other hand, often benefit from increasing, rather than decreasing, the amount of padding between the contents and the cell walls. It should be noted, however, that text rarely runs up against the right side of a cell, anyway, since the vagaries of word size and word wrap often result in a gap of some size between the end of the final word in a line and the right edge of the cell's border. Thus, the primary effect of increased cell padding is to set off the left side of the text from the cell border.

BORDERS, CELL SPACING, AND CELL PADDING

Cell spacing and padding matter most when the borders of the cells and table are visible. If you set the border size to zero, the lines separating cell contents from one another will become invisible. Note that you'll still see a dotted line in the Normal view of FrontPage, but this is to assist you in your design process, and will not appear on a Web page viewed in a browser. This doesn't mean, however, that cell padding and spacing are of no value when going with a zero border width. On the contrary, it's still a valuable addition to your Web design toolbox. The separation of page elements doesn't always have to depend on visible guidelines showing up between them.

CROSS-REFERENCE
See Chapter 6 for more information on Web graphics.

FIND IT ONLINE
A good article on cell padding and spacing is located at **http://builder.cnet.com/Authoring/Htmltips/ss02i.html**.

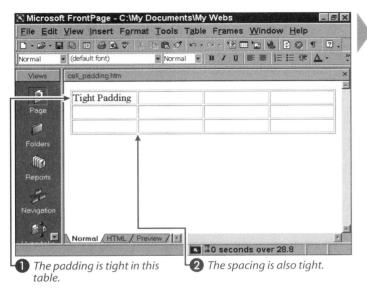

1 The padding is tight in this table.

2 The spacing is also tight.

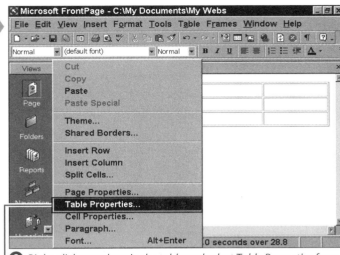

3 Right-click anywhere in the table and select Table Properties from the popup menu.

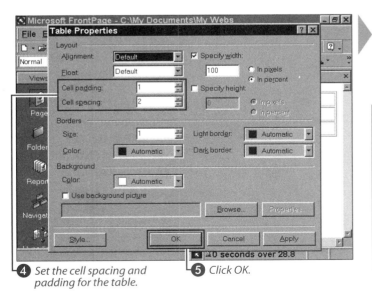

4 Set the cell spacing and padding for the table.

5 Click OK.

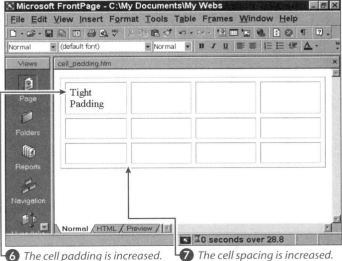

6 The cell padding is increased.

7 The cell spacing is increased.

273

Merging and Splitting Cells

Although you can affect quite a bit of change in a table by inserting and deleting cells, rows, and columns, or by monkeying about with the various settings such as row span, it is often easier to either merge or split cells. You can quickly and easily achieve the same table design results as the more cumbersome methods, and with fewer steps involved, too.

If you have a table consisting of three rows by four columns, for example, and you wish to make the first row one large cell, you could, if you wished, delete three of the top row's cells. Then, in a separate operation, you could set the size of the remaining cell to 100 percent of the table's width. Once you'd done that, you'd be ready to go. On the other hand, you could simply select all four of the top row's cells and merge them in one quick operation. The final appearance of the table after both approaches would be the same, yet the latter technique requires a lot less work.

Similarly, you can save time by using cell span to make a cell cover multiple columns or rows. The simple act of merging the cells involved automatically creates one large cell that covers many columns or rows and keeps the contents intact as well. It's a worthwhile alternative approach. Using cell merge can also save you from having to endlessly cut and paste contents from one set of cells to another cell

because the contents of all the cells involved in the merge operation are automatically dumped into the one cell that results from the operation, as shown in the lower-left figure of the facing page.

Continued

TAKE NOTE

▶ POPUP MENU DIFFERENCES

You may note that, in the upper-right figure of the facing page, you have the option of both splitting and merging cells. In the lower-right figure, however, the only choice is to split the cell. In the first instance, multiple cells are selected while, in the second instance, only a single cell is selected. While multiple cells can be either split or merged, a single cell can only be split, not merged, since there is nothing to merge a single cell with.

▶ YOU CAN ONLY MERGE RECTANGLES

Although it is possible to select oddly shaped cells in a table, or even to select totally discontiguous cells if you click them while holding down the Ctrl button, you cannot merge them. The selected cells must be contiguous and form a pure rectangle in order for the merge option to appear on the popup menu.

CROSS-REFERENCE
See the section "Inserting and Deleting Rows, Columns, and Cells" in Chapter 13.

FIND IT ONLINE
You can find D.J. Quad's table tutorial at
http://www.quadzilla.com/tables/tabletutor.htm.

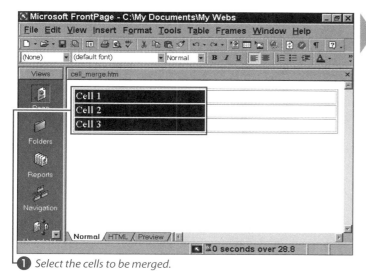

1 *Select the cells to be merged.*

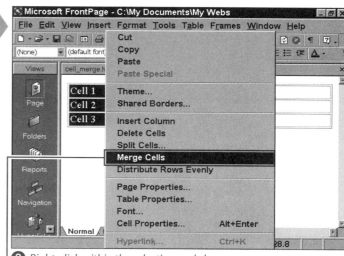

2 *Right-click within the selection and choose Merge Cells from the popup menu.*

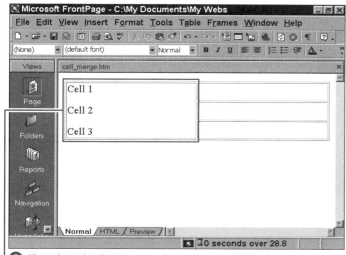

3 *The selected cells are merged.*

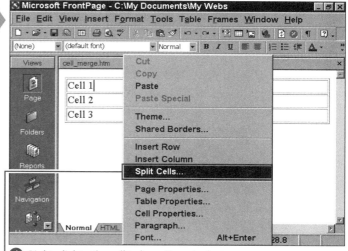

4 *Right-click in the cell to be split and select Split Cells from the popup menu.*

Merging and Splitting Cells

Continued

As with merging cells, there's a shortcut for splitting cells. You could insert more cells and then monkey with the sizing of them, but it's a lot easier to simply create new cells by splitting existing ones. While it's true that you may still need to work with their sizing, you know right off the bat exactly how it's going to fit into the row.

While merging cells is a quick and simple operation — just do it, and it's done — splitting cells demands that you make a couple of choices along the way. Of course, this added complexity makes it a more powerful technique as well. Cells must be split either in rows, which effectively doubles the height of the other cells in that row (as shown in the lower-right figure of the facing page) or in columns. Splitting a cell into more columns does not affect the size of any of the other cells in the table.

There is, however, a limit on cell splitting in FrontPage. You must choose a number between 2 and 100. In practice, however, you won't need anywhere close to 100 cells in a single row, so this "restriction" is really not very restrictive at all.

You can, by the way, use the cell splitting option with more complex cell structures than you can with the cell merge operation. There is no requirement that multiple cells selected for splitting be either rectangular or contiguous; as long as you can select them, you can split them.

TAKE NOTE

WHAT IF YOU MERGE, THEN SPLIT?

When you merge multiple cells, the contents of all the cells becomes the contents of the single cell that results from the operation. If, on the other hand, you attempt to reverse that operation by splitting the new cell back into its component parts, you'll find that you end up with one cell still containing all the contents. All the new cells that are created by splitting are empty by default. If you want them to have contents, you'll have to add it. If you want to actually reverse the operation, re-create the original cell structure, and restore the original contents to the old cells, your best option is to simply use the Undo button on the standard toolbar.

SPLITTING MULTIPLE CELLS

If you select more than one cell at a time and then split them, the same settings apply to all the selected cells at once. As with splitting a single cell, any contents in the selected cells remains in them, whereas the newly created cells are empty.

MAKING A LONG TABLE

Although there are very few situations in which you'd need dozens of columns, there are some situations in which you could use dozens — or even 100 — rows. A convenient way too set up a large table with just the settings you want is to create a table composed of a single row. Then, select all the cells in that row, choose the background color settings and so forth that you want, and then — without doing anything else — split them into as many rows as you need.

CROSS-REFERENCE

See the section, "Setting Cell Width, Height, and Span," earlier in this chapter.

FIND IT ONLINE

Jonny's Crashcourse in Tables is located at
http://www.webhelp.org/tables/.

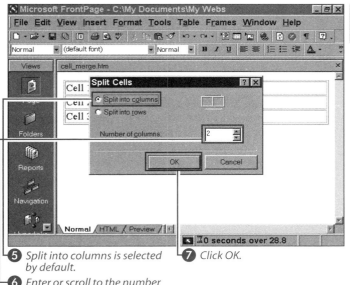

5 Split into columns is selected by default.

6 Enter or scroll to the number of columns to split by.

7 Click OK.

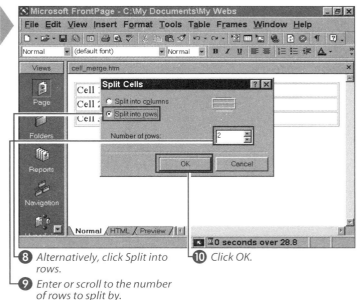

8 Alternatively, click Split into rows.

9 Enter or scroll to the number of rows to split by.

10 Click OK.

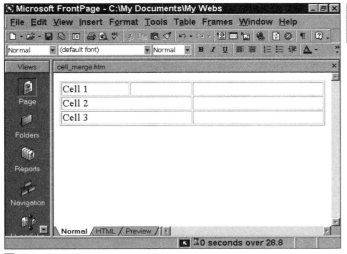

■ The first cell is split into two columns.

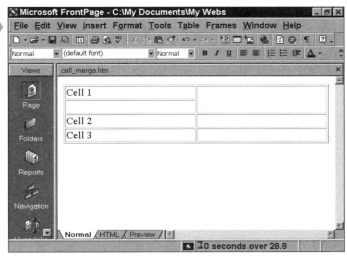

■ The first cell is split into two rows.

Drawing Tables

As an alternative to *inserting* a table, the drawing method works out best for some people. However, it's not the best technique for everyone. In order to get the most out of the table drawing approach, you must be one of those people who can easily visualize a finished Web page before you ever start it. If, on the other hand, you find yourself terrified by the blank screen and would rather stumble along step by step, you'll probably be better off skipping this technique and using the more standard table insertion approaches.

FrontPage will meet you halfway, though, showing a dotted outline of the table as you draw it. This interactive display is very useful, especially when trying to determine the overall size of a table in relation to other Web elements already in place on the page. Once you release the mouse button, and the final table outline is in place, the dotted line is replaced by a solid border. At this point, the table is actually on the Web page (see the lower-right figure on the facing page). What if you make a mistake or change your mind? Just click the Undo button on the standard toolbar and redraw the table outline.

Once you've drawn the table, what you have appears to be just the outer border of a table with no cells in it. Actually, what you have is a full table, complete with one row that contains a single cell (take a look at the HTML source code to see this). By drawing more cell borders within that initial cell, you are,

in effect, splitting it up into more rows and columns. You could, in fact, stop the drawing process at this point and just use the standard cell splitting approach to create more and more cells from the initial one.

Continued

TAKE NOTE

THE TOOLBAR IS STILL USEFUL

Even if you don't want to use the table drawing approach, you should still take a good look at the Tables toolbar. Since it can be called up independently of table drawing, and it has many features that are useful to Web page designers, it's worth taking the time to explore. Just place your mouse pointer over each button and wait a moment for an explanation of the button's purpose.

THE FLOATING TOOLBAR IS STILL ANNOYING

Floating toolbars, such as the Tables toolbar, have one really annoying feature. They tend to block your view of the Web page you're working on, especially if you're working at lower screen resolutions. Of course, you can grab the toolbar by its title bar and drag it around on the screen to reveal what was under it, but that just means that you're covering something else up. Fortunately, you can change a floating toolbar into a docked toolbar. Just drag it to any edge of the screen until it locks into place. You can put it at the top, along with most of the other toolbars, or drop it onto the sides or bottom. To remove it when you're done using it, just right-click any toolbar and deselect the one you want to get rid of.

CROSS-REFERENCE
See Chapter 13 for more information on table creation.

FIND IT ONLINE
Check out the Killer Tables overview at
http://www.killersites.com/tutorial/index.html.

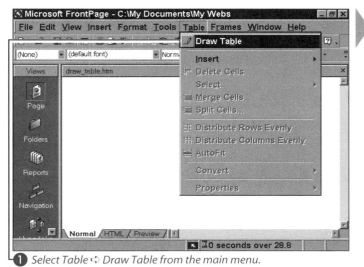

① Select Table ➪ Draw Table from the main menu.

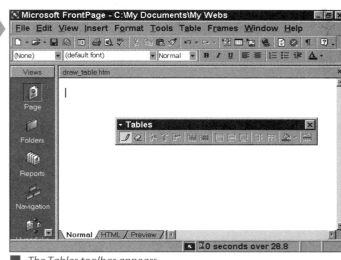

■ The Tables toolbar appears.

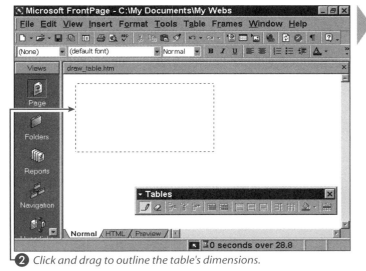

② Click and drag to outline the table's dimensions.

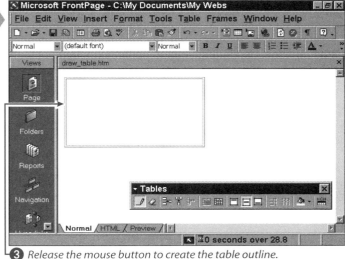

③ Release the mouse button to create the table outline.

Drawing Tables
Continued

Of course, what we think of as the table outline is really the outline of the first cell in the table. The table at this point is nothing but one very large cell, which will be further subdivided as the rest of the table is drawn.

The dotted-line approach also comes into play as you begin to sketch in the locations of the various cells in your table, as shown in the upper-left figure of the facing page. Although you're technically drawing only one side of the cell, the other three are already in place from the moment you draw the table outline. It's a moot point whether you're drawing the top border of the bottom cell or the bottom border of the top cell in this example; what's important is that you are able to simply hack the one cell into two with one stroke of your mouse. Unlike cell splitting, which will evenly divide the existing cell, you get to choose where the line goes (but see the caution in the Take Note section).

You cannot *draw* a table within a table the way you can *insert* one within one. In fact, if you attempt to use the table drawing approach with an existing table, you'll find that you're able only to draw new cells within it.

In the normal course of events, even with the technique of using tables as the underlying structure for other Web page elements, the table insertion technique will do just fine. Table drawing is definitely an advanced feature for power users with unique Web design requirements.

TAKE NOTE

THE LINE GOES WHERE IT WANTS TO

Although you theoretically have full control over the placement of the lines in your tables when you draw them, you'll find that FrontPage will snap one line into alignment with another one if it exists, regardless of what you have in mind. There is no remedy for this, either. While you can indeed drag the line where you want it to be, the other line that FrontPage associates it with will be dragged along with it, even if there is an empty cell between the two.

DISPLAYING THE TABLES TOOLBAR

If you want to use the Tables toolbar, but don't care to use the table drawing approach, you can get it on the screen by right-clicking on any toolbar and selecting Table from the popup toolbar listing. You can also use the main menu to locate it by selecting View ⇨ Toolbars ⇨ Tables.

GETTING RID OF THE PENCIL

When you're done with your table drawing, the pencil doesn't seem to want to go away. You can get rid of it by clicking the pencil icon on the Tables toolbar, or by using the same menu option (Table ⇨ Draw Table) you used to start the drawing. It's easier, however, to just hit the Esc key to return your pointer to normal.

CROSS-REFERENCE

See the section "Inserting Tables" in Chapter 13 for information on how to put a table within a table.

FIND IT ONLINE

Another tables tutorial is located at
http://www.jps.net/nonnnbg/htmlhelp/tables.htm.

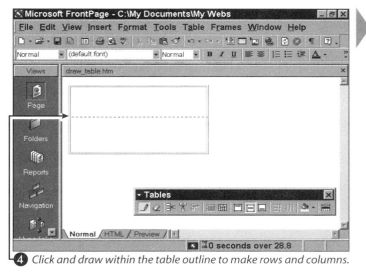

④ Click and draw within the table outline to make rows and columns.

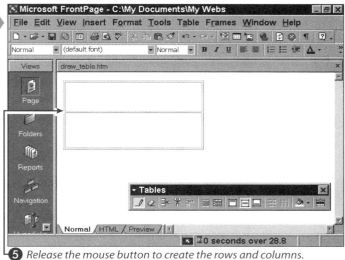

⑤ Release the mouse button to create the rows and columns.

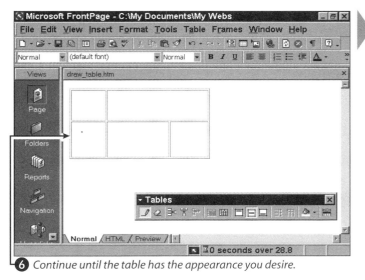

⑥ Continue until the table has the appearance you desire.

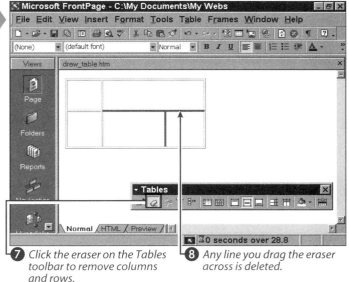

⑦ Click the eraser on the Tables toolbar to remove columns and rows.

⑧ Any line you drag the eraser across is deleted.

Personal Workbook

Q&A

1 What is *cell padding*?

_____

_____

_____

2 What happens to the contents of merged cells?

_____

_____

_____

3 What happens to the contents of split cells?

_____

_____

_____

_____

4 What two measures can be used to set cell width or height?

_____

_____

_____

5 How are the contents of cells arranged when a table is converted to text?

_____

_____

_____

6 What does *CSV* stand for?

_____

_____

_____

7 What happens to the other cells in a row when you make one cell wider?

_____

_____

_____

8 What happens to the other cells in a row when you make one cell taller?

_____

_____

_____

ANSWERS: PAGE 331

EXTRA PRACTICE

① Create a table via insertion and modify the cell structure by using the drawing tool.

② Experiment with various settings for cell spacing before you need to so that you'll be comfortable with the procedure.

③ Adjust the width of a cell by both pixels and percentage.

④ Select and split discontiguous cells in a table.

⑤ Compare merging a row of cells with resizing one and deleting the rest.

⑥ Place some text and images into a table, and then alter the cell padding to see what effect it has on the appearance of each.

REAL-WORLD APPLICATIONS

✔ You need to adjust the width of one cell so that it matches the two under it. Use cell span rather than cell width for a precise fit.

✔ You want to design a table whose cells will cover the same proportions of the screen on all video displays. Use the percentage approach to setting cell size.

✔ You have a table that you don't like. Rather than cut and paste the contents, try merging and splitting cells.

✔ You want to add an existing table from a word processor to your Web page. Save it as CSV and use the text to table conversion feature.

Visual Quiz

How do you get to this dialog box? What is the difference between *cell spacing* and *cell padding*?

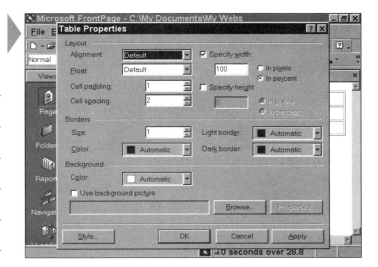

PART

IV

Advanced Issues

The chapters in this section cover how to take advantage of advanced FrontPage features, such as frames, which are covered in Chapter 15. You'll find information on everything from using basic frames templates to saving frames, linking to frames, and editing frames. The chapter covers just about everything you'd ever want to know about frames and includes information on the size and position of frames and nested frames.

The sixteenth and final chapter, "Using Special Effects and CSS," provides instruction on applying the abbreviated Style toolbar and using the Dynamic HTML Effects toolbar. The chapter covers the basics of everything from how to modify basic cascading style sheet files to how to use the more advanced embedded style sheets and inline styles. In addition to information on modifying CSS styles, the chapter includes a discussion of how to link Web pages to external cascading style sheet files.

CHAPTER **15**

MASTER
THESE
SKILLS

▶ **Using Frames Templates**

▶ **Setting the Initial Page**

▶ **Saving Frames**

▶ **Linking to Frames**

▶ **Editing Framed Pages**

▶ **Modifying Frame Size and Spacing**

▶ **Splitting and Deleting Frames**

▶ **Nesting Frames**

Working with Frames

Many, perhaps even most, of the Web pages in existence today are single, stand-alone pages. This does not mean that they are not interconnected with other pages, of course; after all, that interconnection is what makes the World Wide Web work. However, when a Web page is viewed in a browser, that page is all that shows up on the screen.

Frames, however, are radically different. Frames use multiple, separate HTML pages that are all displayed simultaneously in different screen areas, giving the impression that they are a single, integrated page. The magic behind this particular capability is an HTML element called a *frameset*. Framesets provide a structure for holding several Web pages, much as the cells of a table hold different sets of data.

Framesets, in fact, are the replacements for the <BODY> element in normal HTML pages, and although FrontPage places a <BODY> element within the HTML source code for its framed pages, such an approach is not actually required by the HTML standard. FrontPage simply does this as a courtesy to those people who may be using antiquated Web browsers to view your Web pages.

Generally, the largest area of a framed Web site is the one that holds the real content of the site. The smaller areas tend to hold such items as a hyperlinked table of contents, a corporate logo, or footnotes. When the content in the main frame scrolls, the other frames are unaffected. Thus, the logo remains visible at all times, and the contents or footnotes remain accessible regardless of the scrolling.

Depending upon the design of the particular Web site, this main area may be in different areas of the viewable Web site, as seen in a Web browser. And, if you have your own particular designs in mind, the main area may differ radically from that in most of the Web sites currently in use.

FrontPage is one of the Web page design programs that easily accommodates the use of frames and framesets. You have multiple alternatives regarding editing approaches, and FrontPage will give you easy access to the most often used frameset options. And, if you want to change the supplied frameset templates to suit your own personal design needs, the program makes it as easy on you as anything that exists today.

Using Frames Templates

FrontPage comes with several predesigned empty framesets, or "frames pages," as Microsoft calls them. One or more of these framesets may be exactly what you require, or at least close enough to do the job well, but their real purpose is to serve as templates that you can modify to your own needs. Although you can use any of them as the basis for your own frames design, you should start with the one that comes closest to the ultimate design you have in mind. Otherwise, you're just making more work for yourself.

If you find that you're going to need to use the same frameset design repeatedly, and the FrontPage templates don't meet your needs, then you have three basic options. First, you could just keep manually re-creating the frameset from one of the existing templates, but that would be a major waste of time and effort. The second option is to create the design once, reload this earlier effort the next time that you want to use the design, and then change the contents of the frames and resave it under a new name. That approach, however, is fraught with the danger of accidentally altering — or even destroying — the original version. No matter how careful you are in your work, one slip-up can cause you to save over the old version instead of renaming the file.

The third, and wisest, approach is to make your own template. This simply requires you to design the frameset that you want to reuse, and then save it as a template. The latter process is detailed in the section

"Saving Frames" later in this chapter. After you save the frames page design as a template, it is forever available to you, just like one of the original FrontPage templates. It appears on the Frames Page tab (complete with preview image), and you can load it later on as the basis for your new work, following the same procedure as you do for the originals.

TAKE NOTE

▶ NO NEW PAGE BUTTON HERE

You must use the main menu to create a frames page. Simply clicking the New button won't do the job; that only creates a normal, blank page, and doesn't take you to the New Page dialog box in which you can select the Frames Pages tab. You can't use Ctrl+N, either, for the same reason.

▶ YOU DON'T ALWAYS GET A PREVIEW

Normally, when you select a frames template, a visual representation of its structure is shown in the preview window on the right side of the Frames Pages tab. However, some templates lack this feature, in which case all you see is "No Preview Available."

CROSS-REFERENCE

See the section "Saving Frames," later in this chapter.

FIND IT ONLINE

You can find the Frames Tutor at **http://junior.apk. net/~jbarta/tutor/frames/index.html**.

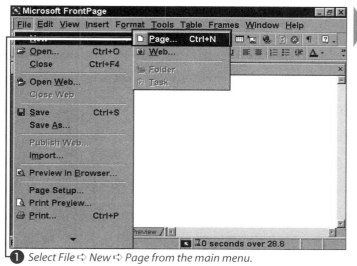

1 Select File ⇨ New ⇨ Page from the main menu.

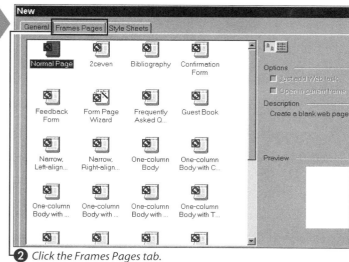

2 Click the Frames Pages tab.

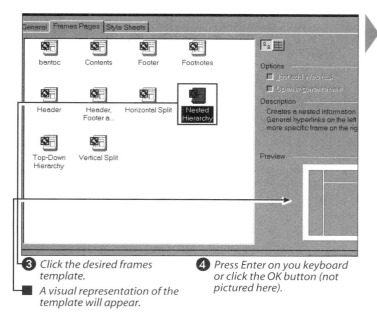

3 Click the desired frames template.

■ A visual representation of the template will appear.

4 Press Enter on you keyboard or click the OK button (not pictured here).

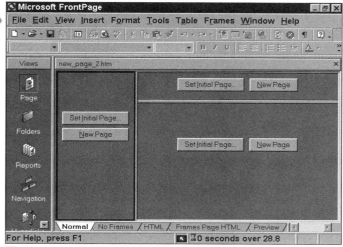

■ The empty frames page appears in FrontPage.

Setting the Initial Page

When a frames page is first created, all the frames in it are totally empty, and your first task is to populate the empty frames with Web pages. You have two basic options when setting the initial page that is displayed in a particular frame. The first option is to set that frame to contain an already existing Web page. This page can be on your own personal computer system, elsewhere on a local area network, or even on the Web. If you do choose this option, by clicking the Set Initial Page button, then, while the page is being loaded into the frame, its location and filename are displayed. This is a relatively quick operation if the file is local, but if it's out on the Web, it may take some time to load, especially if it's a complex Web page with lots of graphics.

The second option is to create a new page in-place in the frame, by clicking the New Page button. You receive a blank Web page, just as though you had created one in a normal FrontPage window. This is, in all respects, a normal Web page. You need to edit that page to add its content, just the same as if you were working outside of a frames situation. Some people find it easier to first design the Web pages that will populate the frames; others believe the only way to do it is to work with the pages in-place in the frames.

TAKE NOTE

PICKING IMAGE FILES FOR THE INITIAL PAGE

You can display files other than HTML in a Web browser. Image files are perhaps the most common example of this. However, if you set an image file as your initial page in a FrontPage frameset, you won't be able to view it in Normal view. Instead, only the path and filename will be listed. However, the image does display in Preview view, or if you view the frames page in a Web browser. Images contained within an HTML page are another matter entirely, because they do show in Normal view when that page is loaded, as demonstrated in the lower-left figure on the facing page.

THE THIRD OPTION

A third approach for initial Web page display, other than using HTML pages or image files, is to do nothing at all, leaving the frame totally blank. Although this isn't a common approach, nothing requires that you absolutely must have a frame filled with content when you initially launch a framed Web site.

THEY'RE NOT REALLY THERE

The frameset doesn't actually contain any Web page or other file at all. What it does hold is just a link. It's the same as when an image is "shown" on a Web page. That image isn't really there, either. In both cases, it's a separate file. Only because the Web page design program or browser creates a composite based on the link information that it appears as a seamless whole.

CROSS-REFERENCE
See the section "Editing Framed Pages," later in this chapter.

FIND IT ONLINE
Take a look at the Frames Demo located at http://wysiwyg.future.easyspace.com/Frames.html.

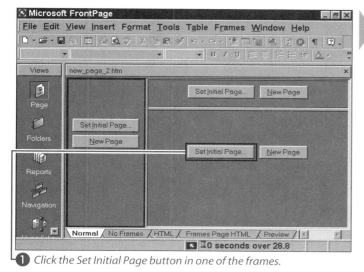

① Click the Set Initial Page button in one of the frames.

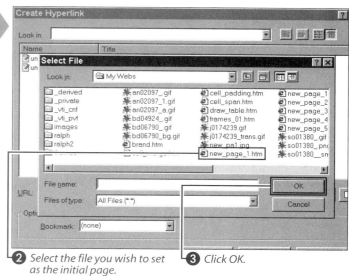

② Select the file you wish to set as the initial page.

③ Click OK.

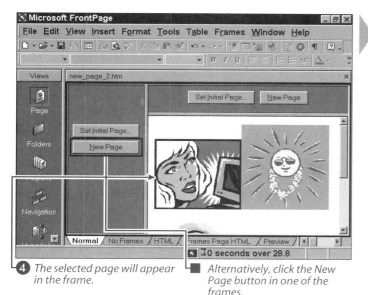

④ The selected page will appear in the frame.

■ Alternatively, click the New Page button in one of the frames.

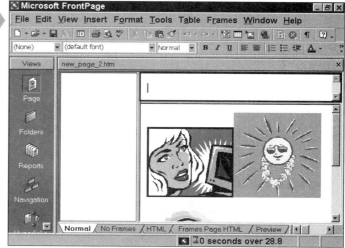

■ New, blank pages will appear in the frame.

Saving Frames

Two different procedures are involved when saving frames and their contents. First, you need to save the frameset itself (the frameset, or "frames page," as you may recall from the introduction, is the overall Web page that contains the actual frame structure). If you do not save it, all of your work will be for nothing. Second, unless the contents of the frames are composed totally of already completed Web pages with no more work to be done on them, you also need to save them from time to time. If you haven't yet saved the overall frameset, you can use one procedure to save all the unsaved or modified Web pages contained within the frames, along with the frames page itself.

A word of warning, though — do not allow the existence of this convenient feature to influence your decision to save or not to save. Unsaved changes are always at risk, whether to the vagaries of electrical power or an unexpected Windows error. The old rule of thumb — save early, save often — still applies, regardless of what handy features a particular program offers.

After you save the frames page, however, this option no longer functions, so you must save the pages individually instead of en masse. Of course, nothing prevents you from saving the frames page itself again, although you shouldn't need to unless you alter its structure.

TAKE NOTE

▶ YOU CAN USE THE MENU, TOO

While in a frame, you can choose Frames ⇨ Save Page or Frames ⇨ Save Page As from the main menu. These two options enable you to either save the currently framed page or to save it and change its name.

▶ MAKING YOUR OWN TEMPLATES

You can alter any of FrontPage's frames templates to suit yourself. After you set the margins, number of frames, placement of frames, and so forth so that the template is exactly the way that you want it, you can save it as a new template. Later, you can use the new template that you designed just as though it were one of the original templates that came with the program (see the Cross-Reference below for sections dealing with altering frameset design). When you reach the stage in saving the frameset that is illustrated in the upper-right figure of the facing page, click the arrow on the right side of the Save As Type dialog box. From the drop-down list, choose FrontPage Template (*.tem). From there, the procedure for saving it is the same as usual, except that you get to enter a name and description for it as well.

CROSS-REFERENCE

See the sections "Modifying Frame Size and Spacing" and "Splitting and Deleting Frames," later in this chapter.

FIND IT ONLINE

You can find Jonny's Crashcourse in Frames at http://webhelp.org/frames.html.

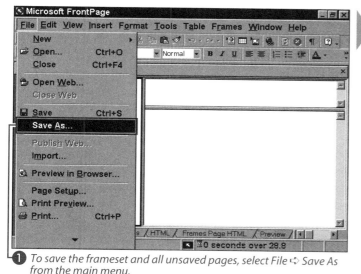

① To save the frameset and all unsaved pages, select File ⇨ Save As from the main menu.

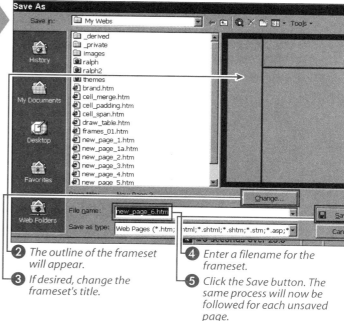

② The outline of the frameset will appear.

③ If desired, change the frameset's title.

④ Enter a filename for the frameset.

⑤ Click the Save button. The same process will now be followed for each unsaved page.

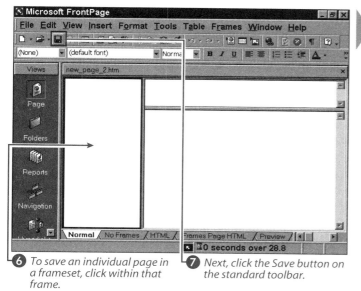

⑥ To save an individual page in a frameset, click within that frame.

⑦ Next, click the Save button on the standard toolbar.

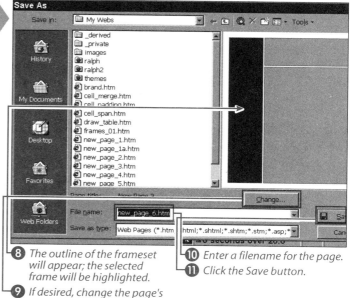

⑧ The outline of the frameset will appear; the selected frame will be highlighted.

⑨ If desired, change the page's title.

⑩ Enter a filename for the page.

⑪ Click the Save button.

Linking to Frames

Generally, the whole idea of using frames is that you can have a set of links in one frame that cause different Web pages (or other Web-displayable files) to be shown in the other frame or frames contained in the master frameset. You don't have to use frames in this exact way, so if you have some unique concept for frames, go right ahead and use it. No hard and fast rules apply in Web page design, and everyone learns through new innovations shared by others.

If you do follow the normal conventions, though, you'll probably want to put in links from one frame to another and specify how those links will be displayed. This is where "targets" come into play in your hyperlinks strategy. Normally, when you follow a link to another page or graphics file, that page or image totally replaces the page from which you clicked the link. With frames, though, you have to decide which frame ends up holding the linked page when it is displayed. That frame is the *target frame*.

Every template in FrontPage has a default target already built in to it. In the Nested Hierarchy frameset template, for instance, the default target is rtop, which is the top-right frame, the smallest one in the frameset. This is manifestly a case of poor Web page design, and the correct target should be rbottom, or the largest frame on the page. The idea of linking to a Web page that is displayed in the smallest portion of the screen is not a great one. Fortunately, Microsoft

built in the ability to alter the default target for a frames page (see the lower-left figure on the facing page), so you can modify this behavior to suit yourself.

TAKE NOTE

▶ USING THE COMMON TARGETS

The Common Targets part of the Target Frame dialog box corresponds to the common notations for such links. The Same Frame approach, for instance, is the _self link in HTML; the Whole Page approach is _top; the New Window approach is _blank; and the Parent Frame is _parent.

▶ ANOTHER USE FOR FRAMES

Although frames typically are used to link to Web pages, some designers use them with online programs. For instance, if you are a JavaScript programmer, you may want to have the user input data in a frame on the top of the Web page, and then make the program's output appear in a frame on the bottom of the Web page.

▶ TARGETS AND BOOKMARKS

Named anchors, which FrontPage calls *bookmarks*, are also misnamed by some other Web design programs. In at least one case, Netscape's Composer, they are known as *targets*, and they should not be confused with the proper use of the term *target* in dealing with frames.

CROSS-REFERENCE
See Chapter 4 for more information on adding hyperlinks.

FIND IT ONLINE
The Introduction to Frames is located at
http://www.markradcliffe.co.uk/html/frame.htm.

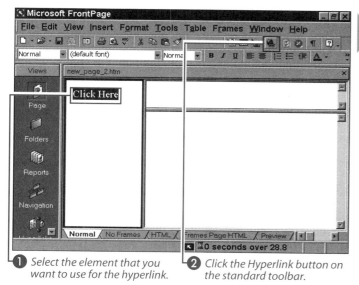

① *Select the element that you want to use for the hyperlink.*

② *Click the Hyperlink button on the standard toolbar.*

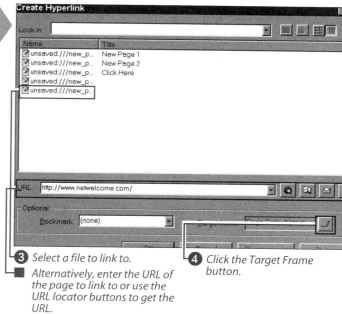

③ *Select a file to link to.*

■ *Alternatively, enter the URL of the page to link to or use the URL locator buttons to get the URL.*

④ *Click the Target Frame button.*

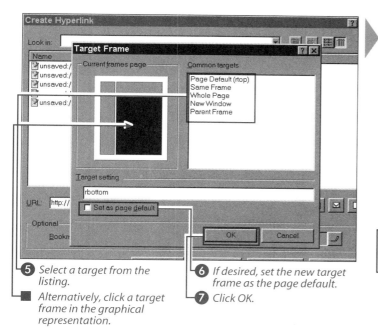

⑤ *Select a target from the listing.*

■ *Alternatively, click a target frame in the graphical representation.*

⑥ *If desired, set the new target frame as the page default.*

⑦ *Click OK.*

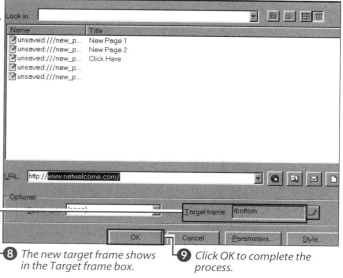

⑧ *The new target frame shows in the Target frame box.*

⑨ *Click OK to complete the process.*

Editing Framed Pages

You can edit the Web pages contained in frames in the same way that you edit Web pages that are shown in their own windows. In this sense, each of the frames showing in FrontPage are separate, fully editable windows of their own. However, frames are just too small to make this a practical alternative in most cases. Fortunately, FrontPage gives you a few alternatives.

The first, and most obvious, approach is simply to open each Web page in its own window, just as though no frames are involved. The second approach is to edit directly the HTML code for the pages. Of course, you can do this in the normal manner if you open the page in a new window, but you can also do it without taking this alternative. This is definitely a toy for power users, but FrontPage enables you to view simultaneously the HTML code for every frame in the frames page (see the lower-left figure of the facing page). Simply click the appropriate frame and start typing. Then click in each frame successively to keep editing every page in the frameset. Of course, it's a good idea, even if you know your way around HTML source code, to switch to normal mode from time to time to double-check that you're getting the exact effect you want.

TAKE NOTE

SEPARATE WINDOWS CAN WORK IN HTML SOURCE CODE, TOO

If you view the framed pages on the HTML tab, you don't give up the ability to open a separate window. The exact same procedure that opens a page in a new window in Normal view works in HTML view also. This means that you can have your cake and eat it, too. To edit the source code in a separate window, just click the HTML tab, right-click the frame that you want to edit, and then select Open Page in New Window from the popup menu.

WHAT IS THE NO FRAMES TAB FOR?

If you look at the HTML code for the frameset itself by clicking the Frames Page HTML tab, you see that the <NOFRAMES> and </NOFRAMES> tags contain the same message that is displayed in the No Frames tab. This message is strictly for users of unusual or antiquated Web browsers that don't support the modern HTML standard. Those browsers that cannot properly display framed Web pages respond to the situation by displaying the message within these tags. You can, if you wish, provide your own custom message by editing the source code, either within the No Frames tab or within the Frames Page HTML tab. This message will be seen by all users who visit your site with Web browsers that lack support for frames. The "no frames" message isn't required, but it is a courtesy.

CROSS-REFERENCE

See the section "Viewing, Editing, and Printing HTML Source Code" in Chapter 2.

FIND IT ONLINE

The Web Design Group has a good frames tutorial at **http://htmlhelp.org/reference/html40/frames/**.

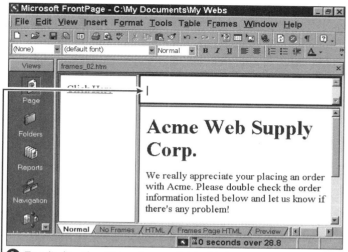

❶ To edit directly within a frame, click inside it.

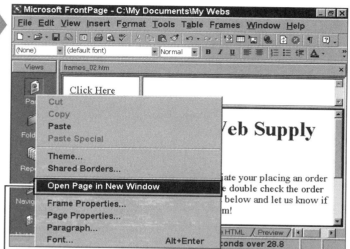

❷ To get a larger window to edit within, right-click inside a frame and select Open Page in New Window from the popup menu.

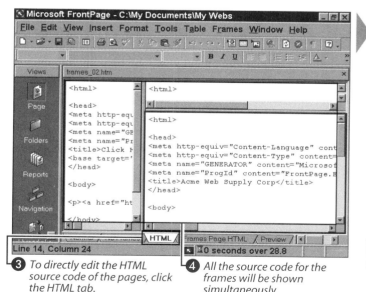

❸ To directly edit the HTML source code of the pages, click the HTML tab.

❹ All the source code for the frames will be shown simultaneously.

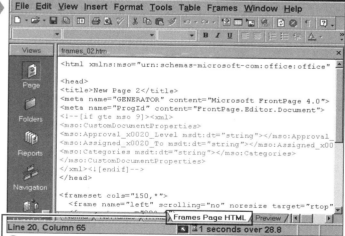

❺ To edit the HTML source code of the frameset, click the Frames Page HTML tab.

Modifying Frame Size and Spacing

The size of a frame is a function of where the borders for it are placed. Everything within those borders is a part of the frame. Thus, the quickest way to change the size of a frame is to simply drag and drop the border. However, you cannot adjust the spacing of frames in this manner.

Spacing refers to the size of the borders that lie between the various frames. The borders don't even have to be visible for their effect to be seen. Although FrontPage automatically sets the border spacing to zero if you take the option to not show borders, you can immediately reset this. The maximum border spacing, by the way, is 1,024 pixels; as with most of the maximum settings in FrontPage, this is much higher than any Web page designer could ever need.

Unless the framed pages have a background color or image, the frames will not be distinct from one another when no borders are showing — if they're viewed in a Web browser, that is. Within FrontPage, in Normal view, simply click within a frame to display the outline of the borders. You can use these outlines in the same way that you use a fully visible border, dragging and dropping them at will.

Remember that borders and spacing are features of the frameset itself, not of individual frames within it. If you change these settings, they affect all the frames.

When manually setting the size of frames, you have to make sure that your percentages or pixel specifications add up properly. FrontPage will not do this for you, and the results of incorrect numbers may be unexpected. Setting the combined percentages of two adjacent frames to over 100 percent, for example, ensures that neither frame will show at the proper size.

Margins in frames function in very much the same manner as cell padding does in HTML tables. In both cases, the purpose of the setting is to determine how close the content of the box comes to the walls.

TAKE NOTE

COLUMN WIDTH OR ROW HEIGHT?

The exact phrasing in the Frame Size panel of the Frame Properties dialog box varies, depending on the orientation of the frame you are dealing with. The example shown in the upper-right figure on the facing page is for a horizontally oriented frame. For reasons known only to Microsoft, this is considered a column rather than a row, so the references are to Column Width and Height. Vertically oriented frames are considered rows instead of columns, and the references in those cases are to Width and Row Height.

CROSS-REFERENCE
See Chapter 14 for more information on tables.

FIND IT ONLINE
Check out the Coolnerds frames demo at http://www.coolnerds.com/html/frames/frames.htm.

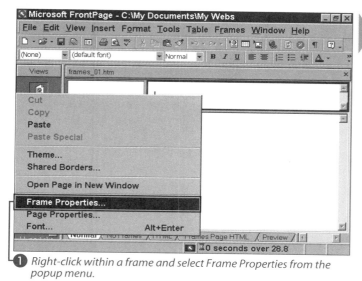

❶ Right-click within a frame and select Frame Properties from the popup menu.

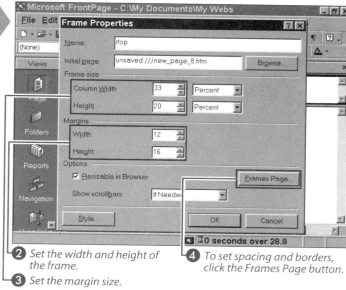

❷ Set the width and height of the frame.

❸ Set the margin size.

❹ To set spacing and borders, click the Frames Page button.

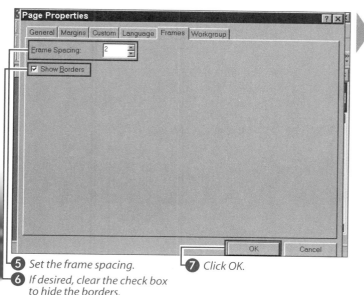

❺ Set the frame spacing.

❻ If desired, clear the check box to hide the borders.

❼ Click OK.

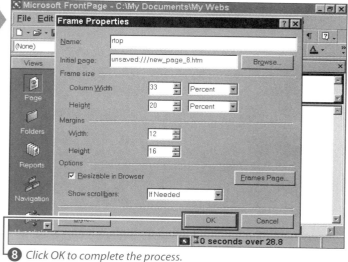

❽ Click OK to complete the process.

Splitting and Deleting Frames

As mentioned in the beginning of this chapter, the frames page templates that FrontPage supplies are really just a starting point for creating your own frames pages. Although some modifications may only require that you move the border of a frame or two, many of them may entail deleting some of the original frames and adding your own along the way.

If, for instance, you have a template that would be absolutely perfect except for the existence of one too many frames — and in the wrong placement, at that — then you simply delete the offending frame. Deleting a frame is very easy. Just select the frame and choose the Frames ⇨ Delete Frame option from the menu (see the upper-left figure on the facing page).

The only way to add more frames in FrontPage is to split the existing ones. Frame splitting, although it begins with the same menu choice as deleting frames, involves making a few more choices, as detailed in the figures on the facing page. Although FrontPage will, by default, be set so that a frame will be divided into columns or rows based on its current orientation, you can change this setting by clicking the appropriate radio button.

When frames are split in this manner, the split happens by placing a new border in the middle of the frame, thus creating two equally sized frames, both of which combined occupy the same space occupied by the original frame. If you want to reposition the border, simply drag it into a new position.

TAKE NOTE

THE OTHER WAY TO SPLIT FRAMES

If you don't want to use the menu approach, you can place the mouse pointer on a frame's border and, while holding down the Ctrl key, drag the border to split the frame. When you have dragged the border to where you want the border of the new frame to be located, release the mouse button. The drawback to this approach is that you don't get to choose whether to split it vertically or horizontally. The split takes place along the same orientation as the border you're clicking has. As with moving borders, you can still use the Ctrl-and-drag approach even if the borders are not visible. Just click within the frame that you want to split so that the border outline appears in Normal view, and then drag the border outline just as though it were a visible border.

WHICH WAY IS UP?

In contradiction to the conventions established in the dialog box for setting frame size in the preceding section, the dialog box for splitting frames considers vertical frames to be columns and horizontal frames to be rows.

UNSPLITTING AND UNDELETING

You can use the Undo and Redo features after frame splits or deletions (use Ctrl+Z and Ctrl+Y for faster action). This feature is particularly useful for flipping back and forth between two or more potential frame designs. It lets you see them one after the other for comparison purposes.

CROSS-REFERENCE

See the preceding section, "Modifying Frame Size and Spacing."

FIND IT ONLINE

The Frames Workshop is located at http://www.idbsu.edu/oit/training/html/frames/.

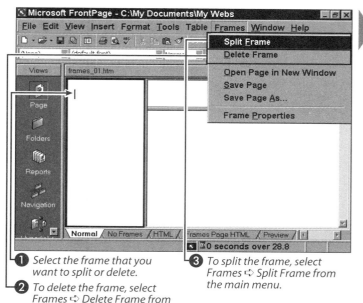

1 Select the frame that you want to split or delete.

2 To delete the frame, select Frames ⇨ Delete Frame from the main menu.

3 To split the frame, select Frames ⇨ Split Frame from the main menu.

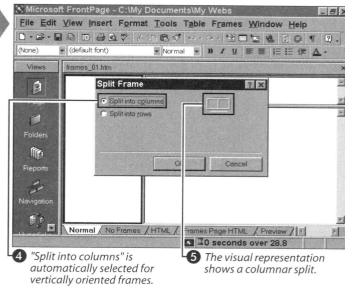

4 "Split into columns" is automatically selected for vertically oriented frames.

5 The visual representation shows a columnar split.

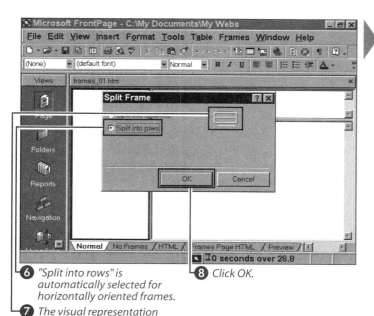

6 "Split into rows" is automatically selected for horizontally oriented frames.

7 The visual representation shows a row-type split.

8 Click OK.

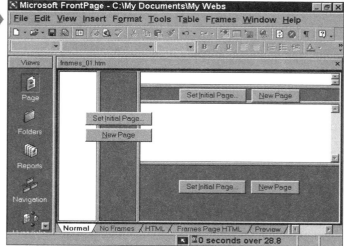

■ This frames page has had each of its three frames split in two.

Nesting Frames

Frames can hold not only regular Web pages, but also other frames pages. Placing one frames page inside another frames page is called *nesting*. This isn't as unusual a situation as it may at first seem. Although Webmasters rarely make a site with nested frames deliberately, this result can happen even unintentionally. For example, suppose that you have a link to someone else's Web page. That page is normal in every respect, but one day the Webmaster at that site decides to use frames. That's all it takes to cause nested frames within your page, and the decisions of other Webmasters normally are totally out of your control. Fortunately, HTML and FrontPage are both flexible enough to take this kind of occurrence in stride.

FrontPage does a pretty good job of handling this type of situation. Although nested frames don't display in Normal view in the same way that a regular HTML page does, nested frames do display in Preview view or in a Web browser just like normal HTML pages do. In Normal view, you simply get a button that reads View Frames Page. Clicking this button, as shown in the upper-right figure of the facing page, causes the nested frames page to be displayed in its own window.

CROSS-REFERENCE

See the section "Viewing, Editing, and Printing HTML Source Code" in Chapter 2.

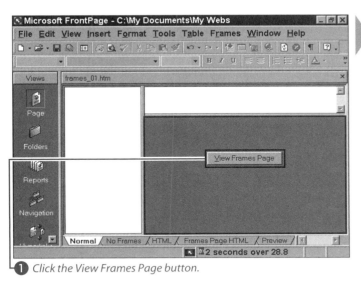

1 Click the View Frames Page button.

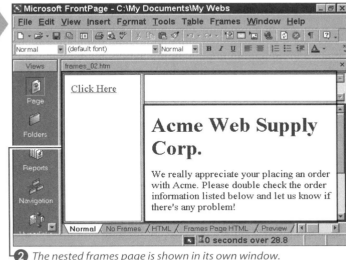

2 The nested frames page is shown in its own window.

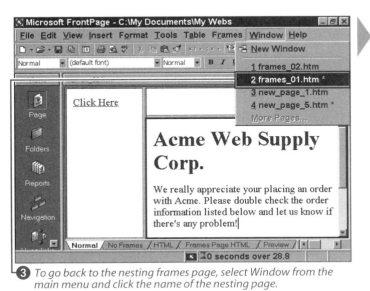

3 To go back to the nesting frames page, select Window from the main menu and click the name of the nesting page.

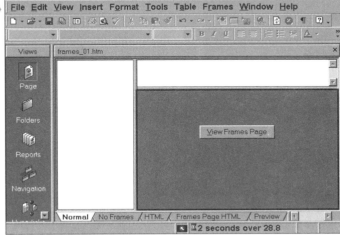

■ You are returned to the original display.

Personal Workbook

Q&A

1 What is a *frameset*?

_____

_____

_____

2 How do you nest frames within frames?

_____

_____

_____

3 What is the only way to add more frames to a frames page?

_____

_____

_____

4 How do you edit the HTML source code of a frames page?

_____

_____

_____

5 What size is a split frame?

_____

_____

_____

_____

6 What are the three options for an initial page in a frame?

_____

_____

_____

_____

7 What is a *hyperlink target*?

_____

_____

_____

8 What is the maximum border spacing?

_____

_____

_____

ANSWERS: PAGE 332

EXTRA PRACTICE

1 Try setting the initial page to something other than an HTML page.

2 Compare editing a framed page in place to editing it in a new window.

3 Alter the default frame to link to.

4 Try linking to _self ("Same Window") and see how it differs from the normal approach.

5 Look at the HTML source code for a normal Web page and a frames page.

6 Create your own frames page template.

REAL-WORLD APPLICATIONS

✔ You want your Web site to be as friendly as possible, even to browsers that aren't frames-capable. Consider using a custom No Frames message.

✔ You may find that the structure of a frames template suits you, but that the default target doesn't. You can change the default target.

✔ You need to make several frames pages that use the same layout. You'll probably want to create a custom template.

✔ You have a company logo that you want to keep visible at all times. One good way to do this is to place it in a separate frame.

Visual Quiz

How do you get to this dialog box? What is the significance of the darkened frame in the Current frames page panel?

_____

_____

_____

_____

_____

_____

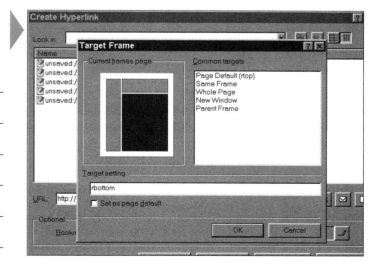

CHAPTER 16

Using Special Effects and CSS

FrontPage provides a wide range of Dynamic HTML effects that you can apply to various elements. You can change one image for another one, make text and other elements float on and off the page, and change the size, color, and background of text. What's significant about these capabilities isn't they can add a touch of pizzazz to your Web page designs. The critical factor here is that these effects can be made interactive. Through the use of events like mouse clicks or even page loadings, these effects can become a part of the experience that people have when they visit your Web site.

Cascading Style Sheets, commonly abbreviated CSS, are pretty much the same thing as FrontPage themes, but they are not an exclusively FrontPage feature. Rather, they are a common standard developed and promulgated by the World Wide Web Consortium (W3C). As such, they are widely used all across the Web. Also, and perhaps more important, they are more versatile than FrontPage themes. Three levels of styles can be applied, including the external CSS files, which can control the appearance of an entire Web site; embedded style sheets, which are contained within one particular Web page and affect only that one page; and inline styles, which are contained within one particular HTML tag, and whose influence does not extend beyond that one element.

FrontPage comes complete with a set of predesigned cascading style sheets, but it can also accept ones that you either design outright or pick up from some outside source. All that is required is that the file adhere to the CSS standard and that you link it to your Web pages. FrontPage will do the rest quite admirably. It should be noted, however, that neither of the major Web browsers fully supports the standard.

FrontPage also has a powerful capability to alter and modify the settings within style sheets. Any item, from embedded style sheets affecting only one page to settings in external CSS files that control entire Web sites, can be modified with precision and ease. You simply use the same old dialog boxes and techniques that you already use to alter fonts, colors, and the like in normal, non-CSS situations. FrontPage takes care of all the details.

Using Dynamic HTML Effects

When Web pages were first introduced, you couldn't really do much of anything with them other than show some text; images were added early on as well. Still, a Web page pretty much just sat there; action and interaction were not a part of the World Wide Web.

As the population of Web surfers began to demand more and more out of Web pages and designers and programmers tried to give it to them, Dynamic HTML (or DHTML) was born. There has been a great deal of debate and acrimony about just exactly what Dynamic HTML actually is. Some people insist that it is absolutely anything that changes a Web page from its basic static nature to one of greater activity. Others hold the more narrow view that it is only the application of scripting languages via the Document Object Model (see the first Take Note). If you look at the HTML source code, you'll see that these dynamic effects are applied via the JavaScript programming language.

The confusion and argument over this is bound to go on for some time, especially in the absence of any specific Dynamic HTML standard. Although some standards exist for parts of what is now known as Dynamic HTML, such as the CSS or DOM standards, a true consensus of professional opinion on the subject does not exist now and is not likely to in the near future.

FrontPage makes the application of Dynamic HTML effects to the elements of your Web pages about as easy as it can get. Although skilled JavaScript programmers have been creating and using such effects for a long time, it is only recently that FrontPage and other such page creation programs have begun to utilize them, making them available to the average Web developer.

Basically, Dynamic HTML works by responding to events. Although a large number of events are available to programmers, FrontPage offers only four of them: the click, double-click, mouse over, and page load events. If you are familiar with JavaScript programming, you'll instantly recognize these as the `onclick`, `ondblclick`, `onmouseover`, and `onload` events. While FrontPage doesn't provide access to the full range of possible events, these four are among the most commonly used, and are certainly more important to most Web designers than more obscure events like `ondragstart`.

Continued

TAKE NOTE

THE DOCUMENT OBJECT MODEL

The Document Object Model (DOM) applies object-oriented programming techniques to HTML. In the DOM, rather than look at the page as a whole, each and every element on the Web page is considered to be a separate object. Thus, each one can be individually accessed and acted upon by programs written in languages such as JavaScript, JScript, or Visual Basic Scripting Edition (VBScript).

CROSS-REFERENCE

See Chapter 6 for more information on creating special effects with CSS.

FIND IT ONLINE

Introduction to Dynamic HTML is located at
http://www.wdvl.com/Authoring/DHTML/Intro/.

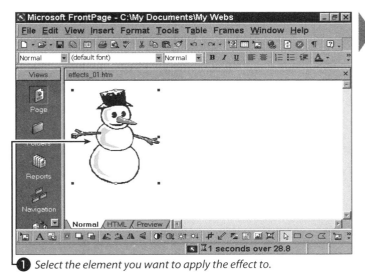

1 Select the element you want to apply the effect to.

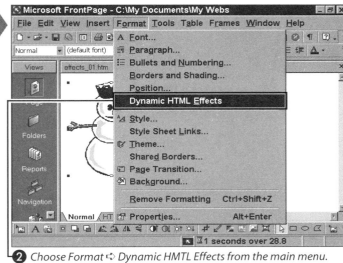

2 Choose Format ⇨ Dynamic HMTL Effects from the main menu.

3 Alternatively, right-click a toolbar and select DHTML Effects from the popup menu.

4 On the DHTML Effects toolbar, click the On arrow.

5 Select an event from the drop-down list.

Using Dynamic HTML Effects

Continued

The *click* and *double-click events* are, of course, the action of pressing and releasing the mouse button either once or twice while the pointer is over the element in question. The *mouse over event* is simply the placing of the pointer over the element; no click is required. The *page load event* is just what it says — an action that takes place the moment the page is first loaded into a Web browser.

Once you've picked an event to respond to, the next step is to choose the type of effect that will be applied when that event takes place. The upper-left figure of the facing page shows the effects available for a click event on an image. The contents of this drop-down list, however, will vary depending upon the particular object and event combination you have chosen. With images, for instance, you'll basically choose between *fly outs* (in which the image moves off the screen) or *swapping* (changing the image file for another one in the same location on the Web page). For text, you'll also have the option to "drop in by word," a nice effect by which one word in the sentence is moved across the page at a time. You'll also be able to change the formatting — including font size, color, borders, and shading — as the result of an event. If the event is a page load, then a larger variety of movement effects, such as hop and fly in, become available.

The final step in applying Dynamic HTML effects to your Web page elements is to choose the settings for the effect you have selected. These setting options

vary widely depending upon the other choices you have made in the first two steps. They may, for instance, specify the direction toward which (or from which) an element will move, or the type of formatting to be applied to text.

TAKE NOTE

▶ MOVEMENT VERSUS ANIMATION

Although many people call the fly out, color changes, and similar effects "animation," the only way to get true animation on your pages is to use either animated GIFs or more sophisticated art techniques via programs like Shockwave. Real animation means that there is a change within the image itself, not just a repositioning of a totally static image, however nicely the movement is done. Likewise, simply changing the color of a font, even if done in response to a mouse click, is not truly animation by any realistic definition of the term. Changing the font's size, on the other hand, does come a bit closer to true animation.

▶ IMAGE DISTORTION

When you're using Dynamic HTML effects to swap images, you should be aware that the second image will not be properly sized unless it is already the exact same size as the first image. The second image will be forced into the size of the first image. If the first image is larger, the second image will be stretched. If the first image is smaller, the second image will be compressed. If they are of significantly different proportions as well as size, the distortion of the second image can be tremendous.

CROSS-REFERENCE

See the section "Changing Text Color" in Chapter 3.

FIND IT ONLINE

There's a good article on browser standards compliance at **http://www.wdvl.com/Authoring/ HTML/Standards/.**

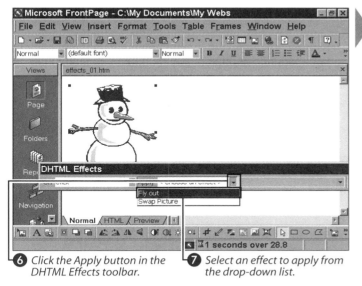

6 Click the Apply button in the DHTML Effects toolbar.

7 Select an effect to apply from the drop-down list.

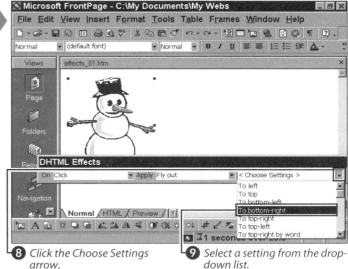

8 Click the Choose Settings arrow.

9 Select a setting from the drop-down list.

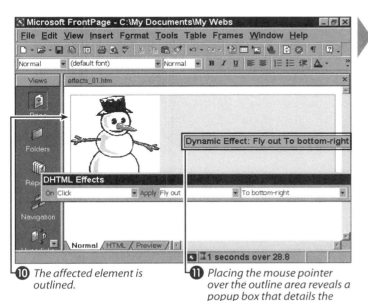

10 The affected element is outlined.

11 Placing the mouse pointer over the outline area reveals a popup box that details the applied effect.

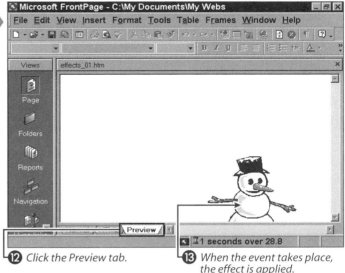

12 Click the Preview tab.

13 When the event takes place, the effect is applied.

Using CSS Templates

Although it's true that you can simply type up a style sheet all on your own, save it, and it will be as useful as one made from FrontPage's CSS (Cascading Style Sheet) templates, the template approach serves an important function. It gives you a basis from which to build. As any planner will tell you, it's always easier to modify an existing plan than to create one from scratch.

You reach the templates for Cascading Style Sheets in much the same way as the ones for frames pages. You must use the main menu to get the proper dialog box and tab because no toolbar button exists (see the upper-left figure of the facing page).

Once you've selected the template you want to use, the source code for it will appear in a FrontPage window (see the lower-right figure of the facing page). Unless you plan on making modifications to the code, there's only one more thing to do: make sure that you save the file when you're finished creating it — and before you make any modifications to it — just in case. Remember, a template is not the same thing as a CSS file. If you don't save your work, it won't be available for linking later on.

When you save your CSS file, make sure that you give it a good, descriptive name. Although you may be confident that you know the difference between 1724lmn.css and 83qrx.css the day you create them, it will be a different story a few months later. Give the files names that tell you what is in them, like red-stripes.css or bordered_headings.css instead. This is not only good programming practice, but it's

absolutely essential if you're dealing with multiple designers working on a single project.

TAKE NOTE

WHY "CASCADING?"

Cascading is used to describe style sheets because of the manner in which the various types of styles are processed. The first style sheet which has an impact on the look of a Web page is the external style sheet. If, however, there is also an embedded style sheet, then that one takes priority in any case where there is a conflicting style assignment. And, finally, the inline style takes precedence over either an external or an embedded style sheet if there is a conflict. Thus, the precedence, like a waterfall, cascades downward.

THEMES AND CASCADING STYLE SHEETS

The first thing you'll notice, no doubt, when you get a look at the Style Sheets tab, is that the style sheets have the same names as some of the FrontPage themes. Oddly enough, however, these do not correspond — at least not in all their elements — to the themes of the same name. Some of them have commonly designed elements, but the overall look is radically different.

WHAT'S THAT LITTLE BUTTON?

The popup element that appears on the screen when you create a style sheet from a template is the Style toolbar. Yes, that's right — an entire toolbar with only one button on it. We cover the use of the Style button in the following section.

CROSS-REFERENCE

See Chapter 15 for more information on working with frames.

FIND IT ONLINE

D.J. Quad's style sheets tutorial is located at **http://www.quadzilla.com/stylesheets/ stylesheets.htm.**

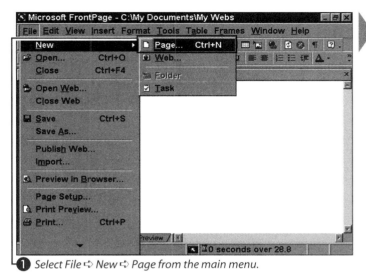

1 Select File ➪ New ➪ Page from the main menu.

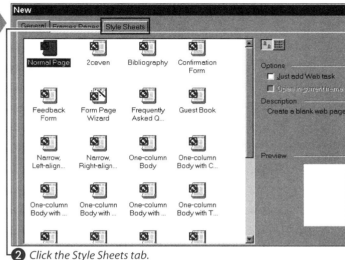

2 Click the Style Sheets tab.

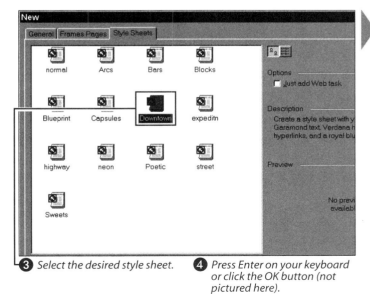

3 Select the desired style sheet.

4 Press Enter on your keyboard or click the OK button (not pictured here).

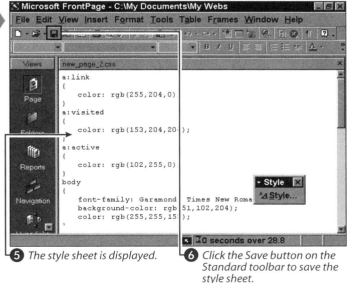

5 The style sheet is displayed.

6 Click the Save button on the Standard toolbar to save the style sheet.

Modifying CSS Styles

You can change anything you want in a Cascading Style Sheet (CSS) file. The simplest way to do this, if you're experienced and confident enough with CSS syntax, is to just type directly into the source code as it shows in the FrontPage window (see the upper-left figure on the facing page). However, you'll find it easier overall to just go ahead and use the program's built-in style modification methods. Not only will your work go more smoothly, but you'll get more precise results that way. Computer programs, at least in theory, are less prone to making mistakes than humans.

Another style formatting technique (Format ⇨ Style on the main menu) confusingly looks like it's duplicating the same efforts we're describing here. Actually, it is technically different although the impact is nearly the same. FrontPage utilizes two other style approaches — the embedded style sheet and inline styles — besides external cascading style sheet files. Embedded style sheets are identical to the style sheets that are found in external CSS files; the only difference is placement. Embedded style sheets are actually a part of the Web page they affect (hence the term *embedded*); they are found in the <HEAD> element of a page. Inline styles, on the other hand, are found within the start tags of the elements they affect. If you take a look at the HTML source code for some of your pages, you'll doubtless see examples of both. Simply do a search for the word "style" to find them. Depending upon the element involved and the formatting applied, FrontPage may create either embedded style sheets or inline styles. Even if you never consciously and deliberately decide to use styles, they will be a part of your Web page design automatically. However, FrontPage will never create an external style sheet file unless you tell it to do so.

TAKE NOTE

▶ NO DIFFERENT APPROACH

The actual modifications of the various elements, such as fonts, are done in the same way when you are using styles as they are done in a regular Web page. You use the same dialog boxes and the same techniques, and you make the same choices as when you change the items on a regular Web page.

▶ WHAT ABOUT NEW?

The New button functions identically to the way the Modify button functions. You receive the exact same dialog box as shown in the lower-left figure of the facing page, and everything in it works identically, too, except, of course, that you are adding a new style to the sheet instead of changing an existing one.

▶ DELETING STYLES

When you use the Delete button, you are removing style specifications from the current style sheet; anything you delete here will be deleted from the .css file as well. If you go to the extent of deleting everything in the current file, then the Styles listing will suddenly fill up again, showing all the standard page elements that are available to you.

CROSS-REFERENCE

See Chapter 3 for more information on font modifications.

FIND IT ONLINE

Visit Inside Dynamic HTML at
http://www.insidedhtml.com/.

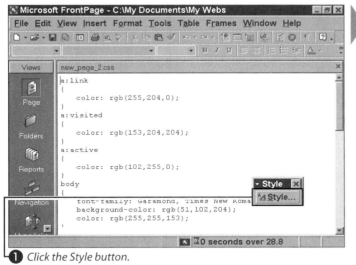

1 Click the Style button.

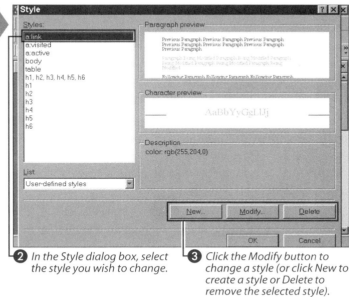

2 In the Style dialog box, select the style you wish to change.

3 Click the Modify button to change a style (or click New to create a style or Delete to remove the selected style).

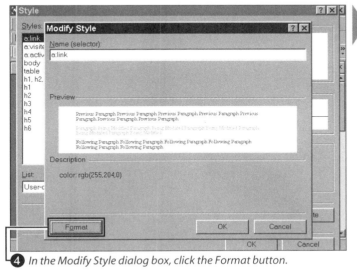

4 In the Modify Style dialog box, click the Format button.

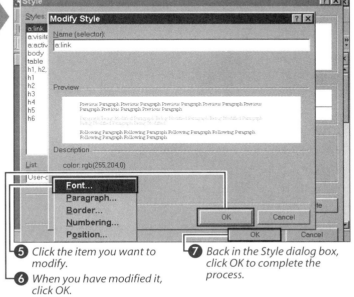

5 Click the item you want to modify.

6 When you have modified it, click OK.

7 Back in the Style dialog box, click OK to complete the process.

Linking to External Style Sheets

There's more to using cascading style sheets than just creating them. Once a style sheet has been made and saved, it then needs to be linked to a particular Web page (or to a series of Web pages) in order for it to be of any practical use.

You can, believe it or not, link more than one style sheet file to a single Web page or Web site. All of them will apply, but not equally. There's an order to it, and that's what "cascading" means when we speak of cascading style sheets. The first style sheet that is applied has the least dominance when it comes to applying styles. If an element is defined in two style sheets, then the second one will override the first one where that element is concerned. If there is an element in the first style sheet that is not found in the second style sheet, then that setting will endure since there is nothing to interfere with it. The importance of a style continues to cascade downward from external style sheets to embedded style sheets. A conflicting setting in an embedded style sheet will override the same settings in any number of external style sheets. And, finally, an inline style will override everything that is above it. It's a case of last come, first served.

Take a look at the dialog box in the lower-right figure of the facing page. If you are using multiple cascading style sheets, then the order in which the pages are listed here is very important. That's because of the cascading nature of the styles themselves.

Remember, whichever is the last one applied will be the one that overrides the others in any style conflicts. That's what the Move Up and Move Down buttons are for. They determine the order in which the style sheets are applied. Of course, if you're just using a single style sheet, you don't have to concern yourself with this issue; in fact, the buttons for changing the style sheets' order won't even be active in that case.

TAKE NOTE

▶ MAKE A LIST

Before you go into the Link Style Sheet dialog box to set the order in which your external CSS files will be linked, it's good practice to create a diagram, or at least a list, showing any conflicting style declarations among the various files. Once you're in the dialog box, there's no way to view those files to double check, so you can save yourself from possible future problems with just a little bit of preplanning.

▶ IT REALLY IS A LINK

When we speak of linking external cascading style sheet files, we're speaking literally. If you take a look at the HTML source code for a Web page that has a CSS file linked to it, you'll see in the <HEAD> element that there is a <LINK> element with an HREF (hypertext reference) attribute just like you'll find in the <A> (anchor) element that is used for a normal hyperlink.

CROSS-REFERENCE

See Chapter 5 for more information on changing fonts, styles, and sizes.

FIND IT ONLINE

Take a look at Technologies Supported by Different Browsers, located at **http://www.coolnerds.com/ html/stats.htm.**

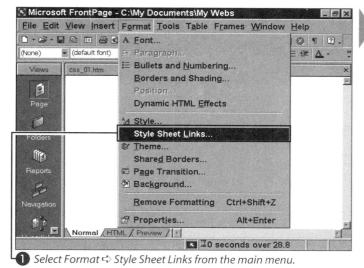

1 Select Format ➪ Style Sheet Links from the main menu.

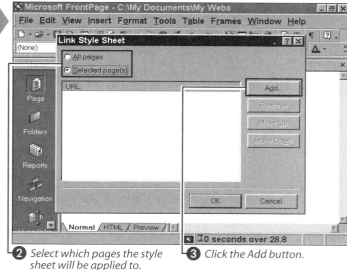

2 Select which pages the style sheet will be applied to.

3 Click the Add button.

4 Select a style sheet.

5 Click OK.

■ Repeat steps 3 through 5 for all the style sheets you want to add.

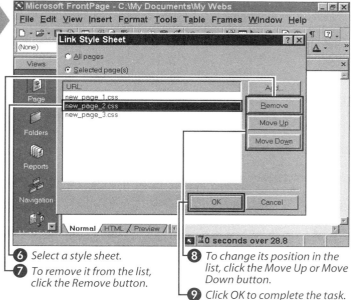

6 Select a style sheet.

7 To remove it from the list, click the Remove button.

8 To change its position in the list, click the Move Up or Move Down button.

9 Click OK to complete the task.

Personal Workbook

Q&A

1 What does CSS stand for?

_____

_____

_____

2 How many events are there on the DHTML Effects toolbar?

_____

_____

_____

3 What are *embedded style sheets*?

_____

_____

_____

4 What order are conflicting style settings resolved in?

_____

_____

_____

5 How are external style sheets linked to a Web page?

_____

_____

_____

6 What is an *inline style*?

_____

_____

_____

7 What does *fly out* mean?

_____

_____

_____

8 What programming language are special effects done in?

_____

_____

_____

ANSWERS: PAGE 333

EXTRA PRACTICE

1 Try out several different effects for the page load event.

2 Link an external style sheet to a Web page.

3 Create CSS files with conflicting settings. Try applying them in varying orders and observe the results.

4 Alter the style settings for the H2 heading element.

5 Study some JavaScript programming to see how it's done.

6 Read the HTML source code before and after altering style settings via the main menu.

REAL-WORLD APPLICATIONS

✔ You have a rather dull Web site. You might want to use some special effects to liven it up.

✔ You need to have a standardized set of rules for a Web site, but don't want to use themes. Try CSS files for greater compatibility.

✔ You're using external CSS files for your Web site, but want one page to be different. Use embedded or inline styles to override the external ones.

✔ You create your own CSS file that you want to be able to modify at will. Try saving it as a template.

Visual Quiz

How do you get to this dialog box? What are the items listed under Styles?

_____

_____

_____

_____

_____

_____

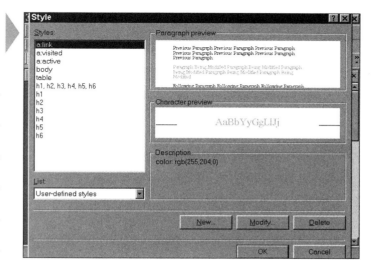

Personal Workbook
Answers

Chapter 1

see page 4

❶ Which view shows link relationships?

A: The Hyperlinks view.

❷ What does *publishing* mean in FrontPage?

A: Publishing is the act of uploading all the files in a FrontPage web to either a remote server or to a folder on a local system or network. Publishing differs from uploading via an FTP (File Transfer Protocol) program in that FrontPage sends all the files in one operation, and you don't have to perform different uploading procedures for text and graphics files. FrontPage is also capable of sending only files that have changed since the last publication of a particular web.

❸ How do you save a FrontPage web?

A: Trick question. You don't. You can, however, save the individual files that make up a FrontPage web.

❹ What is a *wizard*?

A: A wizard is a small program that is designed to walk you through the process of creating a Web page or a FrontPage web by asking you pertinent questions which, when you answer them, provide the basis for the contents and/or structure of the page or web.

❺ What is a *subweb*?

A: A subweb is a FrontPage web that's included within another FrontPage web.

❻ What is a *template*?

A: A template is a predesigned FrontPage web or Web page. It differs from a wizard in that you have no input into its structure or contents until after it's created. Using a template is a one-step process. You just tell FrontPage to use that template, and it creates the web or page without asking you any further questions. Any customization of the results is done by you manually.

❼ Name the three views in which you can create new pages.

A: The Page, Folders, and Navigation views.

❽ What is the name of the default web folder?

A: My Webs.

Visual Quiz

Q: What is this dialog box? Name two ways to navigate to it.

A: It's the New Web dialog box, from which you select a template or wizard to create a new FrontPage web. You can get to it either by clicking on the arrow next to the New button and selecting Web from the drop-down menu, or by selecting File ⇨ New ⇨ Web from the main menu.

Personal Workbook Answers

Chapter 2

see page 30

1 **How do you enter special characters not found on your keyboard?**

A: Choose Insert ⇨ Symbol from the menu. In the resultant Symbol dialog box, click the symbol you want to add, and then click the Insert button. If you need to add more than one symbol in a row, just keep selecting and inserting them. When you're done, click the Close button.

2 **What if special characters are not found in FrontPage either?**

A: You can enter special characters by clicking on the HTML tab and typing in their codes in the HTML source code. The character codes are found at **http://www.w3.org/TR/REC-html40/sgml/entities.html**.

3 **What is the purpose of horizontal lines?**

A: To divide Web pages into sections so they are more readable.

4 **How many sizes of headings are there in HTML?**

A: Six. The largest is H1 and the smallest is H6.

5 **What kind of font does the formatted paragraph style use?**

A: It uses a fixed width, or monospace, font as opposed to the normal variable-width font usually found on Web pages. In HTML, the formatted paragraph style is represented by the <PRE> element.

6 **What are the two most common kinds of lists?**

A: Numbered (also known as ordered lists) and bulleted (also known as unordered lists). The HTML elements for each are, respectively, <OL> and <UL>.

7 **What does red underlining mean on your Web page?**

A: That the underlined term is not found in FrontPage's spell check dictionary. This does not necessarily mean that the term is actually misspelled since the dictionary doesn't include every word in the world.

8 **What does a validation program do?**

A: It processes the HTML code from a Web page and checks it for errors.

Visual Quiz

Q: **What is this screen? How do you get there? What's wrong with it?**

A: It's the source code for the current page in FrontPage. You get to it by clicking the HTML tab. The HTML code in this example has mismatched start and end tags on the heading element.

Chapter 3

see page 46

1 **How does center alignment affect indentation?**

A: A paragraph that is center aligned will not show any effect from indentation no matter how many times it's applied and increased.

2 **How many font sizes are there in HTML?**

A: Seven.

3 **Which font size is the smallest?**

A: The smallest font size is 1. The largest is 7.

4 **What size is the "Normal" font size?**

A: Size 3, which is approximately 12 points.

5 Why shouldn't you use underlined characters?

A: Because hyperlinks are recognized by their underlining, and if other text is also underlined on your Web pages, visitors to your site are likely to be confused.

6 How many standard colors are there?

A: Eight. Several million colors are actually available, but these can only be viewed on high-end systems. The eight "standard" colors come from an earlier day when graphics cards and monitors were more limited than today.

7 What is the meaning of *Document's Colors?*

A: They are the colors that are already in use on a Web page, as opposed to those that are available, but have not been used.

8 What type of text color should be used with a dark background?

A: A light one. If you used dark text against a dark background, it would be difficult to read. By the same token, a light background calls for dark text.

Visual Quiz

Q: What does this drop-down list do? Why are the point listings not necessarily accurate?

A: It enables you to set the size of fonts. The characters must first be selected, and you can select any number of characters, from a single character up to the entire page. The point listings are inaccurate because you cannot control exact font size in HTML.

Chapter 4

see page 64

1 What does *URL* stand for?

A: Uniform Resource Locator. A URL is the address of a file on the World Wide Web.

2 What does a *mailto* link do?

A: It signals the Web browser to open an e-mail message to the address specified in the mailto link, with the addressee already filled in.

3 How do you delete a link without deleting the text or image it's based in?

A: For text, click anywhere within the link and then click the Hyperlink button on the toolbar. For an image, click it and then click the Hyperlink button. With either text or images, you can also right-click the link and then select Hyperlink Properties from the popup menu. In the Hyperlink Properties dialog box, delete the Web address in the URL edit box, and then click OK.

4 What does *HTTP* stand for?

A: Hypertext Transfer Protocol, the method by which files are transferred between Web servers and Web browsers.

5 What is a *bookmark?*

A: Also called a *fragment URL,* a bookmark is a named anchor (<A> element with a name attribute).

6 Do you have to use the "www" prefix in a Web address? If so, why? If not, why not?

A: Not in most cases. Since Web addresses are specified with the prefix **http://** that tells a Web browser that it's to be handled with the Hypertext Transfer Protocol, it's obvious that it's a file on the World Wide Web even without the "www" part, and very few Web addresses really need it.

7 What are the usual colors for hyperlinks on a Web page?

A: Blue for unvisited hyperlinks, purple for visited ones, and red at the moment the link is clicked.

Personal Workbook Answers

8 **What HTML element is common to both links and bookmarks?**

A: The <A> (or anchor) element is used in hyperlinks because a hyperlink, even though it leads the way *out* of a Web page from the point of view of a person surfing the World Wide Web, is one end of a two-way connection between two different files, and both ends of that connection are said to be anchors.

Visual Quiz

Q: **What do you use the four buttons to the right of the URL text box for? How do you get to this dialog box?**

A: The first one launches your default Web browser. Whatever URL you browse to is automatically put into FrontPage. The second button brings up a standard Select File dialog box that lets you find files on your local system. The third button is for a specialized type of URL called a *mailto* link. This link gives an e-mail address and, when accessed, launches the Web browser's associated e-mail client program with a blank message already addressed to the recipient specified in the link. The fourth button actually creates the page you're going to link to. When you click it, you get to the New page dialog box just as if you had selected File ➪ New ➪ Page from FrontPage's main menu. Picking a page from this dialog box under these circumstances both creates the page and establishes the link to it. The newly created page, rather than the page you linked to it from, will be displayed, and you'll need to hit the back arrow on the toolbar to return to your link page.

Chapter 5

see page 88

1 **What is the purpose of a FrontPage graphical theme?**

A: The main purpose is to provide a consistent and pleasing graphical appearance to all the pages in a web.

They can, however, also be used on individual Web pages or series of pages.

2 **How many basic themes are there? How many additional?**

A: There are 13 themes, which are included in the typical installation of FrontPage. There are 54 more that can be loaded afterward, for a total of 67.

3 **How do you create a custom theme?**

A: Working from one of the existing themes, you modify some or all of its elements to suit yourself, and then save the new theme under a different name.

4 **How do you remove a theme from a page or web that has one?**

A: By utilizing the same process by which you apply the theme to begin with. However, instead of selecting the name of one of the themes from the listings, you select the "(No Theme)" option.

5 **How do you delete a theme from the listing?**

A: By selecting its name in the listing and then clicking the Delete button. This can only be done with themes you have created; you cannot delete any of the original themes from within FrontPage.

6 **How many color sets does each theme have? How many graphics sets?**

A: Each theme has two color sets and two graphics sets. The color sets are Normal Colors and Vivid Colors; the graphics sets are Normal Graphics and Active Graphics.

7 **Does each graphics set have its own background image?**

A: No. Normal Graphics and Active Graphics both share the same background image.

8 **Which sets are affected by font modifications?**

A: There are two ways to look at this. The color sets are affected by modifying fonts via the Text button. However, you can also modify the fonts in the graphics sets via the Graphics button. The fonts that are modified via the Text button are only those found in the body and heading elements.

Visual Quiz

Q: How do you get to this dialog box? What do the five-color bars represent?

A: To get to it, you need to right-click on the Web page and select Theme from the popup menu. In the Themes dialog box, click the Modify button. Then, click the Colors button. The five colors in the color bar represent the colors of the Heading 2, Heading 1, Background, Regular Text, and Regular Hyperlink elements, in that order.

Chapter 6

see page 112

1 **What is the *Clip Art Gallery*?**

A: The Clip Art Gallery is a separate program that is a combination of picture database and image viewer. It's a basic feature of Microsoft Office and can be invoked and utilized from within FrontPage.

2 **What is the file format of the images in the Gallery?**

A: Although it can manage images in any popular graphics file format, the Clip Art Gallery comes with images in the Windows Metafile (.wmf) format. The Windows Metafile format uses vector graphics, and is free of the drawbacks of bitmapped images, but this format is not in popular usage on the World Wide Web.

3 **Name at least two image file formats FrontPage can import.**

A: Any of the following: Graphics Interchange Format (GIF), Joint Photographic Experts Group (JPEG or JPG), Portable Network Graphics (PNG), Windows Metafile (.wmf), Windows Bitmap (.bmp), Tagged Image Format Files (TIFF or .tif), Sun Raster (.ras), Postscript (.eps), PCX, Kodak PhotoCD (.pcd), and Targa (.tga) formats.

4 **What are the three image file formats commonly used on the World Wide Web?**

A: GIF, JPEG, and PNG. All three are bitmapped type.

5 **What are the two image alignment settings that work properly with word wrap?**

A: Left and right. All the other image alignment settings are for use with text alignment instead of word wrap.

6 **What is the upper limit for spacing an image?**

A: The highest number you can use in the dialog box settings is 10,000.

7 **What is the purpose of alternate text?**

A: To provide an indication during the downloading of an image what the image is or contains. In addition, alternate text is used to provide vision-impaired Web surfers with information about what they cannot see.

8 **What are some characteristics of good background images?**

A: They tile evenly, do not distract from the rest of the elements on the Web page, and degrade gracefully when viewed at lower color depths.

Visual Quiz

Q: How do you get to this dialog box? What is the purpose of the selected entry?

A: Select Tools ⇨ Options from the main menu. In the Options dialog box, click the Configure Editors tab. The selected entry associates GIF files with the image editor IrfanView.

Personal Workbook Answers

Chapter 7

see page 146

1 What file format is used when you add text to an image?

A: In FrontPage, only the GIF format can be used to add text to an image. In practically any image editor, you can add text to any supported graphics file format.

2 Why can Clip Art Gallery images be resized without resampling?

A: Any of the vector image formats such as Windows Metafiles or Encapsulated Postscript (.eps) defines a mathematical description rather than a bitmap.

3 What is a *thumbnail image*?

A: A smaller image that is substituted for the full image. A hyperlink to the full image is created along with the thumbnail image, so that a visitor to your Web site can click the thumbnail image to view the larger image. The purpose of thumbnails is to speed download time by avoiding the use of a larger graphics file than necessary.

4 Why is the term *z-order* so appropriate?

A: Because it defines the position of an element along the Z axis. There are three axes — X, Y, and Z. The X axis runs horizontally, the Y axis runs vertically, and the Z axis runs perpendicular to the other two, and can be visualized as essentially running from the front of your monitor to the back of it.

5 How many times do you need to rotate an image before it returns to its original position?

A: Four. Each rotation is 90 degrees, so four of them equal 360 degrees, bringing you full circle back to where you started.

6 What is *saturation*?

A: Saturation refers to the amount of white in a color. Colors that have very little white in them are referred to as deeply saturated.

7 What is the default z-order value?

A: Zero. Until a z-order value is explicitly assigned to an element, it has a value of zero. Since all elements initially have the same z-order value, the stacking order along the Z axis is initially determined by the order in which the elements appear in the underlying HTML source code. This same technique is used to determine which element is on top whenever two elements have the same z-order value.

8 What does the Wash Out button do?

A: It decreases both the brightness and contrast values of an image in one operation. Once an image has been washed out, however, further applications of the Wash Out button won't affect it at all.

Visual Quiz

Q: How do you create this thumbnail image?

A: Select the image, and then click the Auto Thumbnail button on the Picture toolbar.

Chapter 8

see page 174

1 What is an *image map*?

A: An image map is an image link that contains multiple links in a single image. Which link is activated depends on what area of the image is clicked.

2 What is a *hotspot*?

A: An area on an image map that is linked to a particular URL.

❸ How many hotspot shapes are there?

A: Three — circle, rectangle, and polygon.

❹ What can a hotspot link to?

A: Anything that has a URL. Although the vast majority of image maps are used to link from one Web page to other Web pages, there is no technical requirement that they be used only for this purpose. Hotspots can link to sound files, video files, and so on as well.

❺ How many hotspots can be used in one image map?

A: Technically, as many as you can possibly fit on one particular image. For practical purposes, however, a good rule of thumb is to use no more than 10 hotspots in a single image map, in order to make it most useful.

❻ What happens when you move a sizing handle on a polygon?

A: The point of intersection of the two lines that meet at that sizing handle is changed. Effectively, moving those two lines changes the shape of the polygon.

❼ What is the main difference between client-side and server-side image maps?

A: Server-side image maps, the first type ever used, depended on the Web server to calculate the location of the mouse pointer and process the hyperlink information. With client-side image maps, the computing burden is shifted to the user's computer.

❽ What is the *default hyperlink?*

A: It's the link that is followed if a user clicks anywhere within the image map except within a hotspot.

Visual Quiz

Q: What are these three shapes? How do you get this display?

A: They are the rectangle, circle, and polygon hotspot shapes. Once the hotspots are in place on the image map, you can click the Highlight Hotspots button on the Picture toolbar to suppress the image and show only the hotspots.

Chapter 9

see page 188

❶ What is a *confirmation page?*

A: The confirmation page is displayed when a visitor to your site clicks on the Submit button of a form. It contains a listing of form fields and their contents.

❷ What are the three environment variables that can be saved along with form data?

A: They are "Remote computer name," "Username," and "Browser type."

❸ What is the HTML name for the scrolling text box?

A: The scrolling text box is the same as the HTML <TEXTAREA> element.

❹ Describe the difference between the way check boxes and radio buttons work?

A: Both check boxes and radio buttons allow several choices to be presented, and both are activated by clicking the one next to the choice, but you can click several check boxes at once, whereas radio buttons represent exclusive choices.

❺ Which fields are displayed to a user on FrontPage's default confirmation page?

A: Every field in the entire form. If you want to change this, you need to create a custom confirmation page and assign it to your form.

❻ Text in a form that responds to a mouse click is called what?

A: It's called a label.

Personal Workbook Answers

❼ What are *hidden fields*?

A: They are fields that don't show up on the form. They do, however, show up in the default confirmation page field listings. Since the hidden fields aren't actually on the visible form, they cannot be changed by someone who's filling out the form.

❽ What is the standard name for the Picture field?

A: FrontPage assigns standard field names that are a single letter followed by a number. The letter is usually the same as the one the form field starts with (for instance, a check box may be called C1 or C2), but the Picture field uses *I* rather than *P*, the *I* standing for the word *image*.

Visual Quiz

Q: How do you get to this dialog box?

A: It's the Advanced Form Properties dialog box, in which you add, modify, or remove hidden fields for your form. To get to it, you right-click the form and select Form Properties from the popup menu. Then, in the Form Properties dialog box, click the Advanced button.

Chapter 10

see page 204

❶ How do you make text in a form respond to a mouse click?

A: You need to select both the text and the element it's related to, and then choose Insert ➪ Form ➪ Label from the menu. The text is now surrounded by a dotted line to signify that it's clickable.

❷ How can you tell if a form field has validation options in place?

A: There is no visual cue. You have to go to the dialog box and look. To do so, either double-click the form field or right-click it and choose Form Field Properties from the

resultant popup menu. Once in the form field's Property dialog box, click the Validate button to view data entry validation settings.

❸ What does a negative tab order value do?

A: It removes the affected form field from the tab order entirely.

❹ Which form field has the most complex validation rule options?

A: Oddly enough, it's the simple text box.

❺ What visual cue tells you a label is assigned to another form field?

A: Normally, text in a form is just plain text. A clickable label (also called a *dynamic label*), on the other hand, is outlined with a dotted line to signify that clicking on it will activate the associated form field.

❻ How does a display name differ from a field name?

A: A field name is assigned to identify the form field within the HTML source code and forms part of the name/value pair that is submitted when the Submit button is clicked. The display name is used only when data entry validation rules are violated and an error message is displayed; it identifies to the errant user which field they need to redo.

❼ How are radio buttons different from the rest of the form fields?

A: Radio buttons work together as a group, representing values that are mutually exclusive. All other form fields work as stand alone elements within the form.

❽ How many form fields have validation options available?

A: Three. The drop-down menu, the radio button, and the text box. None of the other form fields have data entry validation.

Visual Quiz

Q: How do you get to this dialog box? What does the number 9 in the Tab order box mean?

A: It's the Drop Down Menu Properties dialog box. You get there by either double-clicking on a drop-down menu or by right-clicking on it and selecting Form Field Properties from the resultant popup menu. The number 9 is in the Tab order setting, and it means that this form field will fit between whatever other fields have the tab order values 8 and 10.

Chapter 11

see page 218

1 **What is a *hit counter*?**

A: A hit counter is a program that gathers information on how many times a given Web page is loaded into someone's Web browser. It does not distinguish between multiple loadings of a single page by a single user and multiple visits by several users.

2 **What kind of component is background sound?**

A: It's not really a FrontPage component at all, but an HTML extension. Since it's not a part of the HTML standard, it works only in Microsoft Internet Explorer, and users of other Web browsers won't be able to hear the sounds.

3 **What is a *marquee*?**

A: A marquee is a line of text that scrolls or slides from one side of the Web page to the other. When it scrolls, it appears to come from outside the margin on one side of the page and disappear into the margin on the other side. When it slides, it simply appears and then moves across the page until it reaches the far margin and then stops.

4 **Can you alter the fields in a search form?**

A: No, you cannot. The search form is coded as a webbot component, and you can't alter the individual parts of it.

5 **What list do you need to create in order for the search form to work?**

A: This is a trick question. The list of words is actually created by FrontPage whenever you save a page. Although it adds any words to the list that are not already in it, it will not remove any words that disappear when you delete pages. In order to update the word list to handle deleted pages, you'll need to manually select Tools ⇨ Recalculate Hyperlinks from the menu.

6 **On what kind of servers does a FrontPage hit counter work?**

A: Only on those servers that support the FrontPage extensions.

7 **What FrontPage limitation keeps the ad banners from being as useful as they could be?**

A: You can only use a single link, no matter how many banners you add to the rotation.

8 **What is a *time stamp*?**

A: A time stamp establishes the most recent date and time that a Web page was either saved or automatically updated.

Visual Quiz

Q: What requirements are there to use the Custom Picture option in this dialog box?

A: It is the Hit Counter Properties dialog box. The custom picture must be a GIF file with the numerals 0 through 9 reading from left to right, and the digits must be equally divided.

Personal Workbook Answers

Chapter 12

see page 234

❶ What items can be scheduled for display?

A: Images can be scheduled via the scheduled picture component. Web pages can be scheduled via the scheduled include component.

❷ What Web page elements can be used in an include page?

A: Any of them. An include page is just a normal HTML page like any other, and nothing is changed by the fact that it's included in another page.

❸ How many variables can you use on one Web page?

A: There is no limit to the number of variables you can use for substitution.

❹ What is the primary difference between substitution and meta variables?

A: The variables used for substitution are intended for display on a Web page, whereas meta variables are never shown visibly.

❺ What is the purpose of the alternate image in a scheduled picture?

A: Its purpose is to be displayed any time before or after the scheduled image is shown.

❻ What two events does a hover button respond to?

A: A hover button responds to a mouse pointer being placed over it ("hovering") and a mouse click.

❼ What does *HTTP* stand for?

A: Hypertext Transfer Protocol. HTTP is the basic method by which Web browsers and Web servers communicate with one another.

❽ What is the basic function of a hover button?

A: A hover button is used to put a hyperlink on a Web page. Its other functions are primarily for special effects.

Visual Quiz

Q: How do you get to this dialog box?

A: It's the Scheduled Picture Properties dialog box. You get to it either by selecting Insert ⇨ Component ⇨ Scheduled Picture from the menu or by double-clicking an existing scheduled picture.

Chapter 13

see page 250

❶ What kinds of elements can be contained within a table?

A: Any element at all that can be found on a Web page can be contained within a table: images, text, hyperlinks, lists, you name it — even other tables.

❷ How many cells can be inserted into a single row?

A: Theoretically, there is no limit. However, as a practical matter, you'll find yourself running out of room if you have more than about a dozen cells in a row.

❸ Where is a caption placed by default?

A: At the top of the table. It can be moved to the bottom of the table instead, but only after it's created. To move it, right-click it and select Caption Properties from the popup menu. In the resultant dialog box, select Bottom of Table, and then click the OK button.

❹ What happens when you specify both a background color and a background image?

A: If they're both for a table or both for a cell, then the background image will override the background color, just as they do on a Web page. When you use background colors and images for both the table and the cells, things get a bit more complex because a background setting for a cell overrides a background setting for the table, but only within that cell. Thus, for a cell's background color and a table's background image, the background color overrides the background image.

5 **How do you remove the bold formatting in a header cell?**

A: Actually, you can't. Header cells are formatted as bold text, period. You can change the font face, the color, the alignment — you can even make it italic or underlined — but you cannot get rid of the bold formatting no matter what you do.

6 **What is the minimum number of cells you can delete? The maximum?**

A: FrontPage will only let you delete two or more cells at a time. There is no way to delete a single cell, since there is no way to select it. The maximum number of cells you can delete is all of them.

7 **What table elements can be inserted into a table?**

A: Rows, columns, and individual cells can be inserted. Technically speaking, there is no such thing as a column element. Rows are composed of the <TR> (table row) element in HTML, and cells are made of the <TD> (table data) element, but there is no column element. FrontPage lets you treat columns just like vertical rows, though.

8 **What does the No Wrap option do?**

A: Normally, text typed into a table cell will wrap around to form new lines when it reaches the edge of the cell, and the cell will expand vertically to accommodate it. Setting the cell properties to no wrap causes the cell to expand horizontally instead, without any word wrap taking place.

Visual Quiz

Q: **What can you do in this dialog box that we've covered in this chapter?**

A: It's the Cell Properties dialog box. In it, you can set the horizontal and vertical alignment of cell contents, specify a header cell, set the no wrap option, and specify background colors and images.

Chapter 14

see page 264

1 **What is *cell padding*?**

A: Cell padding refers to the distance between the contents of a cell and the edges of that cell. The default cell padding is only one pixel, which works reasonably well for images, but can make text a bit harder to read. You might even try setting the padding to zero for images, but a setting of 2 or more is usually better for text.

2 **What happens to the contents of merged cells?**

A: All the contents of the merged cells are preserved and are placed into the newly created larger cell.

3 **What happens to the contents of split cells?**

A: The contents of split cells remain where they were before the split took place. The newly created cells are empty.

4 **What two measures can be used to set cell width or height?**

A: You can set either cell width or cell height as a percentage of the table size or as an absolute measurement in pixels.

5 **How are the contents of cells arranged when a table is converted to text?**

A: The cell contents are placed into separate paragraphs, with each paragraph following the other.

PERSONAL WORKBOOK ANSWERS

6 **What does *CSV* stand for?**

A: CSV stands for comma separated values. CSV files, also known as comma delimited files, are a common method for preserving table structure.

7 **What happens to the other cells in a row when you make one cell wider?**

A: The other cells in that row move over to make room for the widened cell. This has the effect of making the table asymmetrical.

8 **What happens to the other cells in a row when you make one cell taller?**

A: They also change their height to match the setting of the changed cell.

Visual Quiz

Q: **How do you get to this dialog box? What is the difference between *cell spacing* and *cell padding*?**

A: To get to it, right-click anywhere in the table and select Table Properties from the popup menu. Cell spacing is the distance between the cells themselves, while cell padding is the distance between the cell contents and the cell walls.

Chapter 15

see page 286

1 **What is a *frameset*?**

A: A frameset, also called a *frames page,* is a structure that allows multiple Web pages or other files such as images to be displayed at one time in the screen of a Web browser.

2 **How do you nest frames within frames?**

A: Simply use a frames page as the contents of a frame in another frames page. Since one of them is inside the other, it is said to be *nested.* You can have several levels of nesting, with one frames page holding another frames page, which holds another frames page, and so on.

3 **What is the only way to add more frames to a frames page?**

A: In FrontPage, you add more frames by splitting the existing frames. Technically, there is one other way, which is to directly add frames by entering the appropriate HTML code in the source code for the frames page. The latter approach, however, is not really a FrontPage feature, but simply HTML.

4 **How do you edit the HTML source code of a frames page?**

A: You need to click the Frames Page HTML tab. Once that tab is active, you can type directly into the code for the frameset itself.

5 **What size is a split frame?**

A: If you use the menu approach, it is 50 percent of the size of the frame it was split from because the menu approach divides a frame exactly in half. If you use the click and drag approach instead, the size is determined by where you place the border when you release the mouse button.

6 **What are the three options for an initial page in a frame?**

A: The first approach is to click the Set Initial Page button and select an already existing Web page. The second is to click the New Page button to create a blank Web page. The third is to give it no content at all.

7 **What is a *hyperlink target*?**

A: A hyperlink target specifies which frame in a frameset will be the one to display a Web page reached by clicking on a hyperlink in one of the other frames of that same frameset.

8 What is the maximum border spacing?

A: You can set the border spacing for up to 1,024 pixels. This is an extremely generous range, to put it mildly.

Visual Quiz

Q: How do you get to this dialog box? What is the significance of the darkened frame in the Current frames page panel?

A: To get to the Target Frame dialog box, select the element you want to use for a hyperlink. Next, click the Hyperlink button on the toolbar, which will take you to the Create Hyperlink dialog box, where you click the Target Frame button. The darkened frame represents the currently selected target frame.

Chapter 16

see page 306

1 What does *CSS* stand for?

A: It stands for Cascading Style Sheets.

2 How many events are there on the dynamic HTML effects toolbar?

A: There are four of them. These are the click, double-click, mouse over, and page load events. If you are familiar with JavaScript programming, you'll instantly recognize these as the `onclick`, `ondblclick`, `onmouseover`, and `onload` events. While FrontPage doesn't provide access to the full range of possible events, these four are among the most commonly used, and certainly are more important to most Web designers than more obscure events like `ondragstart`.

3 What are *embedded style sheets*?

A: These are style sheets that, instead of being external CSS files, are contained within the <HEAD> element of an individual Web page. Other than that, the two types are identical in syntax and structure.

4 In what order are conflicting style settings resolved?

A: The last is the first. External style sheets are the last in importance, embedded style sheets are the next in importance, and inline styles are the final arbiters of style settings. If there are multiple external style sheets that are applied, then the first of them has the least importance, and the last of them has the greatest importance.

5 How are external style sheets linked to a Web page?

A: Via the <LINK> element, which is found in the <HEAD> element of a Web page.

6 What is an *inline style*?

A: It is a style setting that is found within the start tag of an element.

7 What does *fly out* mean?

A: An element that flies out is one that leaves its original position on the Web page and moves off the page in one direction or another.

8 In what programming language are special effects done?

A: In FrontPage, they are done in JavaScript, the most common scripting language. They can also be done in any scripting language, including Microsoft's version of JavaScript (which is called Jscript) or in VBScript, the Visual Basic scripting language.

Visual Quiz

Q: How do you get to this dialog box? What are the items under Styles?

A: When a cascading style sheet is displayed, click the Style button on the Style toolbar (the Style toolbar has only the one button on it). The items under Styles are the various Web page elements for which style settings exist in the CSS file.

Glossary

A

alt Short for alternate text. Text that is displayed while an image is loading.

ASCII American Standard Code for Information Interchange. Plain text file format. HTML files are in ASCII format and must be transferred as ASCII files rather than binary files when FTP is used to upload them to a Web server.

attribute A part of an HTML element that provides necessary information or instructions to modify the element in some way. The *href* attribute of the <A> element, for example, gives the URL of a linked file. The *color* attribute, common to many elements, changes the element's color.

B

background color A color underlying the text and images on a Web page, in a table, or a table's rows and cells. Background color on a Web page can be overridden by user preference settings in Web browsers.

background image An image underlying the text and images on a Web page, in a table, or a table's rows and cells. A background image on a Web page can be overridden by user preference settings in Web browsers.

binary file A file that is not plain text, such as a program or graphical image.

BMP A Microsoft Windows graphics file format. Short for bitmap. BMP files are extremely large compared with many other common graphics file formats.

bookmark A named anchor in a Web page that can be linked to so that the page can be loaded into a browser at the position of the bookmark instead of at the top of the page. It is also the term used by some browsers, such as Netscape Navigator, for what is called a *Favorite* in Internet Explorer.

browser *See* Web browser.

bulleted list Also called an unordered list. A list of items each of which is denoted by a bullet, typically a solid circle.

C

caption A title for a table. Unlike other table elements, captions can only contain text, and that text is centered in relation to the table.

Cascading Style Sheets A separate file referenced by Web pages, containing instructions on how Web browsers should display the elements in those pages.

GLOSSARY

cell A part of a table that holds visible information.

cell span The capability of a table cell to cover more than one column or row.

Certificate Authority An organization that issued digital certificates for the purpose of authenticating the identity of a person or company.

CGI *See* Common Gateway Interface.

character code A shorthand method for entering characters that are not found on common keyboards.

client Any program that requests information or processing from a server.

clip art Ready-to-use images for inclusion on Web pages or other programs.

column A vertical grouping of cells in a table.

Common Gateway Interface The usual method of passing form information from a Web page to a program so that it may be processed.

content The material between the start and end tags of an HTML element. The content of a link in an <A> element, for example, may be text or an image.

cookie A file created by a JavaScript program on a Web page you visit. The file is stored on your computer and is referenced when you return to that Web page. Cookies are commonly used to record your personal preferences, name, and other data so that it does not have to be manually reentered.

copyright The right to make copies. Generally speaking, copyright is vested in the author of any work, whether it be text, art, or music.

CSS *See* Cascading Style Sheets.

D

description list A type of paragraph formatting used to differentiate between terms and their definitions. The term being defined is set to the Description Title paragraph format, whereas the definition itself is set to the Description Text paragraph format.

digital certificate An encrypted file used by a certificate authority to validate the identity of a person or company.

dithering The process of rendering an image with more colors than can be displayed on a visitor's computer in a form that approximates the original colors. Dithered images do not show up as well as images that are designed to show the appropriate number of colors, so it is generally better to design images from the start to take advantage of the lowest common number of colors — currently 256 — that are likely to be encountered. If your Web site uses images that call for more than 256 colors, it's advisable to put in a warning to that effect.

domain name The human-readable version of an IP address. For instance, **www.idgbooks.com** is the domain name for the IP address 206.175.162.15. Domain names are assigned after application by authorities such as InterNIC. Each country has its own domain name authority.

downloading The process of receiving a file from a remote server.

E

element The fundamental parts of HTML. Common elements include <IMG> (image elements), <TABLE> (table elements), and <H1> (large heading elements). Elements contain attributes and content and usually have start and end tags, but some of them are forbidden to have an end tag.

emoticon Icons used to signify human emotion. Most emoticons represent the human face turned sideways, showing some expression. One of the most common is the smiley face, which is represented as :-)

FAQ A text file or Web page consisting of Frequently Asked Questions and their answers.

File Transfer Protocol A method for uploading and downloading files.

flame A communication that contains insulting or emotionally charged material.

flame war A prolonged exchange of flames, usually involving several people. Flame wars are destructive to the functionality of discussion groups.

font The total appearance of lettering on Web pages. There are two basic kinds of fonts — proportional and fixed width.

fragment URL *See* bookmark.

frame A separate Web page coexisting on the same Web browser screen with other Web pages, each of which is contained by the same frameset. Frames and framesets are commonly used to present a table of contents or a hyperlink menu to the left of a Web page's screen. Clicking the links in the left-hand frame causes new Web pages to appear in the right-hand frame.

frameset The containing element for frames.

FTP *See* File Transfer Protocol.

GIF Short for Graphics Interchange Format. The most common graphics file format on the World Wide Web. GIF files have two properties that make them very useful in Web pages. *Transparency* allows the background to show through parts of the image. *Interlacing* allows the image to be displayed in gradual increments rather than line by line.

gradient A gradual shading from one color into another.

home page A personal Web page, generally expressing something about the person who created it. Also, the page initially displayed when a Web browser first starts up.

horizontal rule Also called *horizontal line*. A dividing line used on Web pages to separate one section from another. Horizontal rules can vary in width and thickness, and can be either hollow or solid.

HTML *See* HyperText Markup Language.

HTTP *See* HyperText Transfer Protocol.

hyperlink Also called *links*, hyperlinks contain the address of another file on the Internet. Web browsers can navigate around the World Wide Web by using the information contained in hyperlinks. They are usually activated by a user clicking them with a mouse. Hyperlinks can show up on a Web page as text or images, or they can be embedded in an image map.

GLOSSARY

hypertext An approach to presenting information in which linear thinking is discarded in favor of a potentially infinite number of connections between all the material on the Web. Most hyperlinks allow you to follow a trail that only you can create, whereas traditional text methods only allow a reader to proceed from page one to the end of the material.

HyperText Markup Language A derivative of the Standardized General Markup Language. Consists of a group of elements that tells Web browsers how information should be displayed. Since it only offers suggestions, different Web browsers can show the same page in different ways.

HyperText Transfer Protocol The method by which files are sent between Web servers and Web browsers. Browsers send a request to the Web server for particular files; the Web server processes that request and, if the files exist, returns them to the browser. If they aren't there, the Web server returns an error message.

I

icons Small artwork that is representative of an action or concept.

image Any graphical file including digitized photographs or pure art. Most of the image files on the World Wide Web are either GIFs or JPEGs, although PNG (portable network graphics) files are becoming more popular.

image link A hyperlink containing an image element instead of text. Image links are normally surrounded by a border in the same color as the text links on the same page.

image map A single image containing more than one hyperlink. Clicking different parts of the image takes you to different URLs.

index.html The most common name for the root page of a Web site.

interlacing A feature of GIF images. Normal GIF images are displayed in a Web browser one line at a time. This results in a high quality image, but takes some time to accomplish. Interlaced GIFs display every third or fourth line, resulting in a low-quality image at first, which gradually becomes fully realized as all the lines are finally displayed. The advantage is that a visitor to your Web site can get a good idea of the final image long before it has finished downloading.

Internet Short for Internetwork, the Internet is often called the network of networks, because it is a series of networked computers all connected together in a larger supernetwork.

Internet service provider Also called ISPs. A company that provides dialup connections so that you can log on to the Internet. Most ISPs provide a number of common services such as e-mail accounts, Web page space, and newsgroup access.

IP address The location of a resource on the Internet. IP (Internet Protocol) addresses consist of four sets of numbers separated by periods, and are known as a dotted quad.

ISP *See* Internet service provider.

J

Java applet A small program written in the Java language.

JavaScript A programming language that cannot function except within the context of a Web page. JavaScript is commonly used for the creation of cookies.

JPEG A graphics file format. Also known as JPG. JPEG is short for Joint Photographic Experts Group. JPEG images offer high quality and small file size. Technically speaking, it is not properly a file format at all, but a compression method. Different graphics programs may use varying file formats while still holding true to the compression approaches of the JPEG standard.

K

keyword The list of words describing a Web page in metadata for search engines.

L

Link *See* hyperlink.

M

metadata Any information on a Web page that is not displayed to visitors. Typical metadata includes the name of the Web page's author and keywords, which describe the page for the benefit of search engines. However, there are no real standards for metadata, and you can feel free to invent your own.

modem A telephone for your computer. Modem is short for modulator/demodulator.

N

named anchor *See* bookmark.

netiquette A combination of the words Internet and etiquette. The series of customs evolving in Cyberspace to allow tens of millions of people to get along with one another.

numbered list Also called an ordered list. A list of items denoted by numbers.

O

ordered list *See* numbered list.

P

pixel Picture element.

PNG Portable Network Graphics. A new image file format designed for use on the World Wide Web.

publishing The act of uploading all the files necessary for a Web page or Web site to be fully functional.

R

Robot A program used by search engines to surf the Web automatically. Robots bring back information on the Web pages they encounter, and this information is incorporated into the search engine's database.

row A horizontal line of cells within a table.

GLOSSARY

S

search engine A Web site containing a database of information, usually gathered by a robot or a spider, about other Web pages.

secure server A Web server utilizing some method like SSL for encrypting its communications with Web browsers.

Secure Sockets Layer The most common method of establishing secure communications between a Web server and a Web browser.

server Any program or computer providing a service.

Spider A program used by search engines to surf the web automatically. Spiders bring back information on the Web pages they encounter, and this information is incorporated into the search engine's database.

SSL *See* Secure Sockets Layer.

T

table A series of rows of cells within a Web page. Tables are normally used to present data in columns and rows, but can be used to plan and implement page layout.

tag The basic way that HTML elements are delimited in a Web page. Most elements in HTML have both a start tag and an end tag. The start tag states the name of the element or some short form of it. The end tag is identical except for the fact that it starts with a slash.

template A basic Web page design with all the elements in place to serve a particular purpose, but lacking specifics. Templates are used by Web designers to provide a framework within which to develop Web pages with specific references and information.

tiling The process of spreading a single image across a Web page so that it forms a seamless background image. Tiling also occurs in tables and table rows.

transparency The capability of GIF files to allow the background of a Web page to show through one color. Transparency is typically used so that an image appears to be some shape other than rectangular.

U

Uniform Resource Locator *See* URL.

unordered list *See* bulleted list.

uploading The process of sending a file from your local system to a remote computer.

URL Uniform Resource Locator. The address of a file on the Internet or an intranet.

W

Web browser A program that interprets HTML code and allows users to surf the World Wide Web. The two most popular Web browsers are Microsoft Internet Explorer and Netscape Navigator (or Netscape Communicator, depending on which version you're using).

Web page An HTML file that can be read and displayed by a Web browser.

Web server A program designed to handle the processing of requests for files from a Web browser. Also, the computer on which the program and Web pages reside.

Web site A collection of Web pages, all of which are on the same Web server, and all of which are part of a larger design.

wizard A program that walks you through the steps necessary to accomplish some process.

World Wide Web The collection of all the Web pages in the world.

Z

z-order The Z axis is perpendicular to both the X (horizontal) and Y (vertical) axes, and can be visualized as running from the front of your monitor to the back of it. The positioning of elements on the Z axis is called their *z-order*.

Index

Index

Index

INDEX

glossary lists, 38–39
graphical elements, 96–97, 102–105
graphical images. See images
graphical themes. See themes
grayscale images, 170–171

H

<HEAD> tag, 314
header table cells, 256
heading styles, 36–37
hidden form fields, 196–197
hit counters, 220–221
hop and fly in effect, 310
Horizontal Line option, Insert menu, 34
horizontal lines, 34–35
horizontal transition effect, 224
hotspots
    creating, 176–177
    defined, 175
    links, 180–181
    moving, 178–179
    shapes, 176–179
    text, 182–183
hover buttons, 246–247
<HR> tag, 34–35
HTML code, editing, 42–43, 296–297
HTML tags
    <A>, 74
    _blank links, 294
    <BODY>, 287, 302–303
    &copy, 32
    deprecated styles, 38
    <DIV>, 156
    editing source code, 42–43, 296–297
    <FORM>, 190
    <HEAD>, 314
    <HR>, 34–35
    name attribute, 74
    <NOFRAMES>, </NOFRAMES> tags, 296
    <P>, 36
    _parent links, 294

    <PRE>, 36–37
    printing source code, 42–43
    _self links, 294
    <SPAN>, 156
    _top links, 294
    validation programs, 42
    viewing source code, 42–43
    W3C, 38
    World Wide Web Consortium, 38
HTTP (Hypertext Transfer Protocol)
    defined, 65
    headers and meta variables, 244–245
HTTP_USER_AGENT variable, 192
Hyperlink Parameters dialog box, 72–73
Hyperlink Properties dialog box, 70–71
hyperlinks. See links
Hyperlinks View, 80–81
Hypertext Transfer Protocol (HTTP)
    defined, 65
    headers and meta variables, 244–245

I

image editor, configuring, 128–129
Image forms, 194–195
image links, creating, 66–69
image maps
    borders, 178–179
    circles, 176–177
    default hotspot, deleting, 176
    default hyperlinks, creating, 176–177
    defined, 175
    hotspots, 175–183
    polygons, 176–177
    rectangles, 176–177
    and tables, 258
images
    absolute positioning, 154–157
    aligning, 134–135
    alpha channel, 168
    alternate text, 138–139
    animation, 160

Index

J

JavaScript
images, 160–161
special effects, 308–309
JPEG support, 118, 130–133

K

keyboard shortcuts for forms, 208–209
keywords, defined, 222
Kodak PhotoCD (.pcd) support, 118

L

Label form element, 190, 194, 208–209
layering images, 158–161
layout
images, 154–161
using tables, 252
Link Reports, 82–83
Link Style Sheet dialog box, 316
links. See also image maps
banner ads, 224
bookmarks, creating, 74–75
bookmarks, linking to, 76–77
Broken Hyperlinks report, 82–83
colors, 70–71
correcting errors, 70–71
to CSS, 316–317
deleting, 70–71
editing, 70–71
following in Web pages, 78–79
fonts, 108–109
to frames, 294–295
hover buttons, 246–247
Hyperlink Parameters dialog box, 72–73
Hyperlinks View, 80–81

image links, creating, 66–69
inserting in tables, 258
Link Reports, 82–83
mailto links, 68–69
parameters, 72–73
to scheduled images, 238
to search engines, 72–73
Site Summary report, 82–83
table of contents, creating, 76
text links, creating, 66–69
unverified, 80–81
URLs, specifying, 66–67
and variable substitution, 242–243
verified, 80–81
lists, 38–39, 257
low-resolution images, 132–133, 138–139

M

mailto links, 68–69
margins for frames, 298
marquees, 226–227
menu lists, 38–39
merging cells, 274–277
meta variables, 244–245
Microsoft Image Composer, 128–129
midi format, 228
More Colors button, 56–59
mouse over event, 310
multiple CSS, 316–317

N

name attribute, HTML tags, 74
named anchors, 294
nesting
frames, 302–303
tables, 252, 280
New dialog box, 8–9
New Page button, 8

Index

R

Radio Buttons, 190, 194, 212–213
.ras (Sun Raster) support, 118
Recover option, Clip Art Gallery, 116
rectangles in image maps, 176–177
Redo feature, frames, 300
relative positioning, 156
Remote computer name variable, 192
REMOTE_HOST variable, 192
REMOTE_USER variable, 192
removing
    styles, 314
    themes, 92, 100
resampling images, 148
reset button, 190–192
resizing images, 148–149
resource, defined, 65
Rice Paper theme, 92
Romanesque theme, 92
rotating images, 162–163
rows
    frames, 298, 300
    tables, 254–255
rules, 34–35

S

Same Frame option, 294
sans serif fonts, 50
saving
    frames, 292–293
    images, after changing, 164
    themes, 100
scheduled images, 238–239
scheduled include pages, 238
schemes, defined, 65
scrolling marquees, 226–227
Scrolling Text Box, 190, 194
search engine links, 72–73
Search Form Properties dialog box, 222–223

search function, 222–223
select dropper, 56–57
_self links, 294
semicolons, 32
Send Backward button, Picture toolbar, 158–159
serif fonts, 50
server response, defined, 244
Set Initial Page button, 290–291
Set Transparent Color button, Picture toolbar, 168–169
sight-impaired people and images, 138
Site Summary report, 82–83
size
    frames, changing, 298–299
    images, determining, 116
    images, resizing, 148–149
    images, and special effects, 310
    themes, changing, 104–105
sounds, 228–229
spacing
    frames, 298–299
    images, 136–137
<SPAN> tag, 156
special characters, 32–33
special effects
    animation, 310
    DHTML, 308–311
    drop in by word effects, 310
    events, responding to, 308–311
    fly out effects, 310
    hop and fly in effect, 310
    images, 310–311
    JavaScript, 308–309
    swapping effects, 310
    text, 310–311
spell checking, 40–41
spiral notebook background image, 142
splitting
    cells, 274–277
    frames, 300–301
spreadsheet data, converting to table, 266–267
Straight Edge theme, 92
Strong font style, 54
style, modifying
    text, 54–55
    themes, 104–105
Style dialog box, 315

Index

Index

wizards, defined, 8
WMF (Windows Metafile Format), 114, 130–131, 148
word wrapping, 134–136
World Wide Web Consortium (W3C), 38

Z

z-order, 158–161

my2cents.idgbooks.com

Register This Book — And Win!

Visit **http://my2cents.idgbooks.com** to register this book and we'll automatically enter you in our fantastic monthly prize giveaway. It's also your opportunity to give us feedback: let us know what you thought of this book and how you would like to see other topics covered.

Discover IDG Books Online!

The IDG Books Online Web site is your online resource for tackling technology — at home and at the office. Frequently updated, the IDG Books Online Web site features exclusive software, insider information, online books, and live events!

10 Productive & Career-Enhancing Things You Can Do at www.idgbooks.com

- Nab source code for your own programming projects.

- Download software.

- Read Web exclusives: special articles and book excerpts by IDG Books Worldwide authors.

- Take advantage of resources to help you advance your career as a Novell or Microsoft professional.

- Buy IDG Books Worldwide titles or find a convenient bookstore that carries them.

- Register your book and win a prize.

- Chat live online with authors.

- Sign up for regular e-mail updates about our latest books.

- Suggest a book you'd like to read or write.

- Give us your 2¢ about our books and about our Web site.

You say you're not on the Web yet? It's easy to get started with IDG Books' *Discover the Internet*, available at local retailers everywhere.